Teaching
Physical
Education

Teaching Physical Education
Fourth Edition

Muska Mosston
Sara Ashworth

Macmillan College Publishing Company
New York

Maxwell Macmillan Canada
Toronto

Maxwell Macmillan International
New York   Oxford   Singapore   Sydney

Editor: Ann Castel Davis
Production Supervisor: Kelly Ricci, Spectrum Publisher Services, Inc.
Production Manager: Francesca Drago
Cover Designer: HotHouse Designs

This book was set in Optima by Compset, Inc., printed and bound by Arcata Graphics
Fairfield. The cover was printed by NEBC.

Copyright © 1994 by Macmillan College Publishing Company, Inc.

Printed in the United States of America

Earlier edition copyright © 1986 by Macmillan Publishing Company.

Macmillan College Publishing Company
866 Third Avenue, New York, New York 10022

Macmillan College Publishing Company is
part of the Maxwell Communication
Group of Companies.

Maxwell Macmillan Canada, Inc.
1200 Eglinton Avenue East
Suite 200
Don Mills, Ontario M3C 3N1

Library of Congress Cataloging-in-Publication Data
Mosston, Muska.
    Teaching physical education / Muska Mosston, Sara Ashworth.—4th
  ed.
      p.   cm.
    Includes bibliographical references (p.) and index.
    ISBN 0-02-384183-4
    1. Physical education and training—Study and training.
  I. Ashworth, Sara.   II. Title.
  GV361.M75   1994
  613.7'07—dc20   93-2564
                                                                      CIP

Printing: 3 4 5 6 7   Year: 7 8 9 0

To all the students who have studied and practiced the *Spectrum of Teaching Styles* in the past, and those who will study it in the future. Join us in the expanded pedagogy.

Preface

A PERSONAL NOTE: HINDSIGHT, INSIGHT, FORESIGHT

In January 1992, the *Journal of Physical Education Recreation and Dance* (JOPERD) devoted its feature to the Spectrum of Teaching Styles: A Silver Anniversary in Physical Education. Indeed, it was a celebration—a celebration for me and for many colleagues here and abroad who have studied the Spectrum, experimented with its application, and greatly contributed to its growth and dissemination.

I am often asked about the genesis of this idea, the motivation to construct a framework that offers a different paradigm for the theory and practice of teaching. I am taking the liberty—at the publication of the fourth edition—to talk about hindsight related to the genesis of the Spectrum.

I was teaching at Rutgers University at the time the idea of the Spectrum came about, presenting my students with ideas, notions, techniques, and experiences in teaching.

One day, a student approached me and said: "I want to talk to you about the things you are teaching us." "Certainly," I replied. "What is it?" After a slight pause, the student uttered: "I can't be you!" "Thank you," I responded—and began to walk away. "Furthermore," the student said "I don't want to be like you." I was quite stunned. I was upset. It took me some time to recover, but that statement kept gnawing at my mind. Is that what I was doing to my students? Did I impose my ideas on them? Did I demand replication of "me"? It was, indeed, a moment of revelation. I realized that my experiences, my idiosyncracies were mine—solely mine. I realized that they were only a part of the story of teaching. But, what is the other part? Or perhaps other parts? I kept asking myself: What is the body of knowledge about teaching that is beyond my idiosyncratic behavior? Is there such a possibility? Is it possible to identify a framework, a model, a theory that will embrace the options that exist in teaching, or a framework that might embrace future options?

It became clear to me that arbitrary teaching, scattered notions, fragmented ideas, and isolated techniques—successful as they might be—do not constitute a cohesive framework that can serve as a broad, integrated guide for teaching future teachers. The search for a universal structure of teaching had begun.

It has been a search for a "unified theory" that will show and explain the relationship between deliberate teaching behavior and learning behavior, a theory that will identify with consistency the structure of the options in teaching and learning behavior. The search was for a single, unifying principle that governs all teaching—hence, the identification of the axiom: Teaching behavior is a chain of decision making. This statement—simple and universal—led to the insight and discovery of the Anatomy of Any Style. The Anatomy, a universal structure that identifies the decision categories that are made in any teaching-learning episode, opened up the floodgates for the systematic identification and delineation of the individual teaching styles.

The Anatomy has served as guide for the construction of each style and the logical flow from style to style and, thus, the discovery of a *Spectrum of Teaching Styles.*

Each style delineates the specific role of the teacher and of the learner and the relationship between them. This deliberate relationship is the key to understanding the function of each style, the process of the style, and the goals it attains. Regardless of the preferred activity or the curricular design (i.e., gymnastics, fitness, games, outdoor adventure, aquatics, track and field, dance, leisure, etc.), the selection of styles is determined by what we seek to accomplish in a given episode, whether it be a physical performance objective, a social objective, an affective objective, a cognitive objective, or a combination.

Years of experimentation by many colleagues have taught us that the Spectrum is "teachable" and can be learned by anyone who desires to reach for an expanded pedagogy, a pedagogy of alternatives based on a nonversus reality in our schools, a pedagogy that is flexible and mobile, from Command to Discovery.

I would like to acknowledge and thank my colleagues in the United States and in many other countries who have persisted in their contribution to the ideas, theory, and practice of the Spectrum. In particular—Rudy and Sue Mueller, Michael Goldberger, Don Franks, Philip Gerney, Arnold Dert, Don Morris, Jim Stiehl, and Frank Doto of the United States; Wally Mellor of Canada; Risto Telama of Finland; Peter Hill of Scotland; Francisco Carrera Da Costa of Portugal; Lubos Dobry of the Czech Republic; Dircema Krug of Brazil; Carlos Vera Guardia of Venezuela; Marta Picado of Costa Rica; and Santos Berrocal of Spain. I would like to extend special thanks to my co-author, Sara Ashworth.

M.M.

Contents

1 An Overview[1]

THE CONCEPT OF TEACHING

This book is about teaching. It is about the relationships between teacher and learner—relationships that are both ubiquitous and uniquely personal. It is a book about the mastery of this pervasive human behavior.

When teaching takes place, a special human connection evolves, a connection of many dimensions that simultaneously affect the learner and the teacher. Both are subjected to a tacit agreement to share information, to deliver and receive accumulated knowledge, to replicate and reproduce portions of the past, to acquire and discover new information, and to construct and create pathways for the yet unknown. This connection inevitably invites feelings for one another—feelings of cooperation or discord, acceptance or rejection, anger or joy. It invites both the teacher and the learner to participate in a unique social context with special hierarchies, rules, and responsibilities. It inspires aesthetic sensations and seeks to expand the very boundaries of the self. It triggers the brain, stimulates the emotions and, at its best, uplifts the human spirit. The evolution of this connection is an inescapable process that is at the very core of human development. All cultures provide for it, all humans participate in it, and all educational processes and goals rely on it.

How, then, does a teacher translate these educational processes and goals— lofty as some may sound—into daily procedures, daily activities, daily behaviors? What are the practical issues and questions that face *every* teacher, every day? The following are some categorical questions that persist in the mind of every teacher—novice or veteran—when preparing to enter the classroom:

1. What do I want my students to accomplish? What are the objectives of the lesson?
2. What methodology will I choose in order to reach the objectives? What will be my teaching behavior?
3. What is the sequence of the lesson? How do I arrange the materials?
4. How do I organize the class for optional learning? In groups? In pairs? By providing individual activities?

---

[1]Adapted from Mosston, Muska and Ashworth, Sara. *The Spectrum of Teaching Styles.* Copyright © 1992 by Mosston and Ashworth.

5. How do I motivate my class? How do I offer appropriate feedback?
6. How do I create a climate conducive to thinking, social interaction, and good feelings?
7. How do I know that my students and I have reached the objectives? Have we reached all of them? Some?
8. How will I know that the *action* that took place during the lesson was congruent with my prelesson *intent*?

In the course of answering these questions—and, indeed, many others—the teacher must make *decisions* (choices). There are many different ways to answer these questions, and there are many ways of teaching. However, the many options and many idiosyncratic variations in teaching stem from several universal patterns that reflect the *decisions* that are made by the teacher and by the learner during any given episode. Teaching and learning episodes differ from one another because of the decision patterns that take place in the given episode. The decisions made by the teacher define his or her teaching behavior, and the decisions made by the learner define his or her learning behavior. The teaching-learning process is a continuous interaction between the behavior of the teacher and the behavior of the learner.

Teaching Behavior

↕

Learning Behavior

This book describes the options that are available in the interaction between teaching behavior and learning behavior. It offers some answers to the categorical questions just listed by:

1. Identifying the various decision patterns
2. Identifying the specific decisions within each pattern
3. Describing a framework that shows the relationships among the various patterns

The decision patterns are called *teaching styles,* and the framework that holds them together is called the *Spectrum of Teaching Styles.*[2] The Spectrum identifies the structure of *each style* by delineating the decisions that are made by the teacher and those made by the learner. It describes how to shift appropriate decisions from the teacher to the learner as both move from style to style. It describes the influence of *each* style on the learner in the cognitive, affective, social, physical, and moral domains.

---

[2]The phrase *Spectrum of Teaching Styles* was coined in the mid-1960s to designate this particular framework for teaching. The term *teaching style* was selected to differentiate the descriptions of specific teaching behavior from contemporary terms of that time. Terms like *methods, approaches, models,* and *strategies* were used and are still being used in many different ways by different writers. Recently, the term *style* has been used by others in reference to personal style. In this book, as in recent publications by the authors, the term *teaching style* refers to a structure that is independent of one's idiosyncrasies.

What is teaching? It is the ability to be aware of and utilize the possible connections with the learner—in all domains.

It is the ability to behave, in a *deliberate* manner, using a style that is most appropriate for reaching the objectives of a given episode. Skillful teaching is the ability to move deliberately from style to style as the objectives change from one teaching episode to another.

AN OVERVIEW OF THE SPECTRUM OF TEACHING STYLES

The fundamental proposition of the Spectrum is that *teaching is governed by a single unifying process: decision making*. Every act of deliberate teaching is a consequence of a prior decision. Decision making is the central or primary behavior that governs all the behaviors that follow: how we organize students; how we organize the subject matter; how we manage time, space, and equipment; how we interact with students; how we choose our verbal behavior; how we construct the social-affective climate in the classroom; and how we create and conduct the cognitive connections with the learners. All these are secondary behaviors, all emanate from prior decisions, and all are governed by those decisions.

Identifying primary decisions and understanding the possible combinations of decisions opens up a wide vista for looking at the teacher–learner relationships. Each option in the teacher–learner relationship has a particular structure of decisions that are made by the teacher and by the learner. The Spectrum of Teaching Styles defines the available options or styles, their decision structures, the specific roles of the teacher and the learner in each style, and the objectives best reached by each style.

Six Premises of the Spectrum

Figure 1-1 is a schematic overview of the structure of the Spectrum of Teaching Styles. This structure is based on six underlying premises, each of which is described as follows:

1. The Axiom. The entire structure of the Spectrum stems from the initial premise that teaching behavior is a chain of decision making. Every *deliberate* act of teaching is a result of a previously made decision.

2. The Anatomy of Any Style. The anatomy is composed of the conceivable categories of decisions that must be made in any teaching-learning transaction. These categories (which will be described in detail in Chapter 2) are grouped into three sets: the *preimpact set,* the *impact set,* and the *postimpact set.* The preimpact set includes all decisions that must be made prior to the teaching-learning transaction; the impact set includes decisions related to the actual teaching-learning transaction; and the postimpact set identifies decisions concerning evaluation of the teacher–learner transaction. The anatomy delineates *which* decisions must be made in each set.

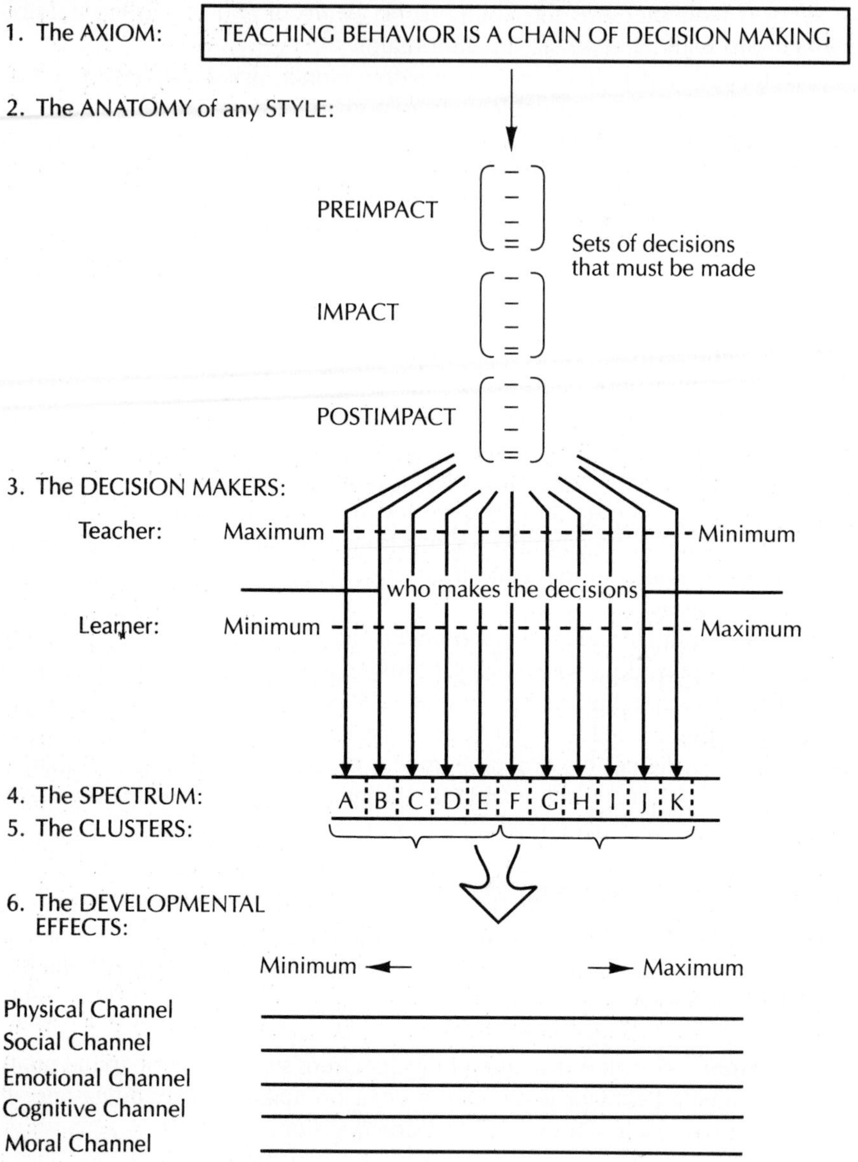

1. The AXIOM: | TEACHING BEHAVIOR IS A CHAIN OF DECISION MAKING |

2. The ANATOMY of any STYLE:

PREIMPACT

Sets of decisions
that must be made

IMPACT

POSTIMPACT

3. The DECISION MAKERS:

Teacher: Maximum ————————————— Minimum

———————— who makes the decisions ————————

Learner: Minimum ————————————— Maximum

4. The SPECTRUM: A : B : C : D : E : F : G : H : I : J : K
5. The CLUSTERS:

6. The DEVELOPMENTAL
   EFFECTS:

Minimum ◄————   ————► Maximum

Physical Channel   _____
Social Channel   _____
Emotional Channel   _____
Cognitive Channel   _____
Moral Channel   _____

FIGURE 1–1   The structure of the Spectrum

3. The Decision Makers. Both teacher and learner can make decisions in any of the categories delineated in the anatomy. When most or all of the decisions in a category are the responsibility of one decision maker (e.g., the teacher), that person's decision-making responsibility is at "maximum" and the other's is at "minimum."

4. The Spectrum. By establishing *who* makes *which* decisions, about *what* and *when,* it is possible to identify the structure of eleven *landmark styles* as well as possible alternative styles that lie between them on the Spectrum.

In the first style (style A), which has as its overriding objective precise replication, the teacher makes all the decisions; the learner responds by adhering to all the teacher's decisions. In the second style (style B), nine specific decisions are shifted from the teacher to the learner and, thus, a new set of objectives can be reached. In every subsequent style, specific decisions are systematically shifted from teacher to learner—thereby allowing new objectives to be reached—until the full Spectrum of Teaching Styles is delineated.

5. The Clusters. The structure of the Spectrum of Teaching Styles reflects two basic human capacities: the capacity for *reproduction* and the capacity for *production.* All human beings have, in varying degrees, the capacity to *reproduce* known knowledge, replicate models, and practice skills. All human beings have the capacity to *produce* a range of ideas and a range of things; all have the capacity to venture into the new and tap the yet unknown.

The cluster of styles A–E represents the teaching options that foster *reproduction* of past knowledge; the cluster of styles F–K represents options that invite *production* of new knowledge—that is, knowledge that is new to the learner, new to the teacher, and—at times—new to society. The line of demarcation between these two clusters is called the *discovery threshold* (see Figure 1-2). It identifies the boundaries of each cluster. Styles A–E are designed for the acquisition of basic skills, the replication of models and procedures, and the maintenance of cultural traditions. Activities in styles A–E engage the learner primarily in cognitive operations such as memory and recall, identification, and sorting—operations that deal with past and present knowledge. This knowledge includes factual data, events, dates, names, computation procedures, rules, and the use of tools. It also includes the knowledge that is required to perform in music, dance, and sports.

The cluster of styles F–G represents the teaching options that foster the *discovery* of single correct concepts. The cluster of styles H–K is designed for the development of *creativity* and *discovery* of alternatives and new concepts.

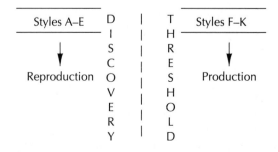

FIGURE 1–2 The clusters of style

Styles F–K engage the learner in problem solving, reasoning, and inventing; they invite the learner to go beyond the given data.

The clusters and each of the styles within them are integral parts of our humanity. Each style contributes to our development, and none seeks (or merits) supremacy over the others. For both teacher and student, the Spectrum serves as a guide for selecting the style appropriate for a particular purpose, and for developing deliberate mobility in moving from one style to another.

6. *The Developmental Effects.* Because *decisions* always influence what happens to people, each style affects the developing learner in unique ways. The Spectrum provides a framework for studying the influence of each style on the learner in the cognitive, affective, social, physical, and moral domains.

Reasons For a Spectrum[3]

There are at least four compelling reasons for developing and using the Spectrum of Teaching Styles: personal; the diversity of the student population; the multiple objectives of education; and the need for a coherent, comprehensive, and integrated framework for teaching.

Personal   Sooner or later, every one of us evolves a favorite way of teaching, a personal style that has been successful in our teaching behavior. Our personal style reflects a unique combination of who we are, how we do things, and what we believe about our relationship with students. One might call this unique amalgamation our "idiosyncratic style." With this personal style, each teacher travels through the vicissitudes of his or her career, succeeding in some lessons, failing in others, but generally staying within the parameters of the personal style.

This realization often evokes two points of view: one is that this is what teaching is about—"I teach my way." The other suggests that being anchored in one's idiosyncrasies (successful as they may be) limits the teacher's options and potential contributions to the students' learning. This point of view raises the question, Is there more to teaching beyond my own experience, my values, my successes?

The birth and development of the Spectrum was motivated by this question. If you have asked yourself the question, then you may add a few more: How many styles do I use in my teaching? Where am I on the Spectrum? Do I know the impact of each style on my students? Am I anchored in a particular style? Am I willing to expand?

Diversity of the Student Population   Students are unique individuals. They learn in different ways and have different needs and aspirations. They come

---

[3]From Mosston, Muska. "Tug-O-War, No More." *JOPERD,* January 1992.

from diverse cultural backgrounds. Our classes are the mirror of this diversity of humanity. In fact, this diversity is the hallmark of our schools. We know it and experience it. We acknowledge it and, at times, we honor it.

Where, then, is the point of entry in teaching diverse students? Assuming for a moment the predominance of personal styles, how can a teacher connect with and reach students who do not "fall" within his or her personal style? Is it possible that this condition invites exclusion of some students? In our teaching is it possible to create conditions that foster inclusion? Any teacher who wishes to reach more students must learn additional points of entry, and to do so, the teacher must learn additional options in teaching styles.

Multiple Objectives   School curricula are rich in goals and objectives, objectives that span a wide range of human abilities. Physical education encompasses objectives that range from uniformity and synchronization of performance in rowing or precise replication of models in gymnastics to individualized forms in freestyle swimming and in modern dance performance. Objectives range from aesthetics in springboard diving to appreciation of nature during hiking, from individual skills and tactics in fencing to group cooperation and strategy in team ball games.

This wide range of objectives requires a range of teaching styles, each with its own structure of teaching behavior that invites a particular learning behavior. When the two successfully interact, the specific objective (or set of objectives) can be reached. Teachers who are willing to expand their teaching repertoire beyond their personal styles and wish to reach more objectives and more students are ready to learn additional teaching styles, experiment with them, and then integrate them with their own.

Need for an Integrated Framework   Teaching styles in the Spectrum represent two basic human capacities: the capacity for reproduction of ideas, movements, previous models, and the capacity for production of new knowledge, the discovery of new movements, and the creation of new models. All humans—in varying degrees of depth and speed—possess these capacities. All subject matter areas emanate and develop from these capacities, and all activities reflect them.

Every activity, every sport, every subject contains aspects that can, and sometimes should, be taught by styles that invite reproduction (replication), and aspects that can and should be taught by styles that invite production (discovery and creativity). The fundamental issue in teaching is not which style is better or best, but rather which style is appropriate for reaching the objectives of a given episode. Every style has a place in the multiple realities of teaching and learning!

For example, in teaching basketball skills, the styles in the reproduction part of the Spectrum are most appropriate. If the episodes focus on developing the psychomotor skills of dribbling, passing, and shooting, the command and practice styles are most appropriate. Practice, repetition, and replication of the correct form of the skills in addition to frequent feedback from the teacher will improve and sharpen the performance. If the social skill of cooperating with a partner is added as an objective of learning, the reciprocal style is most appropriate. When self-learning is to be enhanced, episodes in the self-check style will be introduced. When a task can be designed by the principle of the "slanting rope" (a range of degree of difficulty within the same task), inclusion of all participants becomes the objective.

In physical education tasks, many of the objectives in the physical domain can be reached (by many students, but not all) by implementing the first two styles on the Spectrum (command and practice). However, when other domains and other educational objectives enter the picture, by definition, these two styles cannot accomplish them. The other styles on the reproduction side of the Spectrum need to be called upon. The same is true when teaching all activities (e.g., other ball games, gymnastics, swimming, skiing, scuba).

Every activity provides opportunities for discovering the unknown. There is always a possibility of designing a new strategy in ball games, discovering a new combination of movements in gymnastics, creating new dances. When these learning behaviors become the objectives of an episode, the teaching styles on the production side of the Spectrum must be recruited. The teacher who aspires to reach the objectives of reproduction and production will inevitably learn and experiment with the array of styles and will become mobile along the Spectrum—and, thus, will greatly enrich the experiences of the students. This enrichment includes a wide variety of cognitive involvements that are not possible when only the reproduction styles are activated. The discovery and the creative processes require special conditions that are only possible when the production styles are employed in episodes specifically designed for these objectives. Moreover, specific episodes must be designed for specific cognitive operation such as comparing, contrasting, extrapolating, problem solving, and designing.

The structure of the Spectrum is based on the existence of two clusters of styles: one contains the styles that can be used for reproduction (replication); the other contains the styles that invite production (discovery or creativity). Each style in each cluster has a specific purpose. Each style has an active part in the rich variety of teaching-learning objectives; hence, a nonversus view of classroom realities is created, in which no one style is better or best. Each style is best for the objectives it can reach. Teachers no longer have to struggle with the "tug-o-war" when selecting the teaching style best suited for their needs and the needs of the students.

Our role in using the Spectrum is to understand the structure of each style; learn how to incorporate it into our repertoire of teaching behaviors; experiment with it when teaching different students and different tasks; and refine its operation. It takes time to learn and internalize a new style. It is awkward in the beginning. When trying anything new, one must persist, try several times, identify the discrepancies, correct them, and try it again. There is presently enough evidence that attests to the value of each style, so the main challenge is to learn how to use each style for its own unique purpose.

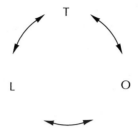

FIGURE 1–3   The T–L–O relationship

THE O–T–L–O RELATIONSHIPS

The previous section presented an overview of the Spectrum and offered the large picture of the entire structure. This section describes the elements that constitute any given episode.

The interaction between teacher and learner always reflects a particular teaching behavior, a particular learning behavior, and particular sets of objectives to be reached. The bond among teaching behavior (T), learning behavior (L), and objectives (O) is inextricable. The T–L–O always exists as a unit, conceived as the *pedagogical unit*. This relationship is diagrammed in Figure 1-3.

Each style is defined by the particular behavior of the teacher (the decisions made by the teacher), the particular behavior of the learner (the decisions made by the learner), and the objectives that this relationship reaches. Hence, each style has its own distinct T–L–O.

There are always two sets of objectives to be reached in any teacher–learner interaction: *subject matter objectives* and *behavior objectives* (Figure 1-4). The first set contains specific objectives that pertain to the particular content of the episode (e.g., citing the capitals of European countries, using the quadratic equation, translating a speech to another language, dribbling the basketball, writing a poem). The second set contains specific objectives of human behavior (e.g., cooperation, accuracy of performance, self-assessment, honesty, replication, creating).

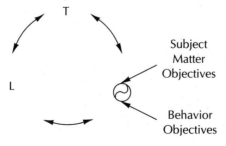

FIGURE 1–4   The two sets of objectives

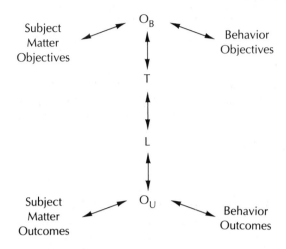

FIGURE 1–5   The pedagogical unit

Subject matter objectives and behavior objectives always exist in teaching. The T–L relationship determines the kind of objectives that can be reached in the subject matter and in the behavior. Conversely, the particular objectives (both in subject matter and in behavior) determine which teaching behaviors and learning behaviors are more likely to achieve them.

One more aspect needs to be considered in this context. *Objectives* are an a priori statement of what is to be achieved in a given episode; at the end of an episode, however, there are always *outcomes*—again, both the subject matter outcomes and behavior outcomes. The entire process of any episode therefore constitutes a flow and an interaction of objectives, teaching behavior, learning behavior, and outcomes. This flow is diagrammed in Figure 1-5.

The objectives of an episode (O_B) affect the teaching behavior (T), which in turn influences the interaction with the learning behavior (L). This interaction culminates with the particular outcomes (O_U), outcomes in subject matter and in behavior. Logically, then, in a successful teaching-learning episode, the outcomes are congruent with the objectives ($O_B \cong O_U$). Stated differently, in a successful episode the intent and the action are congruent:

$$\text{INTENT} \cong \text{ACTION}$$

2 The Anatomy of Any Teaching Style[1]

The single unifying principle (the Axiom) that governs the theoretical structure of the Spectrum of Teaching Styles states that *teaching is a chain of decision making*. Every act of teaching is a result of a previously made decision, and every decision affects the people involved. It affects their thinking, their feelings, and their behavior.

Understanding the decisions, who makes them, how they are made, and for what purpose, provides us with insights into the *structure* of the possible relationships between teacher and learner and the consequences of these relationships.

The Anatomy of Any Style (Table 2-1) is a model that delineates the categories of decisions that must be made (and are being made) in any teaching-learning relationship. The decisions are identified and organized in three sets:

1. *The preimpact set,* which includes all the decisions that must be made prior to the face-to-face transaction. These decisions define the *intent*.
2. *The impact set,* which includes decisions related to the actual transaction and the performance of the tasks. These decisions define the *action*.
3. *The postimpact set,* which includes decisions concerning the evaluation of the performance during the impact set and the *congruity* between the intent and the action.

The three sets together constitute the Anatomy of Any Style. Let us now delineate the specific decision categories in each set.

THE PREIMPACT SET

1. *Objective of the episode.* This decision identifies the episode's goal. It answers the teacher's questions: Where am I going? Where is the learner going? What are the specific expectations for this episode? (O–T–L)

---

[1]Adapted from Mosston, Muska and Ashworth, Sara. *The Spectrum of Teaching Styles.* Copyright © 1992 by Mosston and Ashworth.

TABLE 2–1 THE ANATOMY OF ANY STYLE

Decision Sets	Decision Categories

Preimpact
(Content:
Preparation)
	1. Objective of the episode
	2. Selection of a teaching style
	3. Anticipated learning style
	4. Whom to teach
	5. Subject matter
	6. When to teach (time):
	   a. Starting time d. Stopping time
	   b. Pace and rhythm e. Interval
	   c. Duration f. Termination
	7. Modes of communication
	8. Treatment of questions
	9. Organizational arrangements
	10. Where to teach (location)
	11. Posture
	12. Attire and appearance
	13. Parameters
	14. Class climate
	15. Evaluative procedures and materials
	16. Other

Impact (Content: Execution and Performance)	1. Implementing and adhering to the preimpact decisions (1–14) 2. Adjustment decisions 3. Other
Postimpact (Content: Evaluation)	1. Gathering information about the performance in the impact set (by observing, listening, touching, smelling, etc.) 2. Assessing the information against criteria (instrumentation, procedures, materials, norms, values, etc.) 3. Providing feedback to the learner.

4. Treatment of questions
5. Assessing the selected teaching style
6. Assessing the anticipated learning style
7. Adjustment decisions
8. Other

2. *Selection of a teaching style.* This decision identifies the teaching behavior that will evoke the learning behavior leading the learner to the objective(s) of the episode. (T–L–O)

3. *Anticipated learning style.* This decision can be approached in two ways:
   a. If the selection of a teaching style serves as an entry point for the conduct of the episode, then the learning style anticipated is a reflection of the teaching style in operation.
   b. If the needs of the learner at a given time serve as an entry point, these needs determine the selection of the teaching style. (L–T–O)

This dual approach means that, at times, the learner is invited to behave in correspondence to the teaching style. This approach is based on the "nonversus" foundation of the Spectrum—that is, no style is in competition with any other as the "best" or "most effective" style. Each style has its own assets and liabilities; the goal is for teachers and learners to be able to move from one style to another in accordance with the decided-upon objectives of each episode. The assumption here is that every learner should have the opportunity to participate in a variety of behaviors. In the context of the Spectrum, a learning style is conceived in terms of the learner's ability to make decisions. Therefore, in a given episode, when the teacher is in style X, the learner is also in style X.

At other times, the learning style of the learner invites the teacher to select the teaching style that will correspond to "where the learner is." The interplay between these two approaches, each used for the purpose of an entry point to an episode, represents the most crucial decision determining the success of an episode. (For a detailed discussion of this issue, see "Selecting a Style" in Chapter 16.)

4. *Whom to teach.* A decision must be made about the participants in a given episode. In any given class a teacher can address the entire class, part of it, or individuals. (This decision is separate from the institutional decision concerning who shall attend school, how many will enroll in a given class, etc.)

5. *Subject matter.* This category involves decisions about what to teach and what not to teach. It involves decisions about:
   a. *Type* of subject matter. This decision takes into account the reasons—philosophical or practical—for the use of a given subject matter or task. It answers the questions: Is this subject matter appropriate for the learners? Relevant? Congruent with the objective?
   b. *Quantity* of task(s). There is no human activity devoid of quantity; therefore, a quantity decision must be made that answers the questions: How much? How many?
   c. *Quality* of performance. This decision answers the question: How well? What is expected of the performance in the given task? (See Chapter 9 for a detailed discussion of quantity and quality of subject matter.)
   d. *Order* of performance. This decision answers the question: In what order—sequential or random—will tasks or parts of tasks be performed?

6. *When to teach.* Time decisions must be made about:
   a. Starting time of each specific task.
   b. Pace and rhythm of the activity—the speed of performing the task.
   c. Duration—the length of time per task.
   d. Stopping time per task.
   e. Interval—the time between any two tasks, parts of a task, or episodes (see Figure 2-1).
   f. Termination of the entire episode or the lesson.

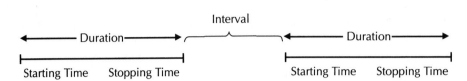

FIGURE 2–1   The interval decision

7. *Modes of communication.* These decisions concern the modes of communication that will be used in the teaching episode.

8. *Treatment of questions.* In varying situations, people ask different kinds of questions, and questions can be dealt with in multiple ways. Decisions must therefore be made about how to treat these questions.

9. *Organizational arrangements.* These are the decisions about various logistical needs and classroom management.

10. *Where to teach.* This decision identifies the exact spot where the task will be done.

11. *Posture.* This decision refers to the relationship among the positions of body parts during the performance of the task.

12. *Attire and appearance.* A decision must be made about clothing, arrangement of hair, makeup, wearing glasses for safety, and so on.

13. *Parameters.* These decisions refer to limits, particularly in conjunction with the categories of location, time, posture, and attire and appearance.[2]

14. *Class climate.* Class climate refers to the affective and social conditions that evolve in a classroom. These conditions result from the sum total of the decisions in categories 1–13.

15. *Evaluation procedures and materials.* Decisions must be made in reference to evaluation that will take place in the postimpact set. What kind of evaluation? What evaluation materials and criteria will be used? How do they relate to the objectives? What is the quality of the performance?

16. *Other.* The Anatomy is an open-ended structure. If another exclusive category is identified, it can be included here.

THE IMPACT SET

1. *Implementing and adhering to the preimpact decisions.* This category includes decisions about how to act on the decisions in categories 1–14.

---

[2]We are fully aware that a *parameter* is "a constant whose value may vary." However, in this context we'll use the more common meaning of "limits." For discussion on the uses of this word, see William Safire's column "On Language" in *The New York Times Sunday Magazine,* May 13, 1979.

2. *Adjustment decisions.* Since planning cannot always be perfect—nor can the performance be perfect at all times—mishaps do occur. When that happens adjustment decisions must be made. There are two options:
   a. Identify the decision that caused the problem, correct it, and continue the teaching episode.
   b. If the problem is severe, terminate the episode and for the time being move on to another activity.
3. *Other.* The model is open-ended.

THE POSTIMPACT SET

The postimpact set includes decisions that deal with evaluating the performance of the tasks done during the impact set and selecting the appropriate feedback offered to the learner. This set also includes decisions about evaluating the congruence between the preimpact and the impact sets (intent ≅ action). This evaluation determines whether adjustments are needed in the following episode. These decisions are made in the following sequence, a sequence that is intrinsic to any evaluative procedure.

1. *Gathering information about the performance in the impact set.* This can be done by observing, listening, touching, smelling, and so on.
2. *Assessing the information against criteria.* Decisions are made in the course of comparing and contrasting the performance against the criteria, the standard, or the model.
3. *Providing feedback to the learner.* Decisions must be made about how to provide feedback, which is the information or judgment given to the learner about the performance of the task, and about the role of the learner in making his or her decisions. Feedback can be either immediate or delayed, and it can be offered by gesture, symbols, or verbal behavior. Regardless of the mode of communication, *all* feedback is presented in one of four forms:
   a. *Value statements.* This form of feedback always includes a word (or symbol) that projects a value or a feeling about the performance. For example: "You wrote a beautiful poem." "The assignment is poorly done." "The experiment was well done."
   b. *Corrective statements.* This form of feedback is used whenever an error is evident and the learner's response is incorrect. Corrective feedback includes one or both of the following:
      i. A statement that identifies the error.
      ii. A statement about how to correct it. For example: "The second and fifth words in this column were spelled incorrectly." "Five times 7 is not 36, it is 35."
   c. *Neutral statements.* This form of feedback is descriptive and factual. It does not correct or judge the performance; it acknowledges what the learner has done. For example: "I see that you have completed the assignment." "You have followed the criteria for writing the. . . ."

    d. *Ambiguous statements.* Phrases like "not bad," "pretty good," or "do it again" can be used for feedback. These words do not convey to the learner precise information about the performance—too much is left to guessing. This kind of feedback is ambiguous.

In addition to being aware of these four forms of feedback and their meanings, one must be aware of the connotation of the tone, as well as the cultural inclination and the idiosyncrasies of the persons giving and receiving the feedback. (For a detailed analysis of the structure of feedback and its impact on teaching and learning behaviors, see Chapter 10.)

4. *Treatment of questions.* Decisions about how to treat questions are made here.

5. *Assessing the selected teaching style.* Decisions are made about the effectiveness of the teaching style used in the completed episode and its impact on the learner.

6. *Assessing the anticipated learning style.* In connection with the decisions made in the previous category (5), a decision is made as to whether the learner has reached the objectives of the episode. Together, categories 5 and 6 provide the information concerning the congruity between intent and action.

7. *Adjustments.* Based on the assessments of the episode, decisions are made about any adjustments needed for subsequent episodes.

8. *Other.* The model is open-ended.

To reiterate, these three sets of decisions—the preimpact, impact, and postimpact sets—comprise the Anatomy of Any Style. These are the decisions that are always made in any teaching-learning relationship and that govern the operation of any teaching. At times these decisions are made deliberately; at other times they seem to represent habits; at still other times some of the decisions are omitted or are made by default. Regardless of the condition, the primary behavior in teaching is the act of making decisions in the sequential three sets of the Anatomy. The Anatomy of Any Style, therefore, is a universal model that is at the foundation of all teaching. It describes *what* decisions must be made in any teaching model, strategy, or educational game.

Several fundamental questions arise now: From this Anatomy how do we identify a specific style? How many styles are there? How do we differentiate one style from the other? And how are the styles related to one another to form a comprehensive framework for all teaching?

3 | The Command Style (Style A)

THE OBJECTIVES OF THIS STYLE

When considering the

as the fundamental unit of relationships, the particular roles of the teacher and the learner in the command style produce a particular set of outcomes (the teacher and the learner reach a particular set of objectives). When a teacher makes all the decisions in the anatomy and the learner follows these decisions, the following objectives are reached:

1. Immediate response to a stimulus
2. Uniformity
3. Conformity
4. Synchronized performance
5. Adherence to a predetermined model
6. Replication of a model
7. Precision and accuracy of the response
8. Perpetuation of cultural traditions via ceremonies, customs, costumes, and rituals
9. Maintenance of aesthetic standards
10. Enhancement of *esprit de corps* (common spirit of the group)
11. Efficiency in time use
12. Safety
13. Others?

If any of these are your objectives, style A—the command style—will reach them. Your action and intent will be congruent. There are many examples of this kind of relationship: a symphonic orchestra, a ballet performance, folk dance, synchronized swimming, crew (sculling), compulsory gymnastics, marching bands, aerobics, drill teams, cheerleaders, choral singing, and many more.

A	
Preimpact	(T)
Impact	(T)
Postimpact	(T)

FIGURE 3-1 The anatomy of the command style (T indicates the role of the teacher in the given set. In the command style, the teacher makes all the decisions in each of the three sets.)

THE ANATOMY OF THIS STYLE

In every teaching-learning transaction there are two decision makers—the teacher and the learner. The *command style,* the first style on the Spectrum, is characterized by the teacher making all the decisions in the anatomy of the style. The role of the teacher is to make all the decisions in the preimpact, impact, and postimpact sets. The role of the learner is to perform, to follow.

The essence of the command style is the direct and immediate relationship between the teacher's stimulus and the learner's response. The stimulus (the *command signal*) by the teacher precedes every movement of the learner, who performs according to the model presented by the teacher. Hence, all the decisions about location, posture, starting time, pace and rhythm, stopping time, duration, and interval are made by the teacher.

Schematically, the beginning of the Spectrum appears in Figure 3-1.

IMPLEMENTATION OF THE COMMAND STYLE

The focal questions for the teacher who wishes to implement an episode (or a series of episodes) in the command style are: What is the "picture" of this kind of a relationship between a teacher and students? How does one translate the theoretical model (intent) into actual teaching and learning behaviors (actions)? How does the teacher determine if the objectives of this style are reached? Let us start with a general description of an episode and then identify the steps needed for implementing it.

DESCRIPTION OF AN EPISODE

An episode in the command style must reflect the essence of this relationship: The teacher makes all the decisions and the learner responds to each decision. In this episode, correspondence between the learner's behavior and the teaching behavior is continuous for every performed movement; the teacher gives the command signal for each movement and the learner performs accordingly. Examples of this relationship can be observed in classes of karate, ballet, aerobics, and folk dances. Sometimes the command signal and the rhythm-support techniques are relegated to other people or to instruments such as the beat of the music in aerobics, the drums in some folk dances, the coxswain in rowing, the student leading a class in warmup exercises, and so on. The essence of the relationship is the same—one person (or surrogate) is making all the decisions for others. When this relationship exists, the objectives for the command style are reached.

A teacher who wishes to use this style needs to be fully aware of the decision structure (the anatomy of this style), the sequence of the decisions, the possible relationships between command signals and expected responses, the appropriateness of the task, and the present ability of the learners (the ability to perform the movements with reasonable accuracy and adhere to the demonstrated model).

HOW TO DO IT

The following steps describe the use of the anatomy of the command style as guidelines for implementation. This process involves the preimpact, impact, and postimpact decisions.

The Preimpact Set

The purpose of the preimpact set of decisions is to plan the interaction between teacher and learner. The teacher's role is to make decisions about the categories identified in Figure 3-2. This is the statement of intent or the lesson plan.

Let us examine the different headings in Figure 3-2.

1. *Episode Number.* An episode is a unit of time during which the teacher and learner are in the same style, heading toward the same objective.
2. *Subject Matter.* (i.e., swimming, soccer, basketball, dance, gymnastics, etc.)
3. *The Overall Objectives of the Lesson.* State in broad terms the overall lesson objectives. What is the expected accomplishment by the end of the lesson?

A lesson (see Figure 3-3) is composed of one or more episodes (see Figure 3-4), each one planned in terms of the style (the T–L–O), the activity, and the supporting logistical arrangements. In most situations a lesson is composed of more than one episode, and the planning that takes place in the preimpact is specific for each episode.

4. *Specific Tasks.* Identify and describe the specific tasks that the learners will engage in to accomplish the overall objective of the episode.
5. *Objectives.* The objective of an episode is, in a sense, the reason for selecting the particular task. These objectives, or reasons, can be in terms of the subject matter (what will be accomplished in the particular sport or the particular dance) and in terms of the learner's role in engaging and developing various qualities such as socialization, cooperation, competi-

FIGURE 3–2 A lesson plan

Subject matter _____

The overall objectives of the lesson _____

_____

| Episode No. | SUBJECT MATTER | OBJECTIVES | | LOGISTICS | | |
	Specific Tasks	S.M. and/or Role	Style	Organization of Learners; Equipment; Task Sheet; etc.	Time	Comments
1						
2						
3						
4						
•						
•						
•						

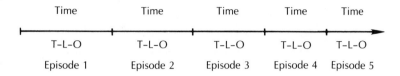

FIGURE 3–3   A lesson

tion, honesty, and so on. In the lesson plan, the role is stated when such objectives are in the episode's focus. Otherwise, the role is implicit in the decision and the identification of the style.

6. *Style.* Identify the style that will accomplish the objectives.
7. *Logistics.* To reach the objectives of the selected activity in the selected style, several decisions must be made about the logistics of the episode. These decisions concern three major aspects.
   a. *The organization of the learners.* In the gymnasium, in the swimming pool, or in the playing fields, there are many options for organizing learners. They can be organized in a variety of random ways, or they can be organized in specific geometric patterns (i.e., lines, circles, squads, etc.). The guiding principle is: Organize learners so that they may efficiently participate in the activity and interact with the teacher.
   b. *The organization of equipment.* Use the same principle as in (a) adding the consideration of maximum participation by each learner. It cannot be emphasized enough that equipment must be organized to facilitate maximum learning for each student if the objective(s) of the episodes are to be reached.
   c. *The task sheet.* A decision must be made as to whether to use a task sheet, which describes and illustrates the specifics of the task(s). A task sheet can be either written or printed (duplicated for each student), a poster, a transparency projected on the wall, and so on. Again, the task sheet must accommodate the objective(s) of the episode.
8. *Time.* Decide a reasonable length for the episode so that all (or most) learners can reach the objectives. This time decision depends on knowing the task, the capability of the learners, and the objective(s).
9. *Comments.* This column is used for statements, questions or suggestions made after the lesson is done. These can include statements about what went well, what needs adjustment for next time, or questions that need to be resolved.

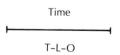

FIGURE 3–4   An episode

The Impact Set

This is the doing time. The purpose of the impact set of decisions is to engage the learners in active participation and to follow through with the preimpact decisions. It is putting the intent into action. In the command style (as in all other styles), it is imperative that the learners know and understand the expectations of the episode. They must know the expectations of the task-performance and of the teacher–learner relationship (roles of the teacher and the learner). When expectations are known, both teacher and learner can be held accountable for their behaviors. Therefore, the teacher must make a sequence of decisions to set the scene for an episode in the command style.

Setting the scene includes these components:

a. Explanation of the roles (the teacher's and the learner's)
b. Delivery of the subject matter
c. Explanation of the logistical procedures

These three components are constants in any episode, and they appear in this order. Explaining the roles sets expectations for the behaviors of the teacher and the learners; delivery of the subject matter establishes what is to be done; and the logistical procedures define the parameters of the task environment.

In the initial stages (the first two or three episodes in this style), the teacher presents the following:

Explanation of the Roles

1. The teacher explains to the students that when a teacher and student are in a face-to-face situation, a variety of decisions can be made by the teacher or the learner.
2. These decisions can be distributed between the teacher and the learners in a variety of ways depending on the relationship's purpose at the particular time and the particular episode.
3. One of these particular arrangements is a relationship where the teacher's role is to make all the decisions and the learner's role is to follow, perform, and respond to each decision—each command (stimulus).
4. The purpose of such a relationship (called *style A* or the *command style*) is to accommodate an immediate response so that certain tasks can be learned accurately and quickly.
5. A series of episodes in this style facilitates the accomplishment of objectives such as replication of a model, precision and accuracy of performance, and synchronized performance. (See the list of objectives cited earlier in this chapter.)

Experience with the Spectrum styles indicates that most students can internalize the structure and operation of the styles within two or three frequent episodes when the introduction to the styles covers points 1 through 5. Therefore, to set the expectations in subsequent episodes, the teacher announces the name of the style and moves on to the delivery of the subject matter.

Delivery of the Subject Matter

1. The teacher demonstrates the whole task, its parts, and its terminology (the order here may vary according to purpose), and thus establishes the model for the performance.
2. The demonstration may be relegated to a film, videotape, pictures, or to a student who can perform the task according to the model.
3. For the value of the demonstration, see Chapter 8.
4. The teacher explains the details necessary for understanding the task.
5. Varying time ratios of demonstration and explanation may be necessary for different tasks.

Explanation of the Logistical Procedures

1. The teacher establishes the preparatory and command signals for the episode. These may change during the episode to accommodate different aspects of the subject matter.
2. Other procedures may be identified depending on the subject matter.

At this point, the teacher and the learners are ready to begin the activity, which is the essence of the impact set. The learners respond according to the command signals and the rhythm support procedures conducted by the teacher.

The Postimpact Set

The postimpact set of decisions offers feedback to the learner about the performance of the task and about the learner's role in following the teacher's decisions. (See the section on feedback forms in Chapter 2).

The command style experience is one of action. The repeated movement in performing each task and replicating the model brings about the contribution of this style to physical development. Passivity is incongruent with this style. In any given episode, a maximum amount of time is used by the learners in active participation. A minimum amount of time is used by the teacher for demonstration and explanation. Time-on-task in this style is very high. Schematically, the time distribution looks like this:

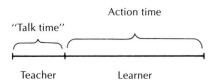

THE IMPLICATIONS OF THIS STYLE

Each style on the Spectrum affects the learner in different ways, as well as affecting the teaching behavior and the subject matter selection and design.

Each style suggests a set of implications. Whenever the command style is used in an episode, it implies that

1. The subject matter is fixed. It represents a single standard.
2. The subject matter is best learned by immediate recall and through repeated performance.
3. The subject matter can be divided into single parts that can be replicated by a stimulus–response procedure and can be learned in a short period of time.
4. The greater the speed of recall, the more proficient the learner will be in moving on to other aspects of the subject matter.
5. Individual differences are not invited; instead, replication of the selected subject matter is sought.
6. Through frequent replication, the group can uniformly perform the task.

STYLE-SPECIFIC COMMENTS

Since each style represents a different teacher–learner relationship, a different reality emerges with the use of a given style. Each style has its own "do's" and "don'ts," its own occurrences, and its own potential difficulties. It is important to be alert to these reality aspects—it helps develop insights into the style's essence and contributions as well as preventing mishaps that might reduce the possibility of reaching the objectives. The following are some style-specific comments regarding episodes in the command style.

1. The teacher must be aware of the sensitive nature of the command style. This relationship of one person making all the decisions for others must be used with full consideration of the emotional state of the learner, the learner's capacity to respond, and the nature and purpose of the task. Young children, for example, enjoy many style A activities such as Simon Says and Follow the Leader. All represent *imitating behaviors*. Emulating, repeating, copying, and responding to directions seem to be necessary ingredients of the early years. Learning to do a task is a part of growing and of becoming socialized into a group. Responding to directions is an important behavior for the young. The objectives of such episodes can be limited to scope, yet satisfying. As the learners get older, more of the objectives of this style must be realized in each episode. Responding and emulating are not enough—the learner must feel the accomplishment and accept this relationship beyond just the act of responding.

    Older learners participate in style A activities for two primary reasons: Personal development and/or participation in a subculture's activities or rituals. An example of such an experience is aerobic sessions, which illustrate all the components and objectives of style A—high time-on-task, repetition, high degree of uniformity, and precision. It is reasonable to assume that the primary purpose and motivation for participating in aerobics are not these components, but the sense of development (fitness, being in shape, losing weight). A style A experience will best accomplish this goal. An equally powerful reason for participating in aerobics is the sense of participating in a socially accepted environment and manner. Another example of a style A experience is karate, primarily the training time. Many of the participants in these activities accept not only the style A behaviors, but the manners and rituals that may not have been a part of their culture or personal conduct. A third type of experience includes high-risk sports. Acquiring some of the necessary skills requires style A relationships and discipline. When safety is paramount, style A is mandatory during training and often during the experience itself. Some of these activities are parachuting, mountaineering, and scuba diving. In such activities, style A episodes focus on the particular physical responses and the appropriate and precise use of equipment and accessories. In addition, deliberate and controlled episodes are designed to teach management of stress and panic. Only when these aspects are learned and integrated (mostly by style A experiences) can participants move on to the real experience of participating and enjoying the sport.

A fourth type of activity representing style A is cultural/aesthetic experiences. The command style is often used to teach various dance techniques. Examples can be found in ballet, certain aspects of modern dance, and in folk dance. In these diverse forms of dance, precise performance and adherence to a predetermined model are important. The dance forms themselves project aesthetic values and the continuity of cultural standards.

The fifth type represents some of the competitive experiences in sports. Synchronized swimming may represent the epitome of style A because of its high-level precision, synchronization, and projection of a particular set of aesthetic values. The compulsory part of competitive gymnastics is another example, and rowing cannot be successful without maximum synchronization and precision.

It is fascinating to realize that such diverse activities of structure and purpose share the same teaching-learning process or teaching style—the command style.

2. The teacher must be aware that style A is one of the options in human interaction; to gain the maximum benefits of this style, an integration of several dimensions must occur when style A is in process. Some of these dimensions are: (1) selection of the subject matter, (2) time-on-task, (3) logistical accommodations, (4) appropriate feedback, and (5) an appropriate affective relationship with the learner. Style A must not be perceived as the "time-efficient style," or the "strict" style. Style A is a combination of all the dimensions just cited. The skilled teacher who also cares for the learners can elevate this relationship to a level of mutual respect and emotional comfort.

3. The teacher must be aware of the emotional context of this style. There are at least two possibilities that can develop in this style. One is the abuse of power by the teacher, who may use this style for control and reprimand

purposes. (When we reprimand someone, we usually take away deci-sions.) When this kind of teaching behavior prevails, negative feelings often result and the learner will reject the teaching style, the teacher, and the subject matter. The second possibility is that the teacher will use style A with affection, charm, and care. Style A does not mean "being mean"; this style can be used to motivate learners, elevate their self-concept, and develop *esprit de corps*.

COMMON PITFALLS TO AVOID

When an episode in the command style is not reaching its objectives, it may be because of one or more of the following reasons:

1. The class is not synchronized in the performance of the movements. The teacher needs to examine the selected pace and rhythm for the episode.
2. The teacher is giving annoying command signals. Sometimes continuous repetition of a signal can cause discomfort. The teacher should consider alternative signals.
3. Excessive repetition of the same task may cause boredom, fatigue, or both.
4. Stopping the action of the entire class because one or two learners are having difficulty stops the flow of the activity and diverts the class's atten-tion to the inadequacies of the individuals.
5. The teacher stays only in one spot. In this style, the teacher does not have to stay in one fixed position when conducting the episode. Moving about (using rhythm-support techniques other than counting) provides the teacher an opportunity for individual and private feedback without stop-ping the action.

There may be other pitfalls, but when something goes awry it can always be traced to a particular decision. The role of the teacher is to examine that decision and make the proper adjustment.

THE DEVELOPMENTAL CHANNELS

Perhaps the ultimate question in education and teaching is: What really hap-pens to people when they participate in one kind of an experience or another? In a broad sense, this question is often answered by various philosophical trea-ties. The specific connection between an educational experience and its out-come is being studied by a multitude of research activities. The questions of *why* and *what for* are paramount in our minds. With the development of the Spectrum of Teaching Styles, these questions are vital in understanding the contributions and boundaries of each style. Because the Spectrum delineates specific and differentiated styles, it is worthwhile to hypothesize, to inquire, and to verify the possible relationships between the experiences in a given style and the place of the learner on various developmental channels.

This section offers a schema for identifying these relationships. What happens, then, to a person along a particular channel when he or she is experiencing a given style? The schema examines four channels: the physical channel, the social channel, the emotional channel, and the cognitive channel.

Each individual can move along these channels from minimum to maximum development. An individual can also be placed at a given point on a channel. This point represents only a relative position between minimum and maximum.

In order to make a reasonable assumption about the relationship between a style and the developmental channels, certain criteria must be used. These criteria can be the degree of independence, the degree of dependence, creativity, group participation, and perhaps others. When a different criterion is used, the individual's placement on the channels will also be different.

Let us examine the criterion of independence. How independent is an individual in the command style to make decisions about each of the developmental channels? Since the role of the learner is to follow, the learner's position in the physical channel is toward minimum independence. The learner does not make decisions about physical development, the teacher does (see Figure 3-5). Social development requires social interaction and exchange. In the command style, the learner has very few opportunities for interaction because all the decisions are made by the teacher. The placement on the social developmental channel, then, is toward minimum. The emotional channel refers to levels of self-comfort; in the context of physical education, it involves the physical concept of the learner and the ability for self-acceptance in pursuit of phys-

	A		
		Independence	
	Minimum ⟵		⟶ Maximum
Physical Channel	—x———————————		
Social Channel	—x———————————		
Emotional Channel	—x———————————		
Cognitive Channel	—x———————————		

FIGURE 3–5 The command style, independence, and the developmental channels*

*This issue of the relationship between the Spectrum of Teaching Styles and the position of learners on the developmental channels is, indeed, a central one in educational concerns. If the differences in teaching behavior matter, then their impact should show when we observe learning behavior.

There are several research studies in physical education that partially substantiate the theoretical assumption presented here. Any future study, however, should take into account two variables—length of time and selection of task. Any behavior study must last long enough for the new behavior to manifest itself, and any task selected for the research, involving physical activity, *must* possess characteristics that the given style seeks to develop. It is quite futile, for example, to use the standing long jump as an activity for studying the placement of the learner on the cognitive channel.

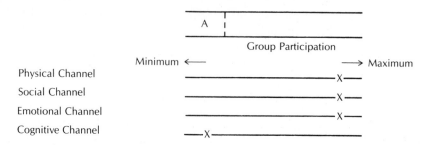

FIGURE 3–6 The command style, group participation, and the developmental channels

ical tasks. The position on this channel may be split. Some individuals prefer being told what to do; they feel very comfortable with it. Their placement is toward maximum on this channel. Others cannot accept decisions made for them by others and are placed toward minimum on this channel.

In the command style, the learner is not involved in a variety of cognitive operations. The main cognitive operation called for is memory. If we were to consider the operation of memory alone, the placement on the cognitive channel would be toward maximum. Cognitive development, however, means participation in many operations such as comparing, contrasting, categorizing, problem solving, hypothesizing, and inventing. The command style does not invite the learner to participate in these operations; therefore, the placement on the cognitive channel is toward minimum.

When we examine this relationship using the criterion of group participation (see Figure 3-6), we can ask: What happens to the individual on each channel when he or she participates in a group activity (sport) representing style A experiences?

The goal of any group sport is to reach the highest and best possible performance. Each individual participant must contribute his or her best. When this occurs, the individual's position on the physical development channel is toward maximum.

The social demands of such participation are high. The individual must integrate his or her own efforts with those of others and must fully cooperate with others, placing the individual toward the maximum on the social channel. (Participating in rowing with two or more rowers is a prime example of this condition. It is an activity that is intrinsically style A, requiring the utmost in social cooperation.)

The high social cooperation demands require a particular emotional pitch. No matter what the consequences of a sporting episode (win or lose), the participating individual must exhibit a certain level of emotional strength and stability to maintain membership in the group. This places the individual toward maximum on the emotional developmental channel. When an individual fails or has a breakdown (minimum on the channel), attempts are made to return to the stable pitch. If these attempts fail, the individual can no longer participate with the group.

Placement of the individual on the cognitive channel depends on the sport and may fluctuate. In sports representing style A behavior, the movements often are repetitive and require relatively little cognitive engagement other than memory and recall, and therefore the placement here is toward minimum.

It is interesting to realize that by using different criteria, a different picture of relationships emerges. Connecting the placement spots on the channels with a line provides a *learner's profile* in the style, in the given criterion. There are a variety of ways of looking at this style and its impact on learners—you are invited to select other criteria for analyzing.

When planning episodes for the day, the week, and the unit, scrutinize the objectives you wish to reach. Identify those portions of the activity that require

FIGURE 3–7   Style A classroom chart

THE COMMAND STYLE

The purpose of this style is to learn to do the task(s) accurately and within a short period of time, following all decisions by the teacher.

ROLE OF TEACHER

- To make subject matter decisions

- To make all impact decisions:

  Subject matter

  Order of task

  Starting time

  Pace and rhythm

  Stopping time

  Interval

  Attire and appearance

  Initiating questions for clarification

- To provide feedback to learner about role and subject matter

ROLE OF LEARNER

- To follow and perform the task when and as described

high-precision performance. The command style will bring the two together—the activity and the objective. Select the parts of the activity that require the relationship of stimulus and immediate response and use style A for efficient teaching and learning, not as a symbol of authority and reprimand.

Using the command style in a spirited manner can create individual and group motivation to participate as well as a sense of achievement. Now that we know the structure, its procedures, and some of the accomplishments of the command style (see Figure 3-7), let's look at the next style.

4 The Practice Style (Style B)

THE OBJECTIVES OF THIS STYLE

The shift of certain decisions from the teacher to the learner (see the next section about the anatomy of the style) creates new relationships between the teacher and the learner, between the learner and the tasks, and among the learners themselves.

The practice style establishes a new reality, offers new conditions for learning, and reaches a different set of objectives. One group of objectives is more closely related to the performance of the tasks, and another group is more closely related to the expansion of the person in his or her role in the style.

Subject Matter

1. To practice the assigned task(s) as demonstrated and/or explained
2. To approximate, as much as physically possible, the performance of the assigned task(s)
3. To realize by experience that proficient performance is related to task repetition
4. To realize by experience that task performance is related to time
5. To realize by experience that proficient performance is related to knowledge of results
6. To realize by experience that this knowledge is obtained from various forms of feedback offered by the teacher

Role

1. To make the nine decisions that are shifted to the learner in the impact set
2. To be accountable for the consequences of the nine decisions
3. To realize by experience that decision making accommodates learning the task
4. To respect the role of other learners and their decisions in the nine categories
5. To experience the beginning of individualization by working individually and privately for a period of time

6. To be able to accept one's performance of a task without constant comparison to others (i.e., accepting the condition for individual decisions in the nine categories)
7. To experience a new, one-to-one relationship with the teacher that includes waiting for private individual feedback
8. To experience episodes in style B that may either follow or precede episodes in style A. To learn the shift of decisions and the transition between these two styles.

THE ANATOMY OF THIS STYLE

In order for us to identify and design the second style on the Spectrum, a change must take place by shifting specific decisions from the teacher to the learner. This shift occurs in the following nine categories of the impact set.

1. Posture
2. Location
3. Order of tasks
4. Starting time per task
5. Pace and rhythm
6. Stopping time per task
7. Interval
8. Attire and appearance
9. Initiating questions for clarification

The decisions in the preimpact and postimpact sets remain as before—the teacher makes those decisions. (See Figure 4-1).

In the anatomy of this style, the teacher's role is to make all the decisions in the preimpact and postimpact sets. In the impact set, the teacher shifts the nine decisions to the learner. The learner's role in this style is to perform the task(s) presented by the teacher and to make the nine decisions in the impact set. This shift of the nine decisions is the beginning of the individualizing process, inviting different behaviors from both teacher and learner. The teacher must learn not to give commands for every movement, task, or activity; the learner has the opportunity to learn how to make these nine decisions within the parameters determined by the teacher.

In the postimpact set of decisions, the teacher observes the performance and offers individual and private feedback to each learner.

	A	B
Preimpact	(T)	(T)
Impact	(T) →	(L)
Postimpact	(T)	(T)

FIGURE 4–1   The anatomy of the practice style

IMPLEMENTATION OF THE PRACTICE STYLE

Style B—*the practice style*—is the first style on the Spectrum that involves the learner in making some decisions during the episode. A new reality evolves in style B episodes where learners actually practice not only the task, but the deliberate process of making decisions in the nine categories. In this style, the focus of the episode changes. A different relationship evolves between the teacher and the learner. The teacher learns to trust the learner to make appropriate decisions while doing the task, and the learner learns deliberate and independent decision making in conjunction with performing the task.

DESCRIPTION OF AN EPISODE

An episode in style B must reflect the essence of this new teacher–learner relationship where the teacher introduces the style (initially, describing to the class the shift of the nine decisions), presents the task(s), accommodates the logistics, and provides feedback to all learners. The role of the learner is to listen to the expectations for the episode, receive the task description, make the nine decisions while performing the task(s), and receive the feedback offered by the teacher.

One of the major differences between the realities of the command style and the practice style is the use of time. As we have seen in the command style, each learner's response is directly connected to the teacher's command signal. In the practice style, a unit of time is available to the learner for practicing the task(s) after deciding when to start each task, the pace and rhythm of performing each task, and so on. This time dimension is essential both for learning the task and for making the decisions. In fact, when a teacher says to learners, "Go practice a given task," the learners will be making the nine decisions. While the learners practice the task(s), the teacher has time to move around, observe individual performances, and offer private feedback to the learners. Episodes in style B are possible in all subject matter areas.

The essence of this style, then, is a particular cycle of relationships between the teacher and the learner. The teacher presents the task, the learner performs it for a period of time, and the teacher observes the performance and offers feedback.

HOW TO DO IT

The following steps describe the use of the anatomy of the practice style as the guidelines for implementation. This process involves making the decisions in the preimpact, impact, and postimpact sets.

The Preimpact Set

As in style A, the teacher's role is to make all the decisions in the preimpact set. The two major differences are: (1) the awareness of the deliberate shift of decisions that will occur in the impact set, and (2) the selection of tasks conducive to this style.

The Impact Set

Since this style's structure defines different roles for the teacher and the learner, the spirit of style B and the shift of the nine decisions must be explained to the learners during the first two or three episodes. After that, only the designation of the style (by name or letter) is needed to picture the ensuing episode—the expectations are clear.

The following is the sequence of events for the episode:

1. The teacher sets the scene by inviting the learners to stand or sit by him or her.
2. The teacher states the style's objectives:
   a. To offer time for each learner to work individually and privately
   b. To provide time for the teacher to offer individual and private feedback to everyone
3. The teacher describes the role of the learner and the shift in decision making. Initially, the teacher actually names the nine decisions (or points to a chart). This procedure clearly identifies the specific decisions shifted to the learner.
4. The teacher describes the role of the teacher:
   a. To observe the performances and offer individual and private feedback
   b. To be available to answer questions by the learner
5. The teacher presents the task(s). The teacher must be aware of the following components of communication and the options within each component.
   a. Content. Each task has a particular content of what is to be done.
   b. Mode. Each task can be presented through different modes: audio, visual, audiovisual, and tactile. The teacher needs to decide which mode is best for a given task.
   c. Action. Each mode has its own form of action; the teacher has a choice of speaking about the task, demonstrating it, or using a combination of both. Each choice depends on the task, on the situation at hand, and on the purpose of the communication. At times, a demonstration of the task conveys a clear image of what is to be done; other times, a few words are needed to clarify the task.
   d. Medium. Various media can deliver the task: the teacher, a film, a video, or a task sheet. A decision must be made about which option to choose.

In addition, the teacher announces the quantity of each task (the number of repetitions per task, or the length of time for the task to be performed) and the order of the tasks (sequence or random).

6. At this point, the learners know the expectations of roles and the subject matter tasks. The teacher, then, establishes the parameters and logistics for the episode. *Parameters* involve decisions about the length of the episode, the general area for performing the tasks, and attire and appearance (if necessary).

An interval decision must be made to establish what the learner will do if he or she finishes the task before the allotted time (transition time).

Logistics involves decisions about equipment and materials. (Parameter and logistics decisions are sometimes referred to as class management.)

7. Once the scene has been set, the teacher may say, "Are there any questions for clarification?" "You may begin when you are ready."
8. The learners start making the decisions that were shifted to them in the impact set. The class will disperse, each learner making his or her location decision, and will proceed with practicing the task and making the rest of the decisions.
9. The teacher observes the initial moments of the episode and then moves about to initiate individual contact with the learners.

The Postimpact Set

10. The purpose of the postimpact time is to offer individual and private feedback to all learners. To accomplish this, the teacher moves about from learner to learner observing both the performance of the task and the decision-making process, then offers feedback and moves on to the next learner. During this process, the teacher needs to consider the following aspects:
    a. Identify, as quickly as possible, the learners who are making errors in either or both the performance of the task or the decision-making process.
    b. Offer corrective feedback to the individual learner.
    c. Stay with the learner to verify the corrected behavior. (In many cases, a few seconds are sufficient for this step.)
    d. Move on to the next learner.
    e. Visit, observe, and offer feedback to those who perform correctly and make the nine decisions appropriately. These students also need the teacher's time. (Often teachers offer feedback only to those who make errors.)
    f. For some tasks, it may take two or three episodes to observe every learner in the class. Learners usually develop the patience needed for such cycles.
    g. Be aware of the options you have in choosing the feedback form. Corrective, value, neutral, and ambiguous feedback are always available to you. Review the section on feedback forms in Chapter 2, and consider the impact of each on the learner in a given instance.

h. The value of one-to-one contact and individual, private feedback have been expounded by educators and researchers for quite some time—the practice style provides for such behavior. The teacher has time to provide this attention, and the cumulative positive effects on the learner and the class climate are quite visible. However, there are times in this style when group feedback is necessary and desirable. For example, when the teacher realizes that a number of learners exhibit the same error, it is efficient to stop the whole class or a part of the class, demonstrate the task again, reexplain the specifics, and then continue with the episode. The structure and the climate of style B, however, must maintain the process of individual and private feedback.

11. At the end of the lesson, assemble the class for a closure. A *closure* is a one-minute "ceremony" for ending the lesson. This can take many forms such as a quick review of the learned content, general feedback to the class, or a statement about the next lesson. A moment of closure provides the teacher and students with a sense of completion.

THE IMPLICATIONS OF THIS STYLE

The reality of episodes in the practice style produce a new set of implications.

1. The teacher values the development of deliberate decision making.
2. The teacher trusts the learners to make the nine decisions.
3. The teacher accepts the notion that both the teacher and the learner can expand beyond the values of one style.
4. Learners can make the nine decisions while practicing the task(s).
5. Learners can be held accountable for the consequences of their decisions as they participate in the process of individualization.
6. Learners can experience the beginning of independence.

SELECTING AND DESIGNING THE SUBJECT MATTER

This section deals with two questions that the teacher must answer while planning episodes in the practice style: What kinds of tasks are appropriate for this style? How does one design and organize a cluster of tasks to accommodate the process of this style?

Kinds of Tasks

The characteristics of an appropriate task for an episode in the practice style are:

1. It is a fixed task that must be performed according to a specific model; no alternatives are sought.
2. It can be assessed by correct/incorrect criteria.

Many activities in physical education consist of fixed tasks. In many cases they form the basis of the activity by defining its structure. For example:

1. When a teacher demonstrates the position at the starting blocks for a short dash, that demonstration becomes the model, the fixed standard. In the practice style, all learners are expected to practice and perform that position as demonstrated without individual variations and adjustments. (Perhaps later, if a variation proves to be beneficial to one runner or another, it will be adopted.)

2. When a forehand stroke in tennis is demonstrated, all the learners are expected to practice the stroke as demonstrated, with the same motion and same foot position (people with preference for left-hand usage performing the opposite stance).

3. When "one-and-a-half, front somersault in tuck position" is the description of the task, all learners are expected to practice according to the accepted standards of this dive.

By delivering and demonstrating these tasks, the teacher has the capacity to offer feedback about the "correctness" of the performance. The teacher compares the performance with the demonstrated model.[1]

At least three sources determine the influence the decision about the fixed standard.

1. Kinesiological or biomechanical principles
2. Past experience of teachers and coaches
3. Aesthetic standard

Kinesiological principles establish the correctness of postures and movement combinations based on scientific analyses. These analyses tell us precisely which posture and which movement is more appropriate for attaining given objectives. Laws of physics, for example, help us determine the degree of difficulty for various exercises.[2] It is futile to produce alternatives when a *specific* posture or movement is sought.

One cannot ignore the accumulation of thousands of observations by teachers and coaches. It is that special and subtle insight into the activity and the appropriate movement that will attain the objective. This, too, serves as a powerful basis for correctness for the standard.

Aesthetic standards generally evolve from cultural agreements and are transmitted and preserved by ceremonies and rituals. Certain postures, movements, and movement combinations are considered attractive, beautiful, and sym-

---

[1] This discussion does not intend to promote fixed tasks, nor is it a statement against alternatives. It is merely emphasizing the importance of precise performance when tasks call for it; it is fixed for *this* task in *this* episode. Another style on the Spectrum develops insights into the process of alternatives.

[2] Mosston, Muska. *Developmental Movement.* Copyright © by Muska Mosston. See the introductory chapter.

bolic. They are used to maintain and project a tradition. In this sense, these movements are correct for this purpose. The actions of cheerleaders, drill teams, marching bands, gymnastics demonstrations, and some dance performances all represent this category of adhering to a particular standard or attaining the predetermined standard by performing the correct movements. Performing these standards is done by style A; practicing for it is often done by style B.

The Design of the Task Sheet

The Purposes of Task Sheets   To increase the efficiency of time-on-task and teacher–learner communication, one could and should use a task sheet (or task card) prepared for the given episode. The *task sheet* is the most useful aid for any of the four organizational formats of this style. (See "Organizational Options" in Chapter 8.)

The purposes of the task sheet are:

1. To assist the learner in remembering the task; what to do and *how* to do it
2. To cut down on the number of repeated explanations by the teacher
3. To teach the learner greater concentration when listening to the explanation the first time
4. To teach the learner to follow specific written instructions and enhance precise performance
5. To record the progress of the learner

It is quite common to see learners in the gymnasium who do not know some details of the task to be performed. This is one of the advantages of the high-visibility factor in physical education—one can see from a considerable distance whether a learner knows how to perform a task. Often, this lack of precise performance is not related to the physical capabilities of the learner, but rather to the learner's inability to remember the details that were previously demonstrated or explained.

Using a task sheet makes clear to learners that part of schooling is listening and observing. It is the learner's role to listen to the explanation and observe the demonstration. Then, during practice time, the task sheet becomes the source of information. This puts the focus on the learner. The learner becomes responsible for following up by using the information on the task sheet.

This technique reduces the learner's manipulation of the teacher. Students who have learned to manipulate ignore the teacher during the initial demonstration and explanation, and then, while the class is dispersed throughout the gymnasium, call the teacher over for an additional complete demonstration, dominating the teacher's time. When this behavior occurs, it reverses the control in the class and reduces the teacher's available time to move about and offer feedback. This is an example of learner manipulation because the teacher must respond when a learner says, "I forgot what you said we should do with the hips during the sit-up." The teacher cannot ignore the request to repeat the explanation nor can the teacher hold the learner accountable for the initial explanation. When this occurs half-a-dozen times during the performance of any given task, a good portion of the teacher's time is used up and the teacher cannot move about and offer feedback initiated by the teacher.

In the gymnasium more than in a classroom there is also the question of distance. There may be a learner in one corner of the gym, another one in the opposite corner, and still a third in another remote spot—all demanding the teacher's attention. These three individuals make the decision for the teacher about where to be, the distance to be traveled, and the amount of time taken from feedback to everyone.

When task sheets are used, however, a learner who requests additional explanation may be asked by the teacher, "What is the description of the movement on the task sheet?" (The teacher has just initiated a different relationship with the learner.) The learner now must resort to the information available on the task sheet. The teacher continues, "Is the description clear?" (The teacher has taken the second step in initiative.) The learner must focus on the description of the task. The learner now has only two options. One is to say, "Yes, it is clear." The teacher then says, "Let me see you perform it," offers the appropriate feedback, and moves on to the next learner.

The learner's second option is to say, "No." The teacher then says, "Which *specific* phrase or word is not clear?" (Again, the teacher initiates.) This question invites the learner to focus on the description of the task and be specific, or *accountable*. The teacher offers the explanation, waits to see the performance, offers feedback, and moves on.

This is a different teacher–learner relationship than the one previously described because it is based on a different notion of how to use verbal behavior that decreases manipulation by learners. It reestablishes the teacher in the appropriate role during postimpact—the role of inviting the learner to participate in understanding and performing the task, and of being available for feedback.

This kind of psychological and effective climate rapidly teaches learners about the assets of the practice style, such as its contributions to their performance improvement and responsibility in making the nine impact decisions.

The Design

1. An effective task sheet contains the necessary information about what to do and how to do it. It always focuses on the task or tasks to be performed during the given episode.
2. It describes the *specifics* of the task.
3. It identifies the *quantity* of the task (number of repetitions, distance, length of time for the particular exercise, etc.).
4. It uses one of two verbal behavior forms:
    a. "Your task is to perform three consecutive forward rolls in tuck position and to finish in squat position." (infinitive)
    b. "Place your left hand on the lower part of the bat and keep your right hand . . . ." (imperative)
5. It has space for notations concerning the learner's progress, feedback comments, and other pertinent information.

FIGURE 4–2   A general sample of a task sheet

Name _____	Style A Ⓑ C D
Class _____	Task Sheet # _____
Date _____	

The general subject matter—the specific topic

To the student:

_____

_____

Task Description [and illustrations]	Quantity of the task	Progress notation; other information	Feedback by:
1. _____			
a. _____			
b. _____			
c. _____			
2. _____			
a. _____			
b. _____			
3. _____			
a. _____			
b. _____			
c. _____			
d. _____			

Figure 4-2, which serves as a general format for a task sheet, includes:

1.   Identifying information (i.e., name, class, date)
2.   Designation of the style that uses the task sheet. In this case it is style B (circled). The same task sheet can also be used for styles A, C, and D.
3.   Task sheet number, indicating the order or sequence of the sheets. This helps keep the sheets organized and available for future use.
4.   The general subject matter refers to the name of the activity or sport (i.e., volleyball, gymnastics, swimming).

5. The specific topic indicates the particular aspect of the sport that will be practiced (i.e., serve, handstand, backstroke).
6. To the student. This space is available for describing the purpose of the activity and any logistical or other relevant information the student might need.
7. Task description. This space is available for describing the tasks and their parts. When necessary, the description should also include an illustration of the tasks and their parts. The illustrations can be drawings or pictures of the desired positions. To illustrate the task in motion, loopfilms or videos can be used in conjunction with the task sheet.[3]
8. Quantity is indicated for every task using units that are relevant to the prescribed task (i.e., the number of repetitions, the length of time for doing the particular task, the number of successful trials out of total number of attempts).
9. Progress notation. This column can be used by the student and the teacher to mark the completed task, to indicate incompletion, to comment on the next session, etc.
10. Feedback. Space is available for feedback comments, which may be provided by different people, depending on the style. In this case, style B, the feedback is provided by the teacher.

For teachers to be able to design tasks with reasonable accuracy and usefulness, they must frequently use the information available from the sports sciences; otherwise, the design of these task sheets are left to anyone's guesses or hunches.

Perhaps this is the place to suggest that sports scientists have an obligation to coordinate a portion of their work and investigation with the teachers who convey that knowledge.

Example of a Lesson Plan If a successful episode is one where intent is congruent with action (Intent $\cong$ Action), than the more we plan the intent, the greater the chances of congruent action. When a lesson is thoroughly planned, it helps in the following aspects:

1. It classifies and specifies the intent of each episode. It answers the question: Where am I gong, and why?
2. It provides guidelines for checking the episode's progress: Am I on the right track? If adjustments are needed, correction can be made.

---

[3]The task description, using line demonstration, printed illustrations, or media demonstrations, establishes the *quality* of the performance. It is the presentation of the model to be attained. It is always bound, however, with the *quantity* of performance. There is always a relationship between the two, and the ratio needed varies with individual learners. The decision about the quantity of repetitions, length of practice time, and so on is often arbitrary. Only with the availability of instrumentation and measurements from the sports sciences has it become more possible to establish quantitative goals for varying individuals.

3. At the end of the episode (and the lesson) when it becomes possible to assess the results, it is quite possible to determine whether the objectives were reached. Was the action congruent with the intent?

Especially for the novice teacher, the more meticulous the planning, the greater the chances of identifying discrepancies that may be corrected in the next episode or lesson. The more experienced teacher uses the planning to visualize the process and to anticipate and orchestrate the events in the lesson.

Planning a lesson, therefore, is a rational activity. It designs a deductive model for the events to come. It is based on a particular sequence of decisions that are related to the teacher's knowledge of the subject matter, the teacher's conception of teaching, and his or her awareness of the learners. The lesson plan transforms the preimpact decisions into action.

The following comments are related to the model of a lesson plan used in conjunction with the Spectrum of Teaching Styles (Figure 4-3). The main principle of this lesson plan is the *planning loop,* which identifies and checks the sequence of decisions throughout the planning; it ascertains that each decision is connected with its antecedent. Thus, some reasonable rationale can be used *before* the lesson takes place.

The starting point of this loop is deciding which aspect of the subject matter will be taught in the lesson: What is the overall objective of the lesson? In this case, the curriculum choice is volleyball; the overall objective for this lesson is to reach some level of competency in tapping and serving. To reach this objective, learners must participate in specific tasks. Success in each task contributes toward the attainment of the objective. In this particular lesson, episodes 2, 3, 4, and 5 are designed for such experiences. (Obviously, episodes 1 and 6 can vary to fit the conditions, the teacher, and the students.) Episodes 2 through 5 are directly connected with the overall objective, and the objective of each episode is directly connected with the overall objective. The next step in the loop is to choose a style that will facilitate the attainment of the stated objectives.

In this case, style B is selected because the T–L–O of style B is appropriate for these episodes. So far, the loop is intact. Next comes the decision about logistics. All the managerial details such as arrangement of equipment, paper work, and so on are taken care of at this point. As previously stated, logistics must accommodate the objective and not vice versa. To conclude the sequence, a time decision is made for each episode—the lesson is ready and the loop is completed. As the lesson progresses (impact), the teacher is available for adjustment decisions, if necessary. At the end of the lesson (as a part of the postimpact), the teacher has the information to assess whether action was congruent with intent.

Subsequent lessons can be planned in the same manner. At times, several lessons may represent a particular theme or topic and should be planned in a sequence that contributes to the continuity of learning. This will be the case here when additional lessons are planned for volleyball (see Figure 4-4).

FIGURE 4-3 A lesson plan

Subject Matter: Volleyball

The overall objective of the lesson: To develop initial competence in the techniques of setting and serving

Episode No.	SUBJECT MATTER Specific Tasks	OBJECTIVES S.M. and/or Role	Style	LOGISTICS Organization of Learners; Equipment; Task Sheet; etc.	Time	Comments
1	Warmup exercises; jogging around the gym; finger tip push-ups; jump and reach a designated spot on the wall	To warm up	B̂*	Identify the marks on the wall	7 min.	
2	Showing a film loop of the setting techniques	To demonstrate the exact model of tapping	B̂*	Film loop; projector; extension cord	5 min.	
3	Practicing setting under different conditions—use attached task sheet no. —, A (1–5)	To develop the initial skills of tapping	B	A ball for each learner; mark the 10′ lines; a task sheet for each learner Reminder: Set time parameters	15 min.	
4	Showing a film loop of the underhand serve	To demonstrate the exact model of this form of serving	B*	Same as episode 2	5 min.	
5	Practicing serving for accuracy—use task sheet no. —, B (1–3)	To develop the initial skills of accurate serving	B	Same as episode 3	15 min.	
6	Closure	General group feedback: To acknowledge what went well and to specify areas to work on next time	B̂*		2–3 min.	

*See the section on the canopy, in Chapter 16.

FIGURE 4–4 A sample task sheet for the practice style in volleyball

Name _____   Style   A Ⓑ C   D
Class _____   Task Sheet No. _____
Date _____

Volleyball—set and serving

To the student:

In order for you to develop better set and serving abilities, a variety of tasks are offered below. Each task represents a different ball control. Record your results.

Tasks	No. Recorded			Teacher's Feedback
	Set 1	Set 2	Set 3	
A. Set				
1. In a slight straddle position, without moving from that spot, record the number of consecutive overhead sets you do. Do 3 sets of 10 each with 15-second intervals between sets.				
2. Do the same as above overhead set except stand with feet together. Don't move from this spot.				
3. Same as 1 except do not restrict your body location to one spot.				
4. Standing behind the 10′ line, tap consecutively against the wall, 3 sets of 10. Record your results. Stay within 1′ of the 10′ line.				
5. Same as 4. Move to 15′ line.				
B. Serving (underhand)				
1. From the 10′ line, serve consecutively to the circle on the wall. Record the hits within the circle. Do 3 sets of 10.				
2. Same as 1 above. From the 10′ line stand on the right, serve to the circle from an angle.				

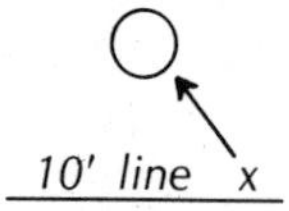

10′ line   x

3. Same as 2 but stand on the left.

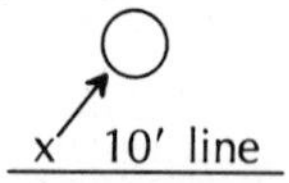

x   10′ line

Which tasks to include in the episodes and what sequence to use is derived from the available knowledge of the particular subject matter. In this example, there is ample knowledge available about the structure and the tasks of volleyball.

STYLE-SPECIFIC COMMENTS

The practice style in operation has revealed several insights that are style-specific; consider and think about the following:

1. The theoretical structure of style B calls for shifting nine decisions from the teacher to the learner; however, there are two decisions that need some commentary, particularly in physical education. *Posture* is the first one. In all other classroom or laboratory subjects, posture is an accommodating feature of the learning situation. Learners can make varying posture decisions to accommodate the performance of the immediate subject matter (i.e., reading, writing, arithmetic, and so on). In physical education, however, posture *is* a part of the subject matter. The description of a task includes the posture to be attained and sustained during the performance. This awareness applies to styles A through F.

    When it comes to specific tasks, then, the posture decision is not shifted to the learner. The second decision that might not be shifted to the learner concerns *attire and appearance*. Situations exist where this is an institutional decision—the school authority makes the decision concerning uniforms. Other institutional decisions concern the necessary safety procedures for a particular sport (protective gear, safety gear) or what attire is appropriate for the rules and procedures of a given sport (particular uniforms for wrestling, Judo, modern dance, or track and field).

2. If a considerable number of learners make the same error when performing the task and/or making the decisions (role error), then an adjustment decision by the teacher is needed. Stop the action of the class, call them around you, repeat the demonstration and explanation and send the students back to continue. This technique of recalling the learners for group feedback has several advantages:
    a. It is time-efficient. The same feedback is given to all those who made the same error. To do it individually wastes time.
    b. The physical proximity of the teacher and the class can create a particular climate of ease different from the climate created when the teacher broadcasts the feedback (and in the gymnasium one must shout).
    c. During this time, learners can ask questions and the teacher can ascertain that most or all learners understood the correction.
    d. It may reinforce those who have performed correctly.

3. Since this style is designed for individual and private practice, communication among or between students must be kept to a minimum. When a student talks to a peer, he or she interferes with the other person's deci-

sions. This must not be perceived as the "no talking" style, but as a style that provides for private time.

4. In the elementary school level, two phenomena may occur in the initial stages of style B. First, individual learners often follow the teacher around to show what they have learned and to seek feedback. Second, learners will stop after one performance and wait for the teacher to get to them for feedback.

   In both situations, the quickest and most neutral way to handle the learner's behavior is to review with the learner the teacher's role in style B. Reassure your learner that you *will* get to him or her, just as you will get to all other learners in the class.

5. Sometimes, because of the different performance levels of the learners, the teacher will assign different groups a different level of the task or a different task. In style B, the teacher makes this decision to accommodate differences in performance.

6. Another situation may call on the learner to select, for example, three out of five available tasks. The teacher has made the subject matter decision about the task design, but the learner makes the decision about which tasks to select for the present episode.

7. At times, learner finish before the allotted time (time parameters). This may occur in all styles except the command style. This *interval time* (also referred to as *transition time*) must be considered when planning the lesson because this interval invites learners to engage in decisions that may not be appropriate for the episode. The teacher should plan an interval activity available for learners who finish their task(s) early. A choice of two or three interval activities could always be available during a certain number of lessons, weeks, or the entire semester.

8. A useful aid in style B (and later in other styles) is the wall chart. A wall chart is a reminder of the series of tasks to be done, the tasks to be done in each station, or the list of decisions in the style. These charts, the task sheets, and the transparencies serve as sources of information for the learner about the tasks and their own role in decision making. The wall chart relieves the teacher from being the only source, allowing more time to provide feedback.

9. By identifying the specific roles of the teacher and the learner, and by doing a decision analysis of various programs, procedures, strategies, and models of teaching, it becomes possible to include these proposals in the Spectrum. For example, "Mastery Learning" is an excellent example of style B in operation—the teacher makes decisions about feedback and the necessary adjustment of the tasks for various learners.

   Some coaching procedures (or coaching behaviors) are excellent examples of style B. With the decision analysis capabilities of the Spectrum, it is possible to more specifically identify what a particular model is or is not. Identifying the boundaries of a given model or program can contribute to an understanding of the objectives that model can achieve. Identifying boundaries develops insights into the particular set of implications of the model in discussion. We will return to this theme later in this book.

THE DEVELOPMENTAL CHANNELS

Now that we know the anatomy of the practice style, the specific behaviors of the teacher and the learner, and the objectives reached when this style is in operation, what can we say about the learner's positions on the developmental channels?

Again, if we use independence as the criterion for relating the style to the developmental channels, we can hypothesize as follows:

1. In the practice style, the learner is more independent in making decisions about his or her physical performance than in style A (see Figure 4-5). The position on this channel, then, moves a bit away from the minimum. One could argue that because the learner practices on his or her own and does not have to wait for the teacher to command every movement, there is a possibility of further physical development.
2. The shift of the location decision to the learner creates new conditions for social contact within the class. Learners can select locations close to or away from other people, so that the position on this channel moves somewhat away from minimum.
3. When physical and social development occur, one can assume that this contributes to new positive feelings about oneself. Hence, the position on the emotional channel is further away from minimum.
4. There is a slight change in the position on the cognitive channel because the learner has to engage in memory as well as adhere to the task description presented by the teacher. There is some mobility from the minimum position because of the learner's involvement in the nine decisions.

The practice style starts the "weaning process" for both teacher and learner. The teacher learns to shift the nine decisions to the learner and trust that the learner will make them appropriately. The learner is given the opportunity to practice these decisions while practicing the task. A new reality in the teacher–learner relationship is evolving that invites the learner to participate in the responsibilities and independence offered by this style.

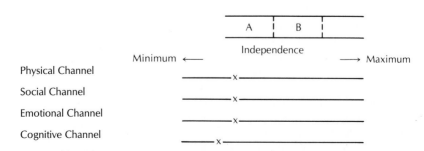

FIGURE 4–5   The practice style and the developmental channels

EXAMPLES OF TASK SHEETS FOR STYLE B

The following pages contain samples of task sheets of various activities for style B (Figures 4-6 to 4-18).

The designation of the styles in the upper right corner indicates that the tasks described can possibly be taught by these styles. These task sheets, however, are for style B.

FIGURE 4–6   A sample task sheet: Basketball—shooting and dribbling

Name _____   Style A Ⓑ C D

Class _____   Task Sheet No. _____

Date _____

Basketball—shooting and dribbling

To the student:

Perform each task as described in the program below and place a check next to the completed task.

Tasks		Dates						Teacher's Feedback
A. Shooting								
1. Set shots—foul line	25 shots							
2. Set shots—45° angle left of basket	25 shots							
3. Set shots—45° angle right of basket	25 shots							
4. One-hand shot—foul line	25 shots							
5. One-hand shot—right side of basket	15 shots							
6. One-hand shot—left side of basket	15 shots							
7. Jump shot—from center, left and right. Do 15 shots from each side—foul line distance.								
8. Repeat No. 7 from greater distance.								
B. Dribbling								
1. Right hand—width of gym	6 times							
2. Left hand—width of gym	6 times							
3. Around obstacle course	10 times							
4. Dribbling sideways—width of gym	6 times							
5. Dribbling backward—width of gym	6 times							
6. Zig-zag dribbling around the obstacles in area 4	10 times							

FIGURE 4–7 A sample task sheet: Basketball—shooting

Name _____   Style A ⓑ C D
Class _____   Task Sheet No. _____
Date _____

Basketball—shooting

To the student:

In developing better shooting, the following are some important aspects:
A. Accuracy from any place around the basket
B. Accuracy from various body positions
C. Accuracy from various distances
D. Accuracy combined with the speed of shooting

The following program provides you with many specific situations designed to help you improve in these four aspects.

Practice each task and record your results. I'll be around to offer you feedback on the execution of the tasks.

Tasks	Quantity	Record Results		Teacher's Feedback
		Set 1	Set 2	
*1. Set shot from foul line	2 sets of 10			
2. Set shot from 45° right (foul line distance)	2 sets of 10			
3. Set shot from 45° left	2 sets of 10			
4. Repeat No. 3 and No. 4 alternating sides—right, left.	2 sets of 5			
5. Set shot from right 30°	2 sets of 5			
6. Set shot from left 30°	2 sets of 5			
7. Set shot from right 10°	2 sets of 10			
8. Set shot from left 10°	2 sets of 10			
9. Combined left and right 10°, alternating sides—Rt, Lt, Rt, Lt	2 sets of 5			
10. From center back to the basket	2 sets of 5			
11. 45° right back to the basket	2 sets of 5			
12. 45° left back to the basket	2 sets of 5			
13. Right 20° right side of basket	2 sets of 5			
14. Left 20° left side of basket	2 sets of 5			
15. Repeat No. 11, 2 yards beyond foul line.	2 sets of 10			
16. Try as many shots as you can, in 60 seconds, from the foul line. (The balls are supplied as rapidly as necessary by a partner.)	2 times Rest 30 sec. between sets			
17. Try as many lay-ups as you can in 60 seconds.	2 times Rest 30 sec. between sets			

*Use available pictures, drawings of the set shot to illustrate the specific technique.

FIGURE 4–8   A sample task sheet: Gymnastics—tumbling

Name _____   Style A Ⓑ C D
Class _____   Task Sheet No._____
Date _____

Gymnastics—tumbling

To the student:

Practice each task as described.

Forward Roll (practice 10 times)
1. Raise the hips as the tucked head is lowered to the mat.
2. Place the back on the mat and push from the toes as the hips move forward.
3. Push from the hands as the shoulders touch the mat.
4. As the hands push off, reach for the shins.
5. Return to a squat position.
6. Return to standing position.

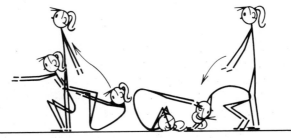

Practice each task as proposed in the program below and place a check next to the completed task.

Tasks	Dates						Teacher's Feedback
A. Forward roll variations							
1. 5 compact rolls (all joints bent)							
2. 5 rolls, one leg bent, the other straight							
3. 5 rolls, both legs together and straight							
4. 5 rolls, both legs straight and apart							
5. 5 rolls, both legs straight; one moves before the other							
6. 5 rolls, the knees at 90° angle							

Tasks	Dates					Teacher's Feedback
B. Backward roll						
7. Repeat the details of No. 1—backward.						
8. Repeat the details of No. 2—backward.						
9. Repeat the details of No. 4—backward.						
10. Repeat the details of No. 4 and end with feet together.						
C. Combinations						
1. Combine roll of No. 2 with No. 9. Repeat 3 times.						
2. Do compact forward, compact backward, compact forward.						
3. Do 2 compact forward rolls followed by 2 compact backward rolls.						
4. Alternate forward and backward straight legs rolls (2 to each direction).						

FIGURE 4–9 A sample task sheet: Field hockey—passing and receiving

Name _____   Style A Ⓑ C D
Class _____   Task Sheet No._____
Date _____

Field hockey—passing and receiving

To the student:

Today there are six stations, each with a task. The first four you can do by yourself; the last two will be done with a partner. You must use a different partner for each one. All tasks are in style B. The equipment you will need is at each station. You may do the tasks in any order. No more than four people per station. I will be available for questions for clarification. I will also offer feedback to each of you.

Task sheet—passing and receiving

Station 1: Push your ball ahead of you, run after it, and hit it forward while you are both moving. Repeat this five times.

Station 2: Place six balls around the outside of a hoop about a stick's length away from it. One at a time, lift (scoop) the balls into the hoop. Replace the balls and try it again but this time run up to the balls as you try to lift them into the hoop.

Station 3: Place three balls at the red pinnie. Dribble around the cones and push or hit the ball into the goal. Come back and do this with the next ball, and the next. Replace the balls at the pinnie for the next person.

Station 4: The balls (8) should be lined up on the line in front of the goal. Starting at the pinnie, put one ball after another into the goal as quickly as you can. Remember not to swing the stick above your shoulders. Your hands should be together at the top of your stick.

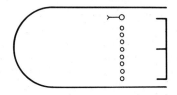

Station 5: With a partner, each stand in front of a cone. Pass the ball back and forth 15 times. You must stop the ball and pass with your stick turned over (reversed).

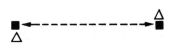

Station 6: One of you (X), stand behind and between the cones. The other (O) has the ball and pushes it to the outside of one cone or the other. X moves to stop it and pushes the ball back to O, then recovers back to the middle as O receives and pushes the ball to the outside of either cone again. This continues until X has received 10 balls. Switch places and repeat. O doesn't move.

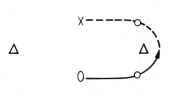

FIGURE 4–10 A sample task sheet: Track—start and short sprints

Name _____   Style   A Ⓑ C   D
Class _____   Task Sheet No. _____
Date _____

Track—start and short sprints

To the student:

Perform each task as proposed in the program below and place a check next to the completed task.

Tasks	Check (√)					Teacher's Feedback
A. The sprint start						
1. 10 starts, as fast as you can, with 3–5 running steps						
2. 10 starts with 10 running steps						
3. 10 starts with 10 fast running steps followed by 10 slow steps, followed by 10 fast steps						
4. 6 fastest starts with 3 fast steps						
5. 6 starts followed by 60-yard sprint						
B. Sprints						
1. Alternate approx. 25 yards fast/slow around the track.						
2. Alternate 60 yards fast running and 30 yards slow running once around the track.						
3. Sprint 60 yards full speed, 15-second interval of rest by walking; 60 yards full speed, etc. Repeat 10 times.						
4. Do 200-yard sprints with half the speed, 60-second rest intervals. Repeat 10 times.						

FIGURE 4–11 A sample task sheet: Track—interval training

Name _____	Style A Ⓑ C D
Class _____	Task Sheet No. _____
Date _____	

Track—increase of speed and endurance in running (interval training)

To the student:

In the following tasks, find out what your maximum is today. Some of the tasks below will be repeated in different quantities.

Tasks	Record Times	Teacher's Feedback
A. Short sprints		
1. Find your maximum speed of 100 yards.		
2. Run the distance 5 times at $3/4$ speed with 30-second rest intervals between attempts.		
3. Run the distance 5 times at $1/2$ speed with 15–20-second rest intervals.		
4. Find your maximum speed of 50 yards.		
5. Run ten 50s at $3/4$ speed with 15-second intervals.		
B. "Longer" distances		
1. Find the maximum distance you can run in 60 seconds.		
2. Run 6 sets in maximum speed $1/2$ that distance with 30-second intervals. (Check your time.)		
3. Try the same half distance in less time.		
4. Rest for a few minutes.		
5. Check your new maximum distance in 60 seconds.		

FIGURE 4–12 A sample task sheet: Swimming—freestyle

Name _____	Style A Ⓑ C D	
Class _____	Task Sheet No. _____	
Date _____		

Swimming—freestyle

To the student:

Perform the tasks as presented in the program below and place a check next to the completed task.

Tasks	Check (√)	Teacher's Feedback
A. Complete stroke		
1. 100 yards, ¹/₂ speed		
2. 25 yards, ¾ speed		
3. 50 yards, ¾ speed		
4. 75 yards, ¾ speed		
5. 50 yards, ¾ speed, 20-second interval of rest followed by 50 yards, ¾ speed. Repeat 4 times.		
B. Arms only		
1. 100 yards, slowly (Rest for a couple of minutes.)		
2. 100 yards, ½ speed		
3. 25 yards, full speed. Repeat 6 times with 30-second rest intervals.		
C. Legs only (with kick board)		
1. 200 yards, comfortable speed		
2. 200 yards, ¾ speed		
3. 50 yards, full speed, 15-second interval. Repeat 4 times.		
D. Complete stroke		
1. 100 yards, full speed, 60-second interval, 100 yards. Repeat 4 times.		

(Task sheets used in the pool should be laminated)

FIGURE 4–13 A sample task sheet: Folk dance

Name _____

Class _____

Date _____

Style A Ⓑ C D

Task Sheet No. _____

Folk dance—Miserlou

To the student:

Practice individually the four sequences of this dance. Later the Miserlou will be performed by (a) standing straight, (b) forming a small line of five or six, (c) interlocking little fingers.

Your first task is to perform the four steps in sequence. I will provide feedback while you are practicing the task.

Music: There are four phases, each with four sequences.

Phase, Sequences, Counts	Description of Specific Steps (Tasks)	Accom-plished	Needs More Time
Phase I			
Seq. 1 Counts 1	Right foot—step forward.	_____	_____
2	Pause.	_____	_____
3	Left foot—point toe of right foot.	_____	_____
4	Pause.	_____	_____
Phase II			
Seq. 2 Counts 1	Left foot—swing leg behind and cross right foot.	_____	_____
2	Right foot—move to the right side of the left foot.	_____	_____
3	Left foot—lift in front of and across the right foot.	_____	_____
4	Pause.	_____	
Phase III			
Seq. 3 Counts 1	Right foot—swing to the side, then in front and to the side crossing left foot.	_____	_____
2	Left foot—place parallel but a little behind the right foot. (Shift weight to your toe.)	_____	_____
3	Right foot—place right toe above the left foot.	_____	_____
4	Pause.	_____	_____
Phase IV		_____	_____
Seq. 4 Counts 1	Left foot—step back one step.		
2	Right foot—step back one step parallel with left foot.	_____	_____
3	Left foot—step in place.		
4	Right foot—lift and touch toe to the ground by the arch of the left foot. Repeat above order.	_____	_____

FIGURE 4–14   A sample task sheet: Developmental movement

Name _____   Style A Ⓑ C D
Class _____   Task Sheet # _____
Date _____

Developmental movement

To the student:

Practice each task in the program below. Place a check next to the completed task.

Tasks	Dates practiced	Teacher's Feedback
A. Agility		
1. High strad- 10 consecutive times dle jumps		

2. High knee   10 consecutive times
    raising
    hops		

3. Repeat No.   10 consecutive times
    1 with turns
    of 90° each
    time you
    land.		

B. Strength
  1. *Legs*
    a. In side lunge shift body weight 20 times.		

Tasks	Dates practiced	Teacher's Feedback

b. In wide straddle position, bend both knees to half squat position 20 times.

2. *Abdomen*
   a. In forearm-supine rest position, lift both legs to 45° off the floor. Perform scissors motion for 25 seconds.

3. *Shoulders and Arms*
   a. Pull-ups (grip: shoulders' width) 7 times (hands supinated)
   b. Push-ups—arms a bit wider than shoulders' width, body in inverted V position, 10 times

C. Flexibility
1. *Shoulder joint*
   a. Straight-arm circles backward 20 slow circles at shoulder level
   b. Repeat No. 1 with larger circles 20 times.

2. *Pelvic joint*
   a. In a wide straddle position, 20 slow bending movements, hands reaching to the floor
   b. Repeat No. 1, hands reaching 10 times to left foot and 10 times to right foot.
   c. In straddle seat position repeat movement of Nos. 1 and 2.

D. Balance
1. Perform a T scale 5 times on each foot.

2. Jump up vertically, turn 180°, and land on the same spot. Repeat 10 times.

FIGURE 4–15 A sample task sheet: Developmental movement

Name _____	Style A Ⓑ C D
Class _____	Task Sheet # _____
Date _____	

Developmental movement

To the student:

Practice each task described below. The teacher will offer feedback.

Tasks	Teacher's Feedback
A. Agility (and endurance)	
1. Consecutive high-knee-raising hops (knees raised to hip level) Start with 3 sets of 10.	
2. Consecutive hops, knees raised to chest level. 3 sets of 10. _____	
3. Consecutive step jumps—long steps in the air. 3 sets of 10.	
B. Strength	
1. Shoulder girdle	
a. Push-ups—straight body, arms at shoulders' width. Intervals between sets: 15 seconds. 3 sets of 10.	
b. Push-ups—straight body, arms wider than the shoulder, at 45° angle between arms and floor. Intervals: 20 seconds. 2 sets of 10.	

Tasks	Teacher's Feedback
2. Abdominal region 　a. Straight-trunk sit-ups with straight arms raised above the head in supine position, legs slightly bent. 2 sets of 15. 　b. In supine forearm support position, raise your straight legs to 60° off the floor and "write" numbers in the air—1, 2, 3, 4, 5. 	

FIGURE 4–16　A sample task sheet: Lacrosse skills

Name _____　　　Style Ⓑ C D
Class _____
Date _____

Lacrosse
Review of cradle, pick-up, catch, pass, pivot, and dodge

1. Cradling
　a. Cradle, jogging around the perimeter of the field.
　b. Standing, cradle 6 times each on R, L, high, and low. Repeat 2 times.

2. Pick-up
　a. Place ball 5 yards away on the ground; run, pick it up, and accelerate to cone, cradling, 10 yards away. Repeat 5 times.
　b. Roll ball away from yourself; run after it, pick it up, and accelerate, cradling, 10 yards. Repeat 5 times.

3. Pivot—cones located 10 yards apart
　a. Cradle and pivot when level with each cone. Repeat 5 times.
　b. Pick up ball, cradle, and pivot when level with cone; accelerate back to first cone. Repeat 5 times.

4. Dodge—cones located 25 yards apart
　a. Run forward and back, cradling on R for 8 steps, and on L for 8 steps. Repeat 2 times.
　b. With 4 cones located along 25 yards, cradle directly towards cone, and at last instant pull L and pass cone, pull R past second cone. Repeat and run course 2 times.

5. Catch—in twos
   Toss 5 balls from R, L, and directly towards partner. Run to meet ball, catch it, and accelerate 5 yards more, cradling.

6. Pass
   Run 5 yards cradling, and pass on move to the hoop from cone located 10 yards away. Repeat 10 times.

7. Pass and catch
   Pass and catch with a partner, standing 10 yards apart, facing one another. Make 30 passes.

FIGURE 4–17 A sample task sheet: Lacrosse skills

Name _____   Style Ⓑ C   D
Class _____
Date _____

Lacrosse
Review of cradle, pick-up, catch, pass, pivot, and dodge

To the student:

This is a review of lacrosse skills. Practice each of these tasks.

1. Cradling
   Cradle for speed for 50 yards. Repeat 2 times.
   Does the ball stay in your crosse the entire time?

2. Pick-up
   a. Place ball 5 yards away on the ground; run, pick it up, and accelerate to cone, cradling, 10 yards away. Repeat 5 times.
   b. Roll ball away from yourself, run after it, pick it up, and accelerate, cradling, 10 yards. Repeat 5 times.
   Record the number of times you pick up the ball successfully out of the 10 attempts.

3. Pivot
   With cones placed 10 yards apart, cradle and pivot when level with each cone. Repeat 5 times.
   Does the ball stay in your crosse the entire time?

4. Dodge
   Set 8 cones in a 50-yard area. Dodge each cone. Repeat 2 times.

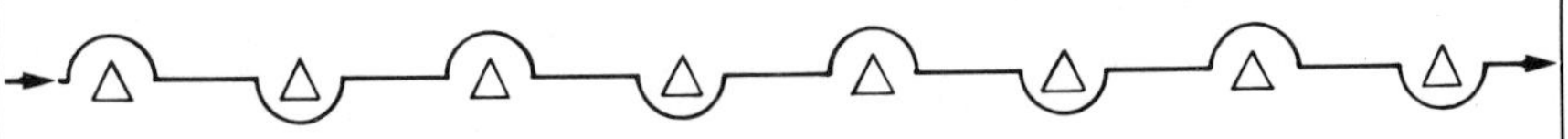

   Does the ball stay in your crosse the entire time?

5. Catch and pass—in twos
   a. Stand 10 yards apart. Record the number of times you pass and catch in succession without dropping the ball. Repeat 3 times.
   b. Run in a 10-yard grid, throwing and catching with partner on the move. Repeat 3 times.

   Record the number of times you catch and pass in succession without dropping the ball.

6. Pick-up, cradle, and pivot
   With cones 10 yards apart, pick up the ball, cradle, pivot when level with cone, and accelerate back to first cone. Repeat 5 times. Does the ball stay in your crosse the entire time?

7. Catch, cradle, and pivot—in twos
   With cones 20 yards apart, toss 3 balls each from R, L, and directly towards partner. Catch ball on move, accelerate to far cone, pivot, and accelerate back to thrower. How many times did you complete the task successfully?

FIGURE 4–18 *Inappropriate* task design

Gymnastics skill sheet

The following task design is not appropriate as a task sheet for style B. The reasons are: (a) There is no specific description of the task or its parts, (b) No quantity is indicated, and (c) The shift of the evaluation decision (can do/cannot do) is the role of the teacher in this style.

	Can Do	Can-not		Can Do	Can-not
Tumbling Skills			Pull-ups		
Forward roll			Hip pullover		
Backward roll			Swan balance		
Dive roll			Back hip circle		
Headstand			Airplane		
Cartwheel			Front knee circle		
Roundoff			Walkout kip		
Back-hand spring					
Hand-stand			*Balance Beam*		
Front-hand spring			Walking		
			Balances		
Vaulting			Front dismount		
Squat on—jump off			Pass		
Courage vault			Squat mount		
Squat vault			V-seat		
Flank vault			Forward roll		
Front vault			Backward roll		
Rear vault			Cartwheel		
Statue vault					
Single leg cut			*Ropes*		
Head spring			Pull to stand		
			Inverted hang		
Horizontal Bar			Climb		
Skin the cat			Climb—hands only		
Forward roll dismount			Climb—upside down		

FIGURE 4–19 Style B classroom chart

THE PRACTICE STYLE

The purposes of this style are:

- To offer the learner time to work individually and privately

- To provide the teacher with time to offer the learner both individual and private feedback

ROLE OF LEARNER

- To do the task
- To make the nine decisions:

  Order of task(s)
  Starting time
  Pace and rhythm
  Stopping time
  Interval
  Posture
  Location
  Attire and appearance
  Initiating questions for clarification

ROLE OF TEACHER

- To be available to answer questions by the learner

- To gather information about the learner's performance and offer individual and private feedback

What, then, is the next set of decisions shifted to the learner? What is the next style on the Spectrum that creates still another reality in the relationship between teacher and learner?

5

The Reciprocal Style (Style C)

THE OBJECTIVES OF THIS STYLE

The structure and implementation of the reciprocal style create a reality that reaches a new set of objectives intrinsic to this style. These objectives are part of the two major aspects of this style—the social relationships between peers and the conditions for immediate feedback.

The objectives are identified in two groups, those that are closely related to the task(s) and those that are related to the role of the learners.

Subject Matter

1. To have repeated chances to practice the task with a personal observer
2. To practice the task under the conditions of receiving immediate feedback from a peer
3. To be able to discuss with a peer the specific aspects of the task
4. To visualize and understand the parts and the sequence of parts in performing a task
5. To practice the task without the teacher offering feedback or knowing when errors were corrected

Role

1. To engage in the socializing process unique to this style—to give and receive feedback with a peer
2. To engage in the steps of this process: observing the peer's performance, comparing and contrasting the performance against criteria, drawing conclusions, and communicating the results to the peer
3. To practice the available feedback options (i.e., to learn how to give corrective feedback that will continue the relationship)
4. To develop the patience, tolerance, and dignity required for succeeding in this process (how to deal with collision and collusion)
5. To experience the rewards of seeing one's peer succeed
6. To develop a social bond that goes beyond the task

THE ANATOMY OF THIS STYLE

To create a new reality in the gymnasium that provides for new relationships between the teacher and the learner, more decisions are shifted to the learner. These decisions are shifted in the postimpact set to heed the principle of immediate feedback. The sooner a learner knows how he or she has performed, the greater the chances of correct performance. Therefore, the optimum ratio providing for immediate feedback is one teacher to one learner. How, then, can the teacher accommodate this goal in physical education classes? Style C, the *reciprocal style,* calls for a class organization that offers this condition. The class is organized in pairs with each member assigned a specific role. One member is designated as the *doer* (d), the other as the *observer* (o). When the teacher (T), in his or her particular role in this style, gets involved with a given pair, a *triad* relationship forms for that period of time. The triad is designated as follows:

d   o

T

In this triad, each member makes specific decisions within his or her specific role. The role of the doer is the same as in the practice style, including communicating only with the observer. The role of the observer is to offer feedback to the doer and to communicate with the teacher. The role of the teacher is to observe the doer and the observer, but communicate only with the observer. Thus, the lines of communication are as follows:

d ↔ o
↕
T

The teacher, then, is making all the decisions in the preimpact set, the doer is making the nine decisions in the impact set, and the *shift* of decision takes place in the postimpact set—the observer makes the feedback decisions. (Schematically, the shift of decisions in style C looks like Figure 5-1).

	A	B	C	
Preimpact	(T)	(T)	(T)	
Impact	(T) →	(L)	(d)	
Postimpact	(T)	(T) →	(o)	

FIGURE 5–1   The anatomy of the reciprocal style

IMPLEMENTATION OF THE RECIPROCAL STYLE

Although the command and practice styles are familiar to everyone in one form or another, the reciprocal style is new to many. The new reality and roles create new social and psychological demands on both the teacher and the learner; considerable adjustments and changes of behavior must be made. All this leads to a new perception of what is possible in the gymnasium. This is the first time in this process of deliberate decision making that the teacher shifts the decision of feedback to the learner. The implicit "power" of feedback that has always belonged to the teacher is now shifted to the learner. The learners, therefore, must learn to responsibly use this "power" when they give and receive feedback with peers. Both teacher and learner need to experience this new reality with trust and comfort; both must understand the value of this style in the growth of the individual learners.

The following section combines the description of an episode with the steps of how to do it. These steps and explanations are needed only during the first two or three episodes. Once the teacher and the learners experience the behaviors and benefits of this style, they can shift into it swiftly when the teacher announces the name of the style at the beginning of a lesson or episode.

DESCRIPTION OF AN EPISODE AND HOW TO DO IT

As in the previous two styles, the anatomy of the style guides the implementation—a process of making decisions in the preimpact, impact, and postimpact sets, and setting new expectations.

The Preimpact Set

In addition to the decision made by the teacher in style B, the teacher in style C prepares and designs the criteria sheet (or criteria card) that the observer uses. (See the following section on designing the criteria sheet.)

The Impact Set

The major task for the teacher here is to set the scene for the new roles and new relationships. Following is the sequence of events in the episode.

1. Tell the learners that the purpose of this style is to work with a partner and learn to offer feedback to that partner.
2. Identify the triad and explain that each person has a specific role; each learner will be both the doer and the observer.
3. Explain that the role of the doer (d) is to perform the task(s) and make the same nine decisions as in the practice style. The doer communicates only with the observer.
4. The role of the observer (o) is to offer feedback to the doer based on the criteria prepared by the teacher. This feedback occurs during the performance and after the completion of any task. Thus, while the doer is mak-

ing decisions in the impact set, the observer is making decisions in the postimpact set.

The Postimpact Set

For the observer to fulfill the role in the postimpact set, he or she must complete the following steps:

1. *Receive* the criteria for correct performance from the teacher. (This is usually provided on a criteria card.)
2. *Observe* the doer's performance.
3. *Compare* and *contrast* the performance with the criteria.
4. *Conclude* whether the performance was correct.
5. *Communicate* the results of the doer. This feedback can be offered during the performance or after the completion of the task—it depends on the kind of task involved. During the performance of static tasks, the learner can hear and assimilate the feedback. During some tasks in motion, this is impossible; in such cases, the observer must wait until the task is completed.
6. *Initiate,* if necessary, communication with the teacher.

The first five steps in this sequence are not only imperative for anyone in the role of assessing performance, they are intrinsic to this feedback process. Before any performance assessment can be done, one must have clear criteria or a model of the expected performance. In style C, the teacher provides this in a criteria card.

Once the criteria are known, the next step is observing the doer's performance and gathering data. The observer then compares and contrasts the performance with the criteria. This provides the observer with information about the "correctness" of the doer's performance. The observer is now ready to communicate results to the doer and offer the appropriate feedback. (These five steps are always used when the teacher offers feedback as well. In fact, if one step is out of sequence, the feedback cannot be accurate.)

7. The role of the teacher is:
   a. To answer questions by the observers
   b. To initiate communication only with the observers

The teacher does not communicate with the doer so that he or she will not usurp the observer's role. This is probably one of the most difficult behaviors to learn. It is indeed difficult to be in the proximity of the doer and observe either a correct or incorrect performance without offering feedback; however, it is important to stay within the structure of the style. You must not interfere with the observer's role and the decisions shifted to the observer in the postimpact set.

8. At this point, the learners are aware of the new style's structure, the specific roles, and the lines of communication. The teacher may now present the task(s).

9. Explain to your students the purpose of the criteria sheet and describe the specific item for today's episode. This step cannot be taken for granted. Using criteria as a tool for assessing a partner's performance is quite a new experience for most people. The temptation to resort to idiosyncrasies and personal preferences is very strong. Therefore, it is important to emphasize the criteria as a guide for observation and feedback.

10. Specify the logistics and the parameters for the episodes (i.e., where to pick up the criteria sheet, time parameters, etc.).

11. Say to your class: "Select your partner, decide who will be the doer and observer first, then begin."

12. The process of selecting partners will take a minute, the pairs will disperse, and the activity will begin.

13. Doers will perform the tasks, and observers will take the necessary steps for giving feedback while making the decisions in the postimpact set. Concurrently, the teacher will move about observing the performances of both the doer and observer, and will communicate with the observer. (For some specific communication procedures, see the section titled "Verbal Behavior" later in this chapter.

14. When the doer completes the task, the doer and the observer switch roles (reciprocal style).

When one observes a well-functioning class in the reciprocal style, all these roles and decisions come alive. One can actually see the relationships budding and developing. New dimensions evolve that go beyond the mere performance of the physical tasks such as social interaction, giving, receiving, trying out ideas, correcting, and succeeding.

IMPLICATIONS OF THIS STYLE

Just as the previous two styles have implications affecting the teacher and the learner, so does this style. The new relationships produce a new set of implications unique to the reciprocal style. Style C implies that:

1. The teacher accepts the socializing process between observer and doer as a desirable goal in education.

2. The teacher recognizes the importance of teaching learners to give accurate and objective feedback to each other.

3. The teacher is able to shift the power of giving feedback to the learner for the duration of style C episodes.

4. The teacher learns a new behavior that requires refraining from direct communication with the performer of the task (the doer).

5. The teacher is *willing* to expand his or her behavior beyond styles A and B and takes the needed time for learners to learn these new roles in making additional decisions.

6. The teacher *trusts* the students to make the additional decisions shifted to them.

7. The teacher accepts a new reality where he or she is not the only source of information, assessment, and feedback.
8. The learners can engage in reciprocal roles and make additional decisions.
9. The learners can expand their active role in the learning process.
10. The learners can see and accept the teacher in a role other than those intrinsic to styles A and B.
11. Learners can spend time learning (by use of the criteria sheet) in a reciprocal relationship without the constant presence of the teacher.

SELECTING AND DESIGNING THE SUBJECT MATTER

When selecting and designing the task(s), follow the same procedures described in the practice style. The teacher's additional task in this style is designing the criteria sheet (see Figures 5-2 and 5-3).

The Criteria Sheet

The single factor that can determine the success or failure of an episode in style C is the criteria sheet (or criteria card). It determines the parameters for the

FIGURE 5–2 A criteria sheet in tennis (the forehand stroke)

Name _____   Style   B Ⓒ D
Class _____
Date _____
Partner _____

Tennis—the forehand stroke

Doer:
1. Use the forehand stroke to bounce and hit 10 balls over the net, as demonstrated.
2. Switch net sides, retrieve the balls and hit 10 more balls over the net.

Observer:
1. Observe the performance, use the criteria (below) to analyze the performance, and offer feedback to the doer.
2. At the end of 10 strokes, record the results.
3. At the completion of the task, switch roles.

Sample verbal behavior for the observer: First, acknowledge what was done well, and then offer corrective feedback about the errors.
1. "Your stance was correct, your weight was on the right foot."
2. "Your swing was at hip level, but you did not keep your eyes on the ball."
3. "The transfer of weight was correctly done."
4. "You need to keep your wrist firm."
5. "Your follow through was in the proper direction."

FIGURE 5–3 A criteria sheet in tennis

Acc. = Accomplished
n.t. = Needs more time

	doer 1				doer 2			
	1st set		2nd set		1st set		2nd set	
Task/Criteria*	Acc.	n.t.	Acc.	n.t.	Acc.	n.t.	Acc.	n.t.
1. Stand with left side turned to the net, with weight on the right foot. (If left-handed, do the opposite.)								
2. Swing the racket back at about hip height, after you throw the ball upward. Keep eyes on the ball.								
3. Transfer your weight onto the front foot, and swing the racket on a fairly straight line to the ball.								
4. Watch the ball until it is hit by the racket. Bend the knees slightly through the stroke.								
5. The racket contacts the ball when it is even with the front foot.								
6. Keep wrist firm and swing with the whole arm, from the shoulder.								
7. Rotate the trunk so that the shoulders and hips face the net on follow through.								
8. Follow through with the racket, upward and forward in the direction of the hit.								

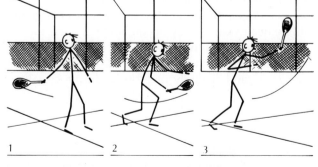

*In some tasks, the specific description of the "parts" constitutes the "points to look for."

observer's behaviors; it keeps the doer accurately informed about the performance; and it provides the teacher with a concrete base for interacting with the observer.

A criteria sheet includes five parts:

1. Specific description of the task—this includes breaking down the task into its sequential parts.
2. Specific points to look for during the performance—these are potential trouble spots in performance that the teacher recognizes from previous experiences.
3. Pictures or sketches to illustrate the task.
4. Samples of verbal behavior to be used as feedback. This is useful in the early experiences of style C.
5. Reminder of the observer's role—this is useful in the first few episodes. Once the learner demonstrates the appropriate behaviors, it is no longer necessary to include the reminder in the criteria sheet.

Comments

1. Initially, preparing criteria sheets for style C does take time; however, many tasks in sports and dance remain fairly constant over the years—in the long run the criteria sheet is a time-saving device for the teacher. Collect and organize your criteria sheets so that you can use them repeatedly.
2. Style C is very useful for review purposes, but it is particularly useful for introducing a new task. Properly designed criteria sheets ensure a more accurate initial performance.

STYLE-SPECIFIC COMMENTS

The following sections and comments reflect the particular events, dimensions, and issues that emerge when style C is in operation. Some emerge immediately during the initial episode and disappear after the teacher resolves them; others emerge more often because of the new social-emotional nature of this style. These should be dealt with as they occur. Some of these dimensions are permanent because they are intrinsic to the structure of this style. The more familiar you become with all these possibilities, the more you will be able to anticipate behaviors and skillfully orchestrate the process for the benefit of everyone.

Verbal Behavior

One of the major dimensions of human interaction is verbal behavior. We communicate ideas and feelings through words. In the classroom or the gymnasium, verbal behavior is a major form of communication affecting the teacher, the learner, and the relationship between the two. From a linguistic standpoint, words have meanings and connotations—both meanings and connotations affect the people involved in the interaction. Let us focus, then, on some insights concerning the teacher's verbal behavior with the observer in the reciprocal style. We will identify several conditions that occur in this style and then suggest a sample dialogue.

1. There is always a need for an entry point. How do you start communication with the observer? What are some possible phrases that will focus on the observer, inviting him or her into a dialogue? The general principle here is to ask questions. For example:

    T: "How is your partner doing?"

    o: "Fine!"

    T: "What does *fine* mean? What is your partner doing specifically?"

    o: "My partner is keeping the legs, hips, and back in the correct position."

    T: "Your observation is accurate; you know how to follow the criteria sheet." The teacher continues,

    T: "Did you give this feedback to your partner?"

    o: "Yes."

    The teacher may either stay a while longer with this pair or move on to the next. If the observer says: "No, I have not told my partner," then say:

    T: "Part of your role is to offer feedback to your partner. Using the criteria sheet, what can you say to your partner?"

    Usually the observer will pause and look at the criteria, going through the process of comparing and contrasting and then offering feedback to the doer.

2. A condition that may occur is when the observer offers inaccurate feedback to the doer. In this case, the teacher must go through the criteria step by step with the observer.

    T: "Let's go over the criteria together. What is the first point on the criteria sheet?" This question invites the observer to focus on the criteria and the process of assessing the performance of the task.

    o: "The first point refers to the . . ."

    T: "Did the doer do it?"

    o: "No."

    T: "Offer him the correction according to the criteria."

    The observer continues with this step and offers the feedback.

3. There are situations when verbal abuse is used by the observer ("You're a dummy!"). In this case, the teacher resorts to statements rather than questions. The teacher's role must be to introduce parameters and to protect the integrity of both the doer and the observer.

    T: "I can't let you talk to your partner in this manner, just as I will not let her talk to you in this way. Your role is to follow the criteria and offer feedback to the doer."

4. At times, observers are silent; they do not offer feedback.

    T: "How is your partner doing?"

    o: "Fine."

    T: "Have you told him?"

    o: "No."

T: "Why not?"

o: "He knows how to do it."

T: "Tell him so. Your partner needs to know that he is doing well."

These examples focus on the spirit of communication and the role of the observer. In different instances you may need to adjust the wording, but the essence should remain.

This process may sound trivial, or perhaps unnecessary, but most learners do not know how to use appropriate verbal behavior while offering feedback. Many shy away from this part of their role because it has not been a part of their past behavior. Offering specific, objective feedback to a peer and using criteria for doing so is a new experience for most people. This new behavior creates a new social-emotional relationship between the two partners, usually a relationship of honesty and mutual trust. People need time to practice it.

Initially, this condition is also new for the teacher. As mentioned before, it is very difficult to relinquish the power of feedback by communicating only with the observer. However, the focus of this style is the appropriate behavior of the observer. Style C only seems strange during the first few episodes; once the style's assets are realized, it becomes one of several styles that the teachers and learners have available to them.

5. During closure, the teacher offers feedback to the entire class by addressing their performance as observers. The verbal behavior might be: "We will need more time to learn how to use the criteria sheet," or "You have performed your roles as observers well." This kind of closure is necessary in the initial few episodes in this style. As the learners internalize the new behaviors, this kind of closure will be needed less frequently.

Pairing Techniques

There are many ways that can be used to organize the class in pairs:

1. Lining up the class and counting off by twos
2. Alphabetically
3. The teacher selects the partners.
4. Students select each other (self-selection).
5. Pairing by height
6. Pairing by weight
7. "Pair up with the person next to you."
8. Skill level
9. And many more ways—do you know any?

Each of these techniques can be used for its own purposes, but to accommodate the purpose of style C (developing the communication between the doer and the observer) the most appropriate technique is self-selection. Usually people enjoy working with someone they know and prefer. Thousands of episodes in this style have verified this assumption.

Initially, when learners select the partners they want to work with, the episode begins more swiftly and continues more productively. It is more comfortable to give and receive feedback with a person one likes and trusts.

The first objective to reach in the first few episodes is the appropriate behaviors in the roles of the doer and the observer. This is the focus of the initial episodes. Self-selecting partners reach this objective faster and more safely with minimal social-emotional conflicts. If a partnership is selected by any other pairing technique, friction between the partners may delay the initial success of the episode. The teacher will have to deal first with the conflict and then with the new roles—usually it will not work! Partners who begin in conflict often refuse to continue together. If the first experience in this style is negative and unrewarding, learners usually resist participating in it. Often the negative feeling spills over to the activity. For example, students who were introduced to tumbling in style C and had a negative experience will often say, "I don't like tumbling!"

It is imperative to create conditions that are conducive to the successful introduction of the style—in this case, be aware of the appropriate pairing technique. After several episodes, when the teacher ascertains that all participants are skilled in both roles, doer and observer, the teacher can announce at the beginning of a subsequent episode, "Now that you know the roles and the decisions in style C, for today's episode select a new partner!" The new partnerships can be sustained for one, two, or three episodes; then, again, a new selection of partners takes place, expanding the social dimension.

Perhaps one of the most outstanding results of this procedure is the increase in social tolerance and communication among the members of the class. You can actually see the growth of patience and tolerance in receiving and giving feedback. It is, indeed, an extraordinary development for the teacher and the learners to reach this level of social-emotional climate while learning to perform tasks successfully!

SOME THINGS TO THINK ABOUT

The experiences that evolve in this style are many and varied—most of those described were observed by many teachers in many episodes. The following comments are for you to consider. Obviously, it is impossible (and perhaps not even desirable) to identify every eventuality. As you encounter a problem in this style, examine it. Examine your behavior, examine the shift of decisions and the roles, and solve the problem within the spirit and purpose of the reciprocal style

1. As you communicate with an observer, keep an eye on the rest of the class by scanning. It takes only seconds to do so, buy you'll have constant information about what's going on.
2. If you observe that there is some deviant behavior by a given pair, complete your feedback to the present observer and then deal with the issue

at hand. Do not ask, "What's the problem?" You will be flooded with statements and accusations by both partners.

Try not to get involved in this type of manipulative behavior by learners. Do not take the position of an arbiter or judge; instead, refocus the learners on their roles. Ask who is the doer and who is the observer, unless you can identify them by who is holding the criteria card. Proceed by saying, "Let me see the doer perform the task and the observer use the criteria card." This will invariably curtail the bickering and conflict. Each is back within his or her role. Your role is to stay with the pair and listen to the feedback. You proceed, then, as previously described.

3. When you move about from pair to pair, do so randomly. Avoid patterns such as clockwise, counterclockwise, pairs closest to you visited first, and so on.

4. Since learners can ask questions for clarification when needed, establish a procedure or a signal for this occurrence. As you scan the class, you will notice the signal and know who needs your attention. Otherwise, you may sometimes be surrounded by several learners—some doers and some observers—all needing your attention about different questions. These learners, knowingly or not, are manipulating you by making decisions for you. These decisions are not theirs to make in this style. If this "gathering of the eager to learn" happens during the episode, stop all activities to assemble the entire class near you. Then remind the class about the specific roles in this style and that you will come to the individual observer. If the doer has a question, it must be addressed to the observer. Ask the learners to return to their activities. Watch for a while before going to an observer. Again, visit and communicate with all observers, not only with those who indicate that they have some difficulties. It is fascinating to observe the patience style C learners develop with each other and with waiting their turn to receive feedback from the teacher. This patience increases with the security of knowing that the teacher will eventually come to them. This security reduces and eventually eliminates the need to vie for the teacher's attention (particularly in the earlier grades; in later grades, students often try to avoid the teacher's attention). In the reciprocal style, all learners receive attention in their respective roles as doers and observers. At the end of the episode, offer your learners feedback about how they performed in their roles.

5. Several misconceptions about style C occasionally emerge in the minds of teachers.

    a. "The smart one working with the dummy." Style C is not designed to differentiate levels of "smartness." On the contrary—the major contribution of this style is creating a condition where both partners are equal in their roles. Both partners have the opportunity to use their capacities within the social context of this style and to adjust their emotions to accommodate the interaction process.

    b. "In style C, the teacher is not working." On the contrary, the teacher is very much working to teach the learners the new behaviors of being an observer and the receiver of feedback from a peer. Nor is the notion that "the observer is doing my job" appropriate. The teacher is constantly engaged in giving feedback, but about a different aspect of the educational process. The teacher is still accountable for the events and the processes in the lesson.

c. "This style is not for the learner who has difficulties in comparing and contrasting performance with criteria." On the contrary. This style is excellent for learners who need more time in these cognitive operations. They need practice, and what better opportunity than with a partner who is "equal" in role and supportive in behavior? Learners with "deficits" are often excluded from competitive situations. The cooperative nature of style C invites most learners, sooner or later, to participate.

d. "The observer cannot evaluate the doer." Style C is not an evaluating style. The roles are confined to offering feedback by criteria to improve the performance of the task.

e. Style C is also not a "work with your partner" style, where learners pair up to do a task and give idiosyncratic feedback to each other.

6. Most students appreciate this equality of roles and usually follow through with appropriate behavior and enjoyment. At times, the superior performer who has always been singled out, reinforced, and perhaps unduly praised demonstrates impatience in style C. (A similar behavior can be seen in the classroom by learners who have been labeled "bright," "talented," "gifted.") Since one of the highlights of this style is social interaction and development, all students need to experience episodes taught in this style.

7. In general, most problems you will encounter between partners in style C fall into two broad categories: collision and collusion. As previously suggested, isolate the problem or issue and deal with it according to the style. Do not abandon the style—tackle it!

8. As with most new experiences, particularly when new behaviors are called for, there is a phase of awkwardness or discomfort that accompanies not knowing what to do or how to do it. This phase occurs in the initial episodes of this style, but you have options in how to ease the discomfort.

a. Introduce the style to a small group of learners first. (The rest of the class will be in style B without feedback from you.) Let the learners experience the new role under your observation and feedback. Go through the class group by group; after a few short episodes, the entire class will be familiar with the style.

b. For these first few episodes, select a task that is not particularly demanding so that the focus will be on the new roles. Keep emphasizing and reinforcing the criteria process of comparing, contrasting, and giving feedback. The internalization of this style will pay off in future lessons.

c. You might choose to introduce the style to the entire class (or to a small group) by demonstrating the process with only one pair. Ask the learners to gather around. (Select a pair of learners in advance who feel secure enough to learn a new idea in public.) Introduce the style step by step while each partner experiences his or her role. All learners, criteria sheet in hand (or projected by a transparency), observe each step and listen to the verbal behavior of the observer. If needed, stop the action. Clarify, emphasize, and reexplain; then the pair continues. When the doer has completed the task, the pair switches roles and the episode goes on. This demonstration serves as a *model* for your students. In time, you and your students will reach the specific objectives for this style.

THE SMALL GROUP

In physical education classes, one often sees small groups engaged in an activity. These groups are usually formed for one of two reasons:

1. The group is necessary to facilitate the performance of a particular task. For example, to develop skill and offensive strategy in soccer, sometimes three players are needed to pass the ball among themselves; hence, various drills in threes have been designed. In tumbling, to facilitate a safe, initial performance of the back handspring, two spotters kneel at the performer's side and help the performer by using various techniques. There are other instances of working in small groups that are intrinsic to the task itself.
2. The group is formed due to organizational needs, usually when there is not enough equipment for the number of participants. One often hears in the gymnasium, "Group one work on the balance beam, group two on the parallel bars," and so on. This situation is really not working in a group, but a group of people organized around a piece of equipment so that each individual can use it with some frequency. (It is, therefore, the Practice style.)

In the context of style C, the term *small group* does not refer to either condition. It refers to the *role* of the participants in decision making, not to the activity.

A small group of three may become necessary when the class has an odd number of students. One way to deal with this is to ask the extra person to join one of the pairs. Under such circumstances, there are two options available to the threesome:

1. Two doers and one observer
2. Two observers and one doer

Each of these options has liabilities. In the first option, it is sometimes difficult for the observer to watch two performers at the same time and identify the specific details of the performance. The threesome is not a particularly disturbing situation, but it makes the episode (for those participants) different from style C done in pairs.

The second option (two observers and one doer) carries more liabilities because it is more difficult to receive feedback from two observers. In addition, most tasks do not have enough points of criteria to justify two observers. Often, the second observer becomes quite bored because he or she does not have an active role in using the criteria and offering feedback.

Another way of dealing with the odd number is to ask the extra person to do the task in style B and have the teacher offer the feedback.

If the class has a permanent odd number of learners, it is imperative to rotate the extra person; it should be a different person in different style C episodes.

There is one more condition that might necessitate using small groups in this style—a given pair may not want to be together due to a social or affective discrepancy. There are, then, two extra people in this episode. Each can join a pair to form two threesomes. Again, it becomes a different condition for the people involved, but these liabilities exist in real classes. The teacher who is aware of any of these conditions can select the most appropriate option for the situation. The focal point here is the deliberate decision made by the teacher in advance. When this is done and the appropriate explanation is offered to the class, chances are higher for a smooth implementation of the episode.

THE DEVELOPMENTAL CHANNELS

In the reality of the reciprocal style, where are the learners on the developmental channels?

If we use independence as the criterion for relating the style to the developmental channels, we can ask: How independent is the learner in making decisions about himself or herself in these channels? This style's structure presents all kinds of possibilities for analyzing interaction and for hypothesizing about a learner's experience (see Figure 5-4).

1. Let us begin with the most powerful dimension—the social dimension. The very act of communicating with each other for a particular purpose demands some social skills that weren't necessary in previous styles. To par-

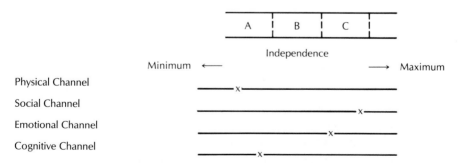

FIGURE 5–4   The reciprocal style and the developmental channels

ticipate in this interaction, one must be reasonably independent in using social skills. Hence, the position of the learner on this channel is toward maximum.

2. The act of giving and receiving feedback from a peer puts the learners in a situation demanding honesty, appropriate verbal behavior (both in words and in tone), considerable patience, and, at times, empathy. All of these behaviors are consequences of choices the learner makes in the affective domain. One must learn to use independence to make the appropriate decisions in this domain; hence, the position on the emotional channel is toward maximum.

3. The position on the physical development channel is similar to that of style B during the role of doer. It is interesting to speculate, however, about the possible difference from style B. Clearly, in style B the doer is practicing a degree of independence in physical development. The task is done within the context of the nine decisions and the role of the teacher in periodically offering feedback. In style C, the doer is independent within the nine decisions, but the physical participation occurs under constant observation and feedback by the observer. Does this make any difference in the performance, development, or rapidity of the development?

4. On the cognitive channel there is a slight change in position—it moves further away from minimum because the observer engages in several cognitive operations such as comparing, contrasting, and drawing conclusions.

If you wish to further analyze the developmental channels, select another criterion, ask the appropriate question concerning the relationships, and move on to seek the answer.

The reciprocal style continues the "weaning process" for both teacher and learner. This style provides the learner the opportunity to make postimpact decisions, and indeed to create a new reality in the relationships between the learner and teacher, a reality that invites the learners to participate in a responsible independence offered by the new decisions shifted to them. It is also a new reality for the teacher who has learned to shift postimpact decisions—a source of power—to the developing learners.

EXAMPLE CRITERIA SHEETS

The following pages present some examples of task/criteria sheets in various activities (Figures 5-5 to 5-20). Note that there are some variations in design and format, but the concept and use are the same. Note also that in some situations there are three participants involved. The third person is needed in some physical tasks for retrieving the ball, catching, tossing, spotting, and so on. This does not change the operation and process of style C. What the teacher needs to add is a rotation system so that the same third person is not stuck as an aide, but can actively participate in the roles of style C.

FIGURE 5–5 Sample criteria sheet: Tennis

Name _____   Style B Ⓒ D
Class _____   Task Sheet No. _____
Date _____
Partner _____

Tennis—the serve

Doer: Serve 10 balls over the net into the left service court.
Observer: Use the criteria, offer feedback to the doer, and record the perform-
               ance after service of 10 balls.
               Switch roles after each set of 10.
               How many balls went successfully over the net into the proper
               service court?
               Doer 1 _____
               Doer 2 _____

	doer 1				doer 2			
	Left		Right		Left		Right	
Things to look for	Yes	No	Yes	No	Yes	No	Yes	No
1. Stand partially sideways to net with forward foot just behind base line and weight on back foot.								
2. Ready position with forehand grip, ball and racket together.								
3. Swing racket down and back as you are extending the hand and arm upward for the "ball toss."								
4. Cock wrist holding racket so that racket is in a "back scratching" position.								
5. At the same time release the ball from the hand straight in air at racket height, 6 to 8 inches in front of forward foot.								
6. With extended arms bring racket up and over to contact ball. Transfer weight to front foot.								
7. Follow through by bringing racket down to opposite side of body and rotating trunk.								

Note: There are a variety of tennis books available in which appropriate pictures can be
selected.

FIGURE 5–6　Sample criteria sheet: Skiing

Name _____　　Style　B　Ⓒ　D
Class _____　　Task Sheet No. _____
Date _____
Partner _____

Skiing—straight running

Doer:　　　Perform the task as demonstrated. If you have any questions, ask your observer.

Observer:　Offer feedback to your doer. Offer the positive feedback first, then corrective comments.

Task:　　　Glide down a gradual slope in a straight running position. Length of slope is _____

Quantity:　　　　　_____

Criteria:

Starting Position
a. Skis parallel at shoulders' width apart _____
b. Skis flat on the snow, equally weighted _____
c. Ankles, knees, and waist slightly bent _____

Straight Running
a. Arms held at the sides of the body _____
b. Hands held forward of the hips _____
c. Body relaxed, not piked or superstraight _____
d. Head up _____

Overview
a. Doer should go straight down fall line _____
b. Knees are apart, not touching _____
c. Tilt should not be exaggerated backward, forward, or straight _____

Note: 1. If used on the slope, the criteria sheet should be laminated and a string provided for keeping the criteria attached to the observer.
　　　　2. To accommodate the feedback, the doer and observer should ski a certain distance and then stop for feedback.

FIGURE 5–7   Sample criteria sheet: Badminton

Name _____   Style   B Ⓒ D
Class _____
Date _____
Partner _____

Badminton—forehand overhead clear

To the students:	This task is performed in groups of three: doer, tosser, and observer.
The tosser:	Throw a high, clear service to the doer.
The doer:	Practice the forehand overhead clear 10 times.
The observer:	Analyze the doer's form by comparing the performance to the criteria listed below. Offer feedback about what is done well and what needs to be corrected.
	Rotate roles after each inning of 10.

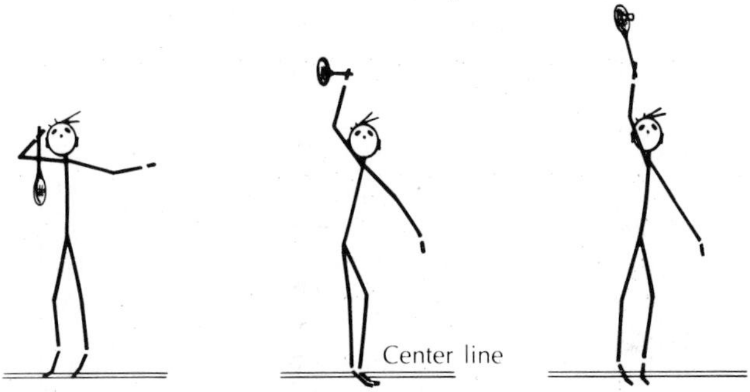

Center line

Task—Criteria:

1. Backswing taken with racket, as if to throw it. _____
2. Left side of the body turned to the net as weight shifts to back leg. _____
3. Shuttle struck overhead but in front of body, with arm fully extended. _____ Racket head contacts bird form below. _____
4. Body weight put into shot, as weight shifts onto front leg. Strong wrist action. _____
5. Follow through in direction of intended flight of bird. _____

FIGURE 5–8 Sample criteria sheet: Archery

Name _____   Style B Ⓒ D
Class _____
Date _____
Partner _____

Archery task and criteria sheet

Instructions for the observer:

1. Communicate to the doer about how he or she is performing the task (use the "Things to look for" column).
2. Offer corrective and neutral feedback.
   Examples of feedback statements:
   "You are gripping the bow correctly, but remember not to grip it too tightly."
   "You are nocking the arrow exactly as the criteria describe."
   "The elbow of your drawing arm is in line with the arrow."
   "Now I will check to see if you are using the same anchor point."

Task 1: Each doer should shoot six arrows.
Switch roles after each round of six arrows.

Things to look for		Yes	No
STANCE	Stand astride shooting line, feet apart at shoulder width, body in comfortable position with straight posture.		
GRIP	Fit handle in V formed by thumb and index finger, bow felt in upper part of hand. Grip should not be tight.		
NOCKING	Nock arrow with cock feather facing away from bow, arrow between first and second fingers, string resting along first joint of all three fingers that grip string.		
DRAW	Keep bow arm and wrist straight without being rigid, using arm, shoulder, and upper back muscles do the drawing. Keep elbow of drawing arm in line with arrow.		
ANCHOR	Draw until string touches another point on face (check to ensure that anchor point is the same each draw).		
RELEASE	Release by relaxing fingers, allowing string to roll off the fingers. Hold bow hand relaxed but steady during release and follow through.		

FIGURE 5–9 Sample criteria sheet: Weight training

Name _____   Style B Ⓒ D
Class _____   Task Sheet No. _____
Date _____
Partner _____

Weight training—Big Four

Doer: Complete one set of the Big Four exercise in 24 seconds. (Do 10 sets each).

Observer: Analyze the doer's performance according to the criteria. Offer feedback to the doer.

             Switch roles after each set.

Task: Big Four

		doer 1		doer 2	
Diagram	Criteria	Yes	No	Yes	No
1	Assume deadlift position. Grasp handle with palms back and pull isometrically for 10 seconds.				
2	Keep arms straight, rotate hips forward, and press with legs to standing position (4 seconds). *Do not lift with back.*				
3	Raise handle to chin, clean (4 seconds).				
4	Rotate hands, palms outward, complete military press (4 seconds). Stretch upward on toes after arms are fully extended overhead.				

BIG FOUR—24 seconds

Possible comments observer can offer doer:	Hold your position. Don't raise your hips. Keep knees bent forward. Pull for 10 seconds.	Keep your head up. Pull to a straight standing position.	Pull handle to chin. Keep head up. Elbows high.	Hold your grip on handle. Rotate hands. Keep going until elbows are straight. Complete toe raiser.

FIGURE 5–10   Sample criteria sheet: Javelin throw

Name _____   Style   B Ⓒ D
Class _____   Task sheet No. _____
Date _____
Partner _____

Javelin throw—the throwing motion

To the Student:

There are several components that make up the javelin throw: the approach run, the cross steps, the throwing position, the throwing motion, and the follow through. This program is concerned with the throwing motion. All the mentioned components must operate in perfect harmony to translate the body momentum and power into a sequence of throwing motions that will produce a perfectly forward straight flight of the javelin. To do this, you need to control every part of the motion sequence. The following tasks break down the details involved in the throwing motion.

The doer will perform each task several times, becoming aware of the details. Then combine each task with the previous part, two previous parts, and so on.

The observer is available to offer you subject matter details and feedback in your practice.

Criteria:	Feedback for d_1	Feedback for d_2
A. The throwing stance (for a right-handed person): 1. Stand with your left side toward the throwing direction, feet in a comfortable straddle. 2. Shift your weight to the rear leg (right leg in this case) and bend it slightly so that you can feel its springy action. 3. Slightly touch the ground with the left foot. 4. Bend trunk slightly forward (facing 90° to the throwing direction). 5. Extend the right hand, holding the javelin, to the right side of the body, the javelin across the chest. Its point should be approximately in front of the face and pointing to the direction of the throw. Drop the javelin's tail to the ankle's height and point it to the opposite direction of the throw.		

Criteria:	Feedback for d_1	Feedback for d_2
6. Relax the left arm at the left side of the body or bend it in front of the left shoulder at shoulder height.		
7. Review each part of the position separately so that you can concentrate on the accuracy of each position and become aware of what each part of the body is doing.		
8. Combine 1, 2, and 3 without a javelin.		
9. Combine 1, 2, 3, and 4 without a javelin.		
10. Repeat 8 and 9 with a javelin.		
11. Review 1, 2, 3, 4, and 5 without a javelin. Check the relationship between the body and the throwing arm.		
12. Repeat No. 1 with a javelin.		
13. Add No. 6.		
14. Repeat the whole stance slowly.		
15. Repeat the whole stance fast.		
16. Walk around the field and at different intervals, stop and assume the stance slowly.		
17. Repeat 16 fast.		
B. The throwing motion The sequence of motion is as follows: ankle-knee-hip-trunk-shoulder-elbow-wrist.		
1. Assume the throwing stance—check every detail.		
2. Push off the right foot. The motion is at the ankle and the knee. Repeat several times.		
3. As the knee straightens out, begin to rotate the hips to the left and begin to shift your weight in the direction of the throw. Keep the javelin in its plane! Check its point! Check the direction and height of the javelin's tail.		
4. Complete the hip rotation so that the chest faces the direction of the throw. At this point your right ankle is raised a bit off the		

Criteria:	Feedback for d_1	Feedback for d_2
ground, and your right foot is turning toward the direction of the throw. The left foot is pointing at the direction of the throw, and the back is slightly arched backward. (There is need for great shoulder and upper back flexibility.) Keep the javelin in the direction of the throw. At this point the javelin will move into a new direction if you do not control it!		
5. Bend the left arm at shoulder level and pull to the left, aiding the rotation of the body.		
6. Continue to move the right shoulder forward to complete the trunk's rotation pulling the elbow as close to the ear as possible.		
7. Extend the elbow in a forward direction followed by the wrist's whip to release the javelin.		
8. Follow through in a relaxed manner.		

Note: This is an example of a criteria sheet that is more elaborate and can be used by learners who have been exposed to this style. Consult books on javelin throwing for pictures showing the technique.

FIGURE 5–11   Sample criteria sheet: Tumbling

Name _____   Style   B   Ⓒ   D
Class _____
Date _____
Partner _____

Gymnastics—tumbling

Task 1: Body Wave

Observer:
Give feedback to doer.
Examples of feedback:
"Your arms are too stiff for a body wave."
"Point your toes a little more."
"Your beginning position is correct."
After the 10th performance, record below how the doer performs each step.

Doer:
Perform 10 body waves.

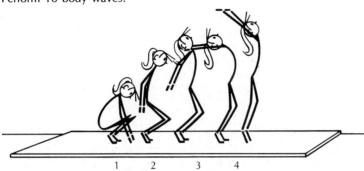

	doer 1		doer 2	
Things to look for	Yes	No	Yes	No
1. Start in squat position with arms straight and in front of the body.				
2. Drop the arms down and back while beginning to straighten the legs.				
3. Circle the arms up behind the body throwing the hips forward.				
4. Arch the back, keeping the shoulders back, and raise both arms as an extension of the body.				

Task 2: Backward Roll

Doer: Perform 6 rolls. Switch roles after the 3rd roll.
Observer: After the 6th roll, record below how the doer performed each of the 5 steps.

	doer 1		doer 2	
Things to look for	Yes	No	Yes	No
1. Start in a squat stand, hands on the mat, fingers pointing forward.				
2. Rock backward onto the buttocks, keeping the head forward and the back rounded.				
3. Reach back for the mat with hands as soon as hips hit the mat.				
4. Keep knees and elbows close to the body.				
5. End stunt in squat position.				

Task 3: Cartwheel:

Doer: Perform 10 cartwheels. Switch roles after 5th cartwheel.
Observer: Record below the performance after the 10th cartwheel.

	doer 1		doer 2	
Things to look for	Yes	No	Yes	No
1. Stand with side to mat. Kick up leg nearest the mat.				
2. Place lifted leg forward as weight is taken on near hand and then other hand.				
3. Keep the arms straight and shoulder distance apart.				
4. Split the legs in the air, and land with first one foot and then the other contacting the mat.				

FIGURE 5–12 Sample criteria sheet: Balance beam

Name _____   Style   B Ⓒ D
Class _____
Date _____
Partners _____

Balance beam—back shoulder roll

Doer and Observer: Follow the roles of style C.
Spotter: Use the demonstrated skill for spotting the task.
Rotate roles after five rolls.

feedback by o to:

Step	Criteria	d_1	d_2	d_3
1	In supine position on the beam, drop the head off to one side of the beam. Grasp the beam in a mixed grip—the hand on the head side gripping the top of the beam, and the other hand gripping the bottom of the beam.			
2	Pike at the hips and, in one motion, carry the legs over the head until the toes touch the top of the beam.			
3	Bend one knee and push up, ending in a knee scale.			

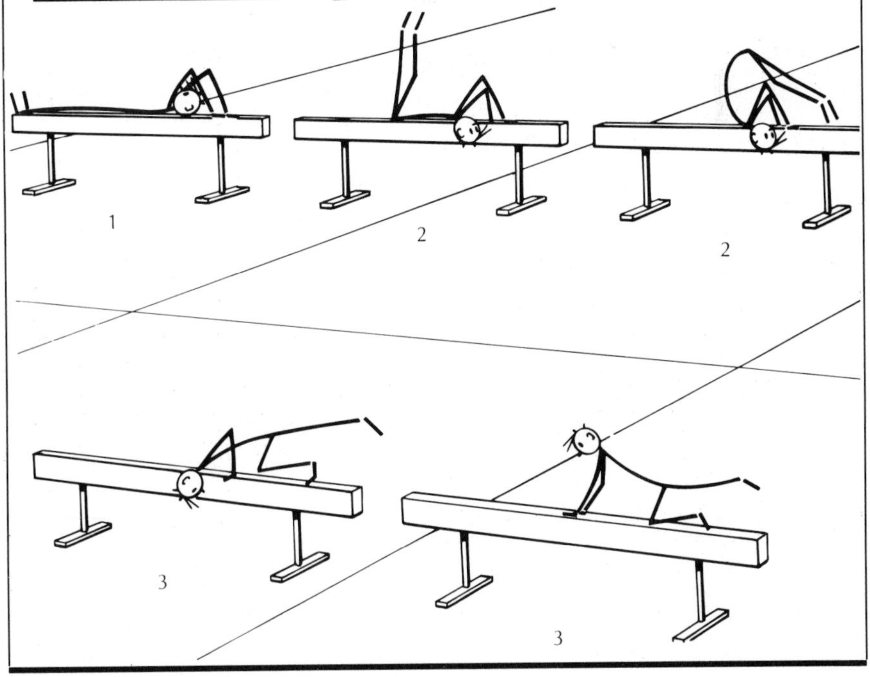

FIGURE 5–13   Sample criteria sheet: Trampoline

Name _____   Style ©
Class _____   Task Sheet No. _____
Date _____
Partner _____

Gymnastics—trampoline

To the student: Doers perform each task 3 times
Observer: Remind the doer of the parts of the task. Offer feedback on each
                          of the points listed. Provide feedback after each performance.

Task:

1. Consecutive bounces—a series of 10 bounces each within one foot
   of the center of the trampoline.
      a. body straight (no parts piked)   _____
      b. arms controlled and even (not swinging)   _____
      c. eyes looking at the fixed spot   _____
      d. toes pointed (while in the air!)   _____
      e. no hesitation between bounces   _____
      f. stopping "on a dime" without taking extra steps   _____
      g. bounces within one foot of the center mat   _____

2. Three consecutive bounces, then a 90° turn, then 3 more bounces
   and a stop—all within one foot of the center mat.
   For the bounce use same seven criteria as above.

     a __   b __   c __   d __   e __   f __   g __

   90° turn
     a.   head moving from spot position "one" to spot position "two"   _____
     b.   arms turning together with the body   _____
     c.   landing after 90° turn with balance (body not bent)   _____
     d.   body parts in line
            before turn   _____
            during turn   _____
            on landing   _____

FIGURE 5–14 Sample criteria sheet: Gymnastics—Triple roll

Name _____ Style B Ⓒ D
Class _____
Date _____
Partner _____

Gymnastics—triple roll (from prone position)

In groups of 3 perform the following task. A fourth person is the observer.

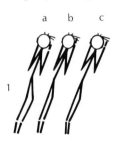

1. The Sequence
   a. The middle person always rolls to the outside.
   b. The left person springs up and over the center person, rolling toward him or her.
   c. The right person springs over the center person coming toward him or her.

2. The Timing
   a. Only two people are in motion at any time.
   b. Roll out, jump back in.

Observer: Read the sequence to the doers and offer them feedback on their performance.
Repeat for 10 cycles, then rotate positions.

FIGURE 5–15 Sample criteria sheet: Headstand

Name _____ Style B Ⓒ D
Class _____
Date _____
Partner _____

Gymnastics—headstand

To the student: Work in groups of three—a doer, a spotter, and an observer. The spotter uses the demonstrated technique.

The doer: Practice the headstand 5 times.
The observer: Use the criteria to offer feedback.
Rotate roles.

Criteria:
1. From crouched position, place hands on floor shoulder width apart.
2. Place forehead in front of the hands (make a triangle) and push off with the feet.
3. Either place thighs on backs of upper arms or straighten legs.
4. Then move hips upwards and forward over base to vertical position.

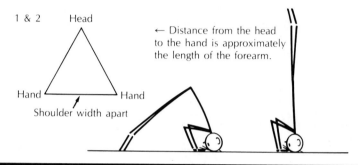

FIGURE 5–16   Sample criteria sheet: Horizontal bar

Name _____   Style   B Ⓒ D
Class _____
Date _____
Partner _____

Horizontal bar—underswing dismount

To the student: This task is performed in groups of three—doer, spotter, and observer.

The spotter stands underneath the bar to the side of the performer. As the dismount begins, he/she places one hand on the small of the doer's back and the other on the shoulder. The spotter must move forward with the doer and, as he approaches the ground, shift one hand across the chest and one hand across the back to be sure that the landing is completed on the feet.

The doer: Practice the task 5 times before everyone rotates to a new role.

The observer: Compare each performance of the doer to the criteria and offer feedback after each performance.

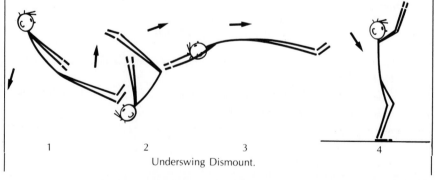

Underswing Dismount.

Criteria:

1. From a front support position, drop head and shoulders backward _____
   with straight legs moving forward under the bar.
2. Keep the arms straight throughout the drop. _____
3. Keep the legs close to the bar and the body in pike position _____
   as the upper body falls backward.
4. Swing the legs forward and slightly arch the body. _____
5. Land with slightly bent knees without additional steps, chest and _____
   arms raised as demonstrated.

FIGURE 5–17 Sample criteria sheet: Soccer

Name _____   Style B Ⓒ D

Class _____

Date _____

Partner _____

Soccer—long throw-in

Work in groups of three—doer, retriever, and observer. Doer executes the task 10 times to a distance of approximately 15 yards. The retriever returns the ball, while the observer offers feedback to the doer by comparing the performance to the criteria listed below.

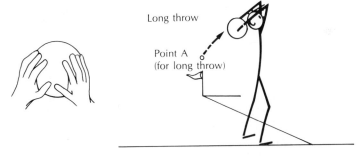

Long throw

Point A
(for long throw)

Criteria:

1. Both hands are used as ball is swung to point A behind the head.

2. Player takes one or two quick steps forward to gain momentum.

3. Body is bent backward, with a slight bend at the knees.

4. A whipping action of the body and a forceful straightening of legs develops thrust.

Note: Both feet must stay on the ground until ball is released and it must be thrown in the direction the thrower is facing.

FIGURE 5–18   Sample criteria sheet: Lacrosse

Name _____   Style   C

Class _____

Date _____

Partner _____

Lacrosse—cradle, pick-up, and catch

Reminder for the observers:

1. Communicate to doer how he/she is doing the task, using "Things to look for" column.
2. Offer corrective and neutral feedback.
3. Examples of feedback statements:
   "Your arms are working together in the cradle, but don't use too much wrist movement."
   "You're doing the pick-up exactly as the criteria describe."
   "You're 'giving' with the catch correctly. Now I'll check your top hand position."

Task 1: Cradling

Doer: While cradling, run around 2 cones located 10 feet apart, 5 times. Repeat this task twice, with 20-second intervals for rest.

Observer: a. Use the criteria (below) to analyze the performance and offer feedback to the doer.

b. Record the performance after the 2nd trial.

		Trial 1				Trial 2			
		Yes		No		Yes		No	
Diagram	Things to look for	d_1	d_2	d_1	d_2	d_1	d_2	d_1	d_2
1	Hands are apart with "throwing" hand at top of stick. V of thumb and forefinger should be even with open face of crosse, stick in upright position.								
1, 2, 3	Swing crosse across body with both hands working together, one directly above the other.								
1 & 3	Wrist action finishes the motion on both right and left side.								
1, 2, 3	Bottom arm is at waist level and parallel to ground during motion.								
1 & 3	Arm and leg motion are the same (cradle R, R leg forward, cradle L, L leg forward).								

Cradling

1   2   3

Task 2: Picking Up

Doer: Put the ball on the ground 5 yards away. Run, pick it up, and accelerate cradling to the cone located 20 yards away. Repeat 5 times.

Observer: Follow your role!

	Trial 1				Trial 2			
	Yes		No		Yes		No	
Things to look for	d_1	d_2	d_1	d_2	d_1	d_2	d_1	d_2
1. Bend knees, with stick low to ground.								
2. Hold head over ball, with R foot even with ball if R-handed (L foot if L-handed).								
3. Move "through" the ball, moving forward with the pick-up.								
4. Cradle immediately, and stay low for 1 or 2 cradles.								

Picking Up   Catching

Task 3: Catching

Observer: a. From 10 yards away, toss 5 balls directly to the doer.
Wait for the doer to "ask" for the toss.
b. Toss 5 balls from the right of the doer.
c. Repeat the task from the left of the doer.

Doer: "Ask" for the toss and catch the balls as demonstrated.

Observer: Using the criteria, offer feedback to the doer.
Switch roles after performing a, b, and c 5 times.

	Trial 1				Trial 2			
	Yes		No		Yes		No	
Things to look for	d_1	d_2	d_1	d_2	d_1	d_2	d_1	d_2
1. Top arm is straight and stick reaches out to "ask" for the ball.								
2. Top hand position is same as in the cradle.								
3. Open face of crosse faces direction ball is coming from. Watch ball into crosse.								
4. The catch *is* a cradle. Bend top arm and "wrap" crosse around head in cradling motion.								

FIGURE 5–19 Sample criteria sheet: Lacrosse

Name _____   Style   C
Class _____
Date _____
Partner _____

Lacrosse—pass, pivot, and dodge

To the observer:

1. Communicate to doer how he/she is doing the task, using "Things to look for" column.
2. Make positive comments to doer first.

3. Examples of feedback statements:
"Your shoulder was turned correctly in the throw, but you pushed forward with your arm rather than coming 'up and over' with the crosse."
"You've transferred your weight in your pivot just as the sheet describes."
"You're protecting the crosse very well with your body in the dodge. Now accelerate."

Task 1: Passing
Doer: Stand 10 yards from a hoop located on the hill, and pass 2 sets of 10 balls at that target.
Observer: Do your role!
Switch roles after each set of 10.

		Trial 1				Trial 2			
		Yes		No		Yes		No	
Diagram	Things to look for	d_1	d_2	d_1	d_2	d_1	d_2	d_1	d_2
1	Cradle to throwing side and pull crosse back as lead shoulder faces direction of pass.								
2	Point handle of stick in direction of pass.								
3	Lever motion with arms and wrists, bottom hand pulling down and top hand lifting up.								
1 & 3	Transfer weight from back to front foot.								

Passing

1   2   3

Task 2: Pivoting

Doer: Cradle between 2 cones located 10 yards apart, pivoting each time you are level with a cone. Repeat 5 times, and do 2 sets.
Switch roles after each set of 5

		Trial 1				Trial 2			
		Yes		No		Yes		No	
Diagram	Things to look for	d_1	d_2	d_1	d_2	d_1	d_2	d_1	d_2
1	To change direction, cradle to side of lead foot with weight well over lead leg.								
2	Cradle across body with a slight lift of the crosse to keep the motion smooth.								
2	Turn on balls of feet.								
3	Push off in opposite direction by transferring weight forcefully from "new" back leg to "new" lead leg—cradle finishes cradling motion.								

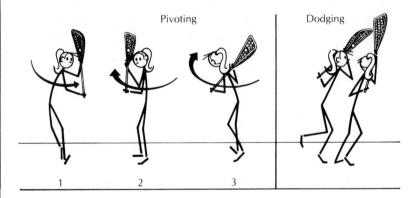

Pivoting   Dodging

1   2   3

Task 3: Dodging

Doer: Cradle (going in forward direction) around 2 cones located 5 yards apart, cradling R as you pass the first cone and L as you pass the second cone. Then accelerate, cradling in front of the body to a line 10 yards away. Repeat 4 times, cradling L, then R the second and fourth times. Do 2 sets of 4.

Switch roles after each set of 4.

Things to look for	Trial 1				Trial 2			
	Yes		No		Yes		No	
	d_1	d_2	d_1	d_2	d_1	d_2	d_1	d_2
1. Pull the crosse well to one side of the body when dodging the cone, and cradle to that side.								
2. Turn the trunk when pulling crosse to side.								
3. Feet and hips should be facing in direction player is running.								
4. Accelerate to finish dodge.								

FIGURE 5–20 *Inappropriate* design of criteria sheet

This criteria sheet is not desirable because of all the value words that have been included in the description. These words prevent precise feedback and may cause conflict between the observer and the learner.

Avoid "value" words in the task description. Be as precise as possible by using neutral words.

Golf—putting

Task/Criteria:

1. Use a stance that is **comfortable** but limits body movement.
2. Do not move shoulders—putting is a wrist and arm stroke.
3. Hold head directly over the ball.
4. Hold club **lightly** but **firmly.**
5. Keep club face square to the line of the putt.
6. Rest putter **softly** behind the ball at the beginning of the stroke. Do not press down on the green at the address.
7. Bring club back **smoothly** and keep it **low, close** to the green.
8. Follow through with a **smooth,** forward **sweeping** movement, keeping club-head on the line of the putt.
9. Keep hands **even** with the ball on impact.

FIGURE 5–21   Style C classroom chart

THE RECIPROCAL STYLE

The purposes of this style are:

- To work with a partner

- To offer feedback to the partner, based on the criteria prepared by the teacher

ROLE OF LEARNER

- To select the roles of doer and observer

- The *doer* does the task (as in style B)

- The *observer* compares the work of the doer with the criteria, draws conclusions, and offers feedback to the doer

- When the task is completed by the doer, doer and observer switch roles

ROLE OF TEACHER

- To monitor the observers

- To give feedback to the observers

- To answer the observers' questions

What, then, is the next set of decisions shifted to the learner? What is the next style on the Spectrum that creates still another reality in the teacher–learner relationship?

6 | The Self-Check Style (Style D)

THE OBJECTIVES OF THIS STYLE

Once again, a new reality is created by the teacher–learner relationships that evolve in the self-check style. More decisions are shifted to the learner, which calls for more responsibility. The self-check style prompts the learner to reach for a new set of objectives.

Subject Matter

1. To develop an awareness of one's performance. A major dimension of development is that of kinesthetic awareness.
2. Kinesthetic awareness can be reached by learning to observe one's own performance and then making an assessment based on criteria.

Role

1. To wean the learner from the total dependence on outside sources of feedback; to begin relying on oneself for feedback
2. To use criteria for self-improvement
3. To maintain honesty and objectivity about one's performance
4. To accept discrepancies and one's own limitations
5. To continue the individualizing process by making the decisions shifted to the learner in the impact and postimpact sets

THE ANATOMY OF THIS STYLE

Now that the learner has practiced using criteria as a basis for feedback to a peer, the next step is to use criteria for feedback to oneself; hence, the name of this style is *self-check*. In this style, each individual performs the task(s) as in the practice style (style B) and then makes the postimpact decisions for oneself. The style C skills of comparing, contrasting, and drawing conclusions are used by each learner to check one's own performance.

Schematically, the shift of decisions and the anatomy of this style appear in Figure 6-1. In the anatomy of this style, the teacher's role is to make all the decisions in the preimpact set, primarily about the subject matter. As in style

	A		B		C		D	
Preimpact	(T)		(T)		(T)		(T)	
Impact	(T)	→	(L)		(d)		(L)	
Postimpact	(T)		(T)	→	(o)	→	(L)	

FIGURE 6–1 The anatomy of the self-check style

B, the learner makes the nine decisions in the impact set while performing the task, but now makes postimpact decisions for one self as well.

IMPLEMENTATION OF THE SELF-CHECK STYLE

Description of an Episode

Perhaps the most striking aspect of a style D episode is the carryover from the two previous styles. Ultimately the learners gain the ability to assess themselves using these techniques. In style B, they learn to do the task. In style C, they learn to use criteria and give feedback to a peer. In style D, the learner uses the same skills for self-assessment. This does not necessarily mean that the learner must move sequentially from B to C to D, but it certainly helps in accumulating skills. It is quite fascinating to observe a class that has experienced all three styles and know both their roles and the appropriate decisions to make.

Episodes in style D actually provide learners the opportunity to become more self-reliant in knowing what they have or have not done in the performance of the task.

When the learners disperse in the gymnasium, playing field, court, dance studio, and so on, they begin performing the task, stop frequently to look at the criteria sheet, compare their own performance with the criteria, and then move on. They either repeat the task, to correct or maintain the performance, or go on to a new task. This is the first style that allows time for these kinds of decisions. For learners to experience these decisions, they must engage in several subsidiary behaviors: They pause to read and internalize the criteria, and they pause after the performance of a task to think about their performance. At times, they may engage in "self-negotiations," expressing concern or joy. These behaviors are overt and observable. Together, they present a different picture of what goes on in the gymnasium. A great deal more than just performing tasks occurs in style D episodes.

This different behavior is possible because the teacher's role has changed. The verbal behavior that is specific to this style develops and maintains the operation and the spirit of such episodes.

Now that you have an idea of what an episode in this style is like, what kind of learner can readily engage in this style? There is a difference in success between learners who are proficient in performing tasks and those who are still in the "awkward phase" of performing tasks. Learners who are reasonably proficient in the physical performance seem to handle the demands of comparing and contrasting their own performance against criteria. However, for learners who have not attained basic competency in a task, this style may not be appropriate. (We return to this topic in the section on selecting and designing the task.)

HOW TO DO IT

The Preimpact Set

The teacher makes all the preimpact decisions in this style—the decisions about which tasks are appropriate and the criteria sheet that the learner will use.

The Impact Set

The sequence of events in this episode is as follows:

1. Assemble the learners around you.
2. Explain the purpose of the style (new expectations).
3. Explain the role of the learner. (Describe the decisions involved in self-checking and point out the time available for self-assessment.) Explain the shift from style C.
4. Explain the role of the teacher.
5. Present the task(s).
6. Explain the logistics.
7. Establish the parameters.
8. Send the student to begin the tasks.

The learners will select their locations and start making style B decisions as they perform the task, adding the new decision of the self-check style.

The Postimpact Set

As each learner performs the task, use of the criteria sheet begins. Each learner will decide when to use the criteria sheet for self-feedback, based on individual pace and rhythm.

The teacher's role in the postimpact set is to:

1. Observe the learner's performance of the task.
2. Observe the learner's use of the criteria sheet for self-check.
3. Communicate with the individual learner about proficiency and accuracy in the self-check process. (See the section on verbal behavior later in this chapter.)
4. Offer feedback at the end of the lesson (closure). This feedback is addressed to the entire class in the form of general statements about their performance of the role.

IMPLICATIONS OF THIS STYLE

Style D implies that:

1. The teacher values the learner's ability to develop their self-monitoring system.
2. The teacher trusts the learner to be honest during this process.
3. The learner can identify his or her own limits, successes, and failures.
4. The learner can use self-check as feedback for improvement.
5. The teacher has the patience to ask questions focusing on the process of self-check as well as the performance of the task.
6. The teacher values the learner's independence.
7. The learner can work privately and engage in the self-checking process.

SELECTING AND DESIGNING THE SUBJECT MATTER

Not all tasks in physical education are conducive to style D. The criterion for task selection is that the learners must have some proficiency in performing the task so that they can engage in postimpact self-assessment. The short duration of many physical tasks does not allow the performer much time to learn a great deal about the performance. Often, when one asks a novice in tumbling, "What was the position of your left shoulder during the backward roll?," the answer is, "I don't know." This is quite understandable because most learners in the early stages of learning are not aware of the details concerning their body's performance. It is difficult, and sometimes impossible, to do an accurate self-assessment when learning a new task. The Reciprocal style will be more appropriate in such situations.

Another hindrance is the lack of accurate "recording" of the performance. The learner is asked to assess performance against precise criteria using memory as the recording device. This is often very difficult to do. When a novice learns a new skill, it is quite unlikely that he or she will remember the detailed conditions of the body parts. The same is true for tasks in many sports. (Two good ways to overcome this hindrance are using a videotape for immediate feedback, and mirrors such as those used in dance studios.)

These difficulties occur when the *focus* of the task and the end results are the body itself, when the criteria for excellence focus on the precise relationships among the parts of the body. This applies to gymnastics, diving, and some branches of dance. All these activities hinge upon kinesthetic sense. Often one hears a gymnast say, "It did not feel right," or "If felt just great." This sense of movement develops with time, experience, and success. Those learning new activities usually cannot use this as an accurate source of information about the performance. The sense of movement may supply a general feeling about the performance, but it does not supply the accurate information needed for improvement. Many tasks in these areas are inappropriate for style D. Style C supplies the feedback needed from an outside source.

There are other physical tasks, however, that are more applicable to style D. These tasks pursue end results external to the body itself. These activities are concerned with the results of the movement, not the movement itself. A prime example of this type of activity is basketball. Any basketball shot, despite the technique, is judged by the *results* of the movement. It is the distance of the javelin throw that counts in track and field, not the specific form used by the athlete. This relationship between body movements and end results provides the performer with immediate feedback and possibilities for self check using particular criteria. (These are situations where the feedback is intrinsic to the task.)

In many self-check tasks, the implements used are the main source of information. For example, a wiggly flight of the javelin shows the learner that the javelin's release was incorrect. The learner can then refer to the section of the criteria card that highlights the details of the release. During subsequent throws, the learner concentrates on correcting this particular aspect. In soccer, when the task is to practice kicking the ball a relatively short distance through a high arc and the ball does not fly accordingly, the learner knows that something in the kick was incorrect. The learner then refers to the part of the criteria that highlights the details of placing the foot under the lower part of the ball.

The purpose of this analysis is not to offer a classification system for various activities nor to interfere with well-established techniques of various sports (these are readily available in kinesiology materials and specific sports books); rather, the purpose is to invite the teacher to analyze tasks in terms of their applicability to style D. There is no need to use this style with a task that can be better accomplished by another style. Your role as teacher is to facilitate efficient learning and reduce frustration.

STYLE-SPECIFIC COMMENTS

Verbal Behavior

The teacher's verbal behavior must reflect the intent of this style and must support the roles of the teacher and the learner. The purposes for communication between the teacher and the learner are:

1. To ascertain that the learner can compare and contrast his or her own performance against criteria
2. To listen to what the learner is saying
3. To lead the learner to see discrepancies (when they exist) by asking questions
4. To tell the learner about the discrepancies if the learner cannot see them.[1]

---

[1]*Note:* Be careful not to increase the learner's frustration by asking questions that the learner cannot answer, or by withdrawing feedback. Now is the time to make an adjustment decision. The learner's feelings are more important than the structure of the style. Momentarily switch to style B and offer feedback to the learner about the performance of the task.

To initiate communication with the learner in this style, the teacher asks a general question: "How are you doing?" The learner has several options in answering it:

1. "Fine!"
2. "I can't do the task, and I'm not sure why."
3. "I can't do the task, but I know how to correct it."
4. "I can do the task and I understand each part on the criteria sheet."

In the case of the first two answers, the teacher should continue to ask questions that invite the learner to focus on the criteria and the performance. (See the verbal behavior examples of communication between the teacher and the observer in style C.) Once the learner can verbalize what he or she is doing, the teacher can verify it by acknowledging the performance with a value statement. If the learner gets stuck in the process and cannot identify or correct the error, the role of the teacher is to tell the learner.

Options in Task Design

Two options are available for task design in style D: (1) a single task for all learners, and (2) a differentiated task. These options were discussed in style B. In the first option, the teacher assigns the same task to all learners; in the second option, the teacher assigns different tasks to different learners. The roles, however, remain within the structure of the self-check style.

Criteria Sheets   The criteria sheets that were designed for style C can be used for style D. The criteria do not change—only the style.

Target Games   Target games are essentially style D experiences. Examples of target games are bowling, archery, darts, and pinball machines. In all these games, the feedback is intrinsic to the activity—it's built in! The degree of success is seen by the participants in the event itself. Many carnival games fall into this category as do many children's games such as jump rope, marbles, and hopscotch. "Do-it-yourself" repair or construction activities represent this style. Since these experiences exist in everyday life, why not initiate these activities in schools?

DEVELOPMENTAL CHANNELS

The positions of a learner on the developmental channels in this style are interesting (see Figure 6-2). On the physical development channel, the position is similar to that of style B. The position on the social channel, however, moves toward minimum. In this style the learner works alone. The individual performance and the high level of privacy in self-check do not provide social interaction with peers or much contact with the teacher.

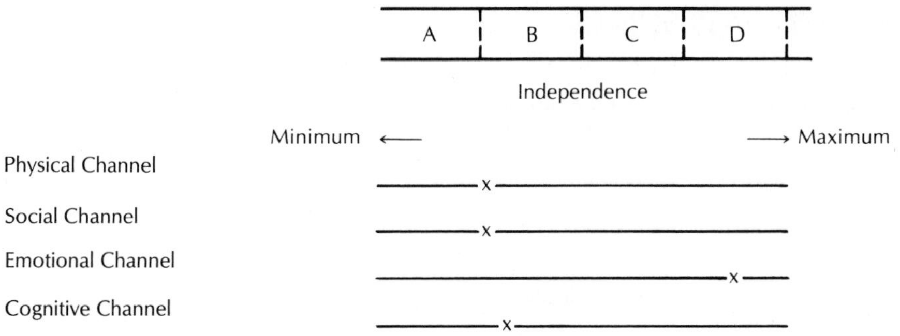

FIGURE 6–2   The self-check style and the developmental channels

People reach a level of comfort in this style at different speeds. There are those who immediately enjoy the demands of individualization and independence implicit in this style, and there are those who need more time to reach this level. A teacher can learn a great deal about students by watching them experience the self-check style. For those learners who are very comfortable with being more independent for the duration of the episode, the position on the emotional channel may move toward maximum.

On the cognitive channel, the learner is engaged in the same style C process of comparing and contrasting against criteria, but here the learner is doing it for himself or herself. This may increase the cognitive demand and the position on this channel may move still further away from minimum.

EXAMPLE TASK SHEETS

FIGURE 6–3 Criteria for self-assessment: Squash

Name _____ Style B C Ⓓ E
Class _____
Date _____

Squash—high lob serve

To the student:

Task: Practice 10 high lob serves from the right service box and 10 from the left service box.

Note the position following the task.
After the performance, check each step of the criteria.

Criteria:

	Service Box	
	Right Side	Left Side
Starting Position		
1. Stand as near to the center "T" as possible, with one foot inside the lines of the service box.	_____	_____
2. Hold the racket low and point the left shoulder at the spot on the front wall where the ball is aimed.	_____	_____
The Swing		
1. Toss the ball up about 2 inches, well in front of the body.	_____	_____
2. Keep wrist firm and swing arm forward to meet the ball directly ahead of the body at about knee level.	_____	_____
3. Contact point is under the ball so it will lift upward.	_____	_____
Follow-Through		
1. The racket, arm, and shoulder all follow the ball, allowing a long, high, deliberate follow-through.	_____	_____
2. Ball should contact the front wall as high as possible and have a rising, arching effect after leaving it.	_____	_____
3. Ball should fall perpendicularly to the length of the court.	_____	_____

FIGURE 6–4   Criteria for self-assessment: Skiing

Name _____   Style B C Ⓓ E
Class _____
Date _____

Skiing—herringbone

To the student:

1. Following the steps listed below, practice the herringbone six times.
2. After the last performance of each step, check in the appropriate space.
3. Practice this task 20 times.

A. Starting Position
   1. Skis are placed in a "v" position with the tips apart facing the hill.

B. Uphill Action
   1. The left ski is moved forward while both poles support the skier.

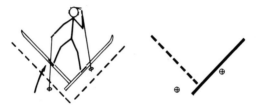

   2. The right ski is set and the right pole is brought forward.

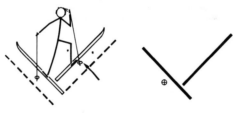

   3. The right ski is moved forward while both poles support the skier.

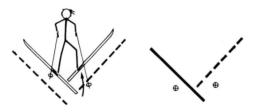

4. The left ski is set on edge and weighted as the left pole is moved forward.

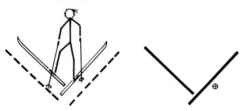

5. The left ski is lifted while the right ski and both poles hold the skier to the hill.

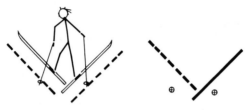

Task performance:
_____ complete
_____ incomplete: difficulty with steps # _____

FIGURE 6–5   Criteria for self-assessment: Gymnastics

Name _____   Style   D
Class _____
Date _____

Gymnastics—apparatus skills review

To the student:

The following tasks are to be practiced 5 times each. After the fifth time, check the appropriate column. Continue to another skill. Complete all skills on the same apparatus before moving to another apparatus.

Parallel Bars	Task Accomplished	Needs More Time
a. Jump to front support.	_____	_____
b. "Walk" length of bar.	_____	_____
c. Swing 6 times from front support position.	_____	_____
d. Swing into straddle seat.	_____	_____

Uneven Parallel Bars
   a. Hang by arms.
   b. L straddle.
   c. Sit and balance on lower beam.
   d. Hang by knees.
   e. Do T scale, holding high bar.

Balance Beam
   a. Jump to one leg balance.
   b. Walk length of bar.
   c. Do T scale (with spotter).
   d. Do V seat.
   e. Do 90° jump turn.

Tumbling
   a. Do forward roll.
   b. Do backward roll.
   c. Do head stand.
   d. Do T scale (hold for 5 seconds).
   e. Do cartwheel.

High Bar
   a. Jump to arm hang.
   b. Swing.
   c. Pull up.
   d. Skin the cat.
   e. Hang by knees.

FIGURE 6–6   *Inappropriate* task design

The following task design is not appropriate as a task sheet for style D. The reasons are (a) since this task keeps the learner in continuous motion, the learner cannot assess each step, and (b) most beginners cannot do this task, and therefore cannot engage in self-check.

Gymnastics—backward hip circle

To the student:

A spotter is required for this task. The spotter's role is to stand to the side and push up on the learner's chest as required for completion of the circle.

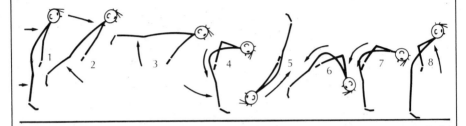

	Feedback
1. The Cast a. From a front rest position with regular grasp, pike slightly, as in diagram one. b. Extend legs backward, lean forward, and raise hips, as in diagram three. 2. The Circle a. Bring legs and hips down forcefully into the bar assuming a pike position, as in diagram four. b. Hold hips into bar during rotation, as in diagram five. c. Extend the legs up over the bar and pull up on arms, diagrams five and six. d. As the upper body rises above the bar, push down on the bar and resume extended position (diagrams seven and eight).	

FIGURE 6–7   Style D classroom chart

THE SELF–CHECK STYLE

The purposes of this style are:

- To learn to do a task

- To check your own work

ROLE OF LEARNER

- To perform the task

- To make the 9 decisions of style B

- To check his or her own task performance

ROLE OF TEACHER

- To prepare the subject matter and criteria

- To answer questions by the learner

- To initiate communication with the learner

The Inclusion Style (Style E)

THE CONCEPT OF INCLUSION

The first four styles have one feature in common—the design of tasks. Every task represents a *single standard* decided on by the teacher. The learner's task is to perform at that level.

Style E introduces a different conception of task design—multiple levels of performance in the same task. This shifts a major decision to the learners that they could not make in previous styles—at what level of performance does one begin?

The following experience illustrates this concept.

Hold a rope about 2 feet off the ground and ask your students to take a few steps and jump over it. Chances are that all of them will clear the rope. Raise the rope a couple of inches and ask the class to jump over it again. Chances are that all of them will clear the rope. They are all successful. As the height of the rope keeps increasing, a particular phenomenon occurs—at each subsequent height, one, two, or more students will fail to clear the rope. They are *excluded* from the experience. As you continue to raise the rope, eventually the number of successful participants will be one, or none!

This particular arrangement of the subject matter—in this case, jumping over the horizontal rope—represents the *single standard* design of the task. All learners participating in this experience were asked to jump over the same height each time. This condition always induces the process of *exclusion*.

If the objective of an episode is to exclude people, this arrangement is appropriate (see Figure 7-1). The objective of excluding participants will be accomplished every time. There are situations when this objective is acceptable and desirable, such as in the competitive high jump.

In contrast, if the objective of the episode is *inclusion* of *all* participants, how can the objective be reached? What adjustments or changes must be made in the task design to shift from exclusion to inclusion?

Can you suggest an alternative? How would you provide each learner the opportunity for successful participation in the same task?

Indeed, several solutions are available. The most succinct one, and perhaps the most dramatic, is to slant the rope—hold one end of the rope at floor level and the other at about your shoulder level (see Figure 7-2). Now ask the learners to jump over the rope once more. Using no additional words, ask them to

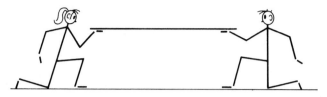

FIGURE 7–1 A task designed for exclusion

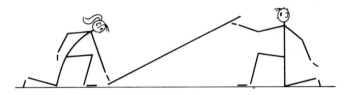

FIGURE 7–2 A task designed for inclusion

jump over the slanted rope.[1] Invariably the class will spread along the rope and people will jump over at varying heights.

Everyone will be successful. Everyone is included! The intent and the action in this episode are congruent because the slanted rope arrangement accomplished the objective to create conditions of inclusion (choice of the degree of difficulty within the same task).

THE OBJECTIVES OF THIS STYLE

The objectives this style strives for are:

1. Inclusion of learners and continued participation
2. A reality accommodating individual differences
3. An opportunity to enter the activity at one's ability level
4. An opportunity to step backward to succeed in the activity
5. Learning to see the relationship between one's aspiration and the reality of one's performance
6. Further individualization than in previous styles because choices exist among alternative levels within each task

THE ANATOMY OF THIS STYLE

Let us now identify the anatomy of style E and then analyze the functional steps in this process (see Figure 7-3).

---

[1] Never say, "Do your best." Why is this verbal behavior inappropriate for this style?

	A		B		C		D		E	
Preimpact	(T)		(T)		(T)		(T)		(T)	
Impact	(T)	→	(L)		(d)		(L)	→	(L)	
Postimpact	(T)		(T)	→	(o)	→	(L)	→	(L)	

FIGURE 7–3 The anatomy of the inclusion style

The role of the teacher in this style is to make the decisions in the preimpact set. The learner makes the decisions in the impact set, including the decision about the entry point into the subject matter by selecting the level of task performance. In the postimpact set, the learner makes assessment decisions about his or her performance and decides in which of the available levels to continue.

Let us examine more specifically the decisions a learner makes when offered the multiple-level conditions of the slanted rope. For the purpose of analysis, let us examine one learner. The sequence of steps is as follows:

1. The learner looks at the options of height made available by the slanted rope.
2. The learner makes a decision of self-assessment and selects the entry point. (You can actually watch the learner going through this selection process; it is almost like a bargaining session with oneself. You will see the learner select a position opposite a given height. This might be followed by a hesitation and perhaps another position choice, and then the learner is ready to approach the rope.)
3. The learner takes a few running steps and jumps over the selected height. Usually it is a height that the learner knows will ensure success. The *initial* choice is always a *safe* choice!
4. The learner knows that he or she was successful in the first choice of height (postimpact decision). Now the learner has three options:
    a. To repeat the same height
    b. To select a higher spot
    c. To select a lower spot

Whichever choice the learner makes is acceptable. The important point is that the *learner* made the decision about further placement in the range of levels. The learner made the choice of where to interact with the task.

5. The learner takes a few steps and jumps over the selected height.
6. The learner assesses the results of this jump (postimpact decision) and whether or not the second jump was successful. Again, the learner has three options—to repeat the height, to select a higher spot, or to select a lower spot.
7. The process continues.

This episode of the slanted rope has been used as an illustration hundreds of times in lessons, conventions, and seminars in the United States and abroad. *All* participants grasp the principle of inclusion without any strain or difficulty. Regardless of age, geographic location, or culture, this episode has been successful in including all types of learners. In one demonstration with 30 fifth graders as participants, one girl with a cast on her leg asked to be excused and sat on a chair nearby. As we reached the end of the first part, the horizontal rope was raised again and again and all but one learner were excluded. I asked the learners, "What can we do with this rope so that all can be included?" After a slight pause, one learner offered, "Why don't you dip it in the middle?" In effect, a double slanted rope was designed where the center dipped and touched the floor. All participants were then engaged in the jump and in making all the decisions previously described. Soon the girl with the cast on her leg stood up, limped to the rope, and walked over its lowest point, where the rope touched the floor. The audience observed that this style is indeed an inviting one.

IMPLEMENTATION OF THE INCLUSION STYLE

Description of an Episode

Style E can be initially introduced to your classes by doing it. Demonstrate the concept using the slanted rope. The transfer to other activities will be quite smooth. It is possible, of course, to hold a rope in your hand and explain the whole idea, but nothing can match the impact of really doing it and feeling included.

After the demonstration is completed, identify the task(s) that will be performed and ask your students to begin. (The next two sections deal with the design of tasks in various activities based on this concept.) As in previous styles, the learners will disperse, pick up their task sheets, and select their locations. Next, they will survey the levels of performance offered and decide their individual entry points. You will see your learners perform the task(s) on different levels, assess their performance, and make decisions about their next steps.

While this is occurring, pause for a while and observe the process; give the learners time to start and experience the initial steps. Then your role is to move about and offer each individual feedback as in style D. Respond to the learner's role in decision making, *not* to his or her performance of the task. Your initial contact with the individual learner should be to ask, "How are you doing in your role?" Most likely, the learner will reply, "I have selected my level and I am now doing . . . " or "I'm doing my bending exercise on level four." Your feedback, then, would be, "I see that you know how to make that decision."

Focus on using neutral feedback; avoid value feedback referring to the selected level. It is not your role to tell the learner whether or not you like the level selected. The learner's role is to select the appropriate level for him or her, not please you. It might be a little difficult to refrain from commenting on the selected level, but patience is mandatory. The objective is to teach the learner to make appropriate decisions about which level in the subject matter he or she is most capable of performing.

If you observe an error in the performance of the task, regardless of the selected level, ask the learner to refer to the task description and check the performance once more. Wait to see if the learner can identify the error; if not, tell him or her, then move on to the next learner.

HOW TO DO IT

The description of style E at the beginning of the chapter and the description of the episode should provide you with an idea of appropriate episodes. Let us summarize the sequence of events in doing this style in your classes.

The Preimpact Set

1. All the decisions in this set are made by the teacher. To introduce the style to a new class, the teacher prepares the "presentation of the concept," reviews its sequence, the appropriate questions and statements, and the use of the rope. In subsequent episodes this preparation will not be necessary. Since the presentation of the concept is usually powerful, learners do not need to see or hear it again. They need to experience it.
2. The teacher prepares the Individual Program for the selected tasks.

The Impact Set

The sequence of events is as follows:

1. Set the scene by presenting the concept. This can be done by telling, or by asking the learners questions that guide them to discover the concept of the slanted rope.
2. State the major objective of the style—to include learners in the task by providing a range of levels (degrees of difficulty) within the same task.
3. Describe the role of the learner, which involves:
   a. Surveying the choices
   b. Selecting an initial level for performance
   c. Performing the task
   d. Assessing one's performance against criteria
   e. Deciding whether or not another level is desired or appropriate
4. Describe the role of the teacher, which involves:
   a. Answering questions by the learner
   b. Initiating communication with the learner
5. Present the subject matter; describe the individual program.

Identify the factor that determines the degree of difficulty. (For an explanation of these terms see "Selecting and Designing the Subject Matter" later in this chapter.)

6. Explain the logistics and establish the necessary parameters.
7. At this point, the class may disperse and begin to engage in individual roles and tasks.

The Postimpact Set

1. Learners will assess their performance using the criteria sheet.
2. Observe your class for a while; then move about making private contact with each learner and offering feedback about the learner's participation in the role. The principle of the verbal behavior is the same as in style D with the added dimension of verifying (not approving) to the learner the appropriateness of his or her selection of level.

IMPLICATIONS OF THIS STYLE

It is true that each style on the Spectrum has its own beauty and its own power in the development of the individual learner. This is particularly true when one keeps the nonversus notion in mind. However, some degree of bias and personal preference can always creep into the way one sees alternatives.

With some degree of bias, it is suggested here that this style has tremendous implications for the structure and function of physical education. If the goals of physical education include providing developmental programs for large numbers of people, then a wide variety of activities must be offered (which is a programmatic condition for choice) and day-to-day conditions for choice should be considered by increasing the frequency of style E episodes in each activity. If inclusion is a true goal of physical education, then what counts is the *frequent* inclusion of all students by creating conditions for successful entry points! The only style that can accomplish this goal is style E. The only design for including everyone is the design reflecting the principle of the slanted rope.

As in previous styles, the objective analysis of style E identifies a cluster of implications:

1. First, when this style is used it implies that the teacher philosophically accepts the concept of inclusion.
2. It implies that the teacher can expand his or her understanding of the nonversus notion by planning some episodes that tend to exclude while others are specifically designed to include.
3. It implies that conditions have been created for the learners to experience the relationship between aspiration and reality.
4. It implies that learners have the opportunity to learn to *accept* the discrepancy between aspiration and reality and, at times, learn to reduce the gap between the two.
5. It implies the legitimacy of doing more than or less than others; this is not a measurement of what *others* can do, but rather "what *I* can do!" The competition during the episodes is against oneself and one's own standards, abilities, and aspirations—not those of others.

6. The last three points are important factors that induce examination of the self-concept. This self-concept includes one's emotional independence from the teacher's decision of where the learner should be in the performance of the task.

At the risk of being redundant, it is important to create *legitimate* options in entry points—this can become the "hallmark" of physical education. Physical education, in particular, must acknowledge the vast differences among people—differences in size, shape, ability, physical attributes, energy levels, and so on.

SELECTING AND DESIGNING THE SUBJECT MATTER: THE INDIVIDUAL PROGRAM

The Concept of Degree of Difficulty

Let us look at the slanted rope example again (Figure 7-4). The gradations in height along the rope present the learner with different degrees of difficulty within the *same* task. The task is to jump over the rope (in a particular way) regardless of the height. The variation occurs in the height, which determines the degree of difficulty.

For any learner, points A, B, and C on the rope represent different levels in the degree of difficulty. Point B is higher than point A and more energy (effort) is *always* required to jump over this point; hence, it is more difficult. The same is true with point C. More effort is always required to jump over the rope at point C than at points A or B. This is true for all jumpers regardless of their ability. In the example of jumping over the slanted rope, the factor that determines the degree of difficulty is *height*. Varying the height creates many levels of difficulty within the same task. How, then, can we identify the factors that affect the degree of difficulty in other activities, in other tasks?

Let us analyze a familiar activity—shooting a ball into a basket (see Figure 7-5). It is imperative to realize that the task is *not* playing the game of basketball within the competitive rules; rather we are taking the particular activity of shooting a ball into a basket and analyzing it in terms of factors affecting the degree of difficulty.

1. Factor 1—Distance. Distance is intrinsic to the degree of difficulty in getting the ball through the hoop. It is more difficult to get the ball through

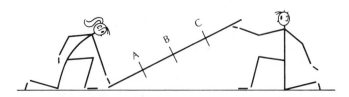

FIGURE 7–4 A task designed for inclusion

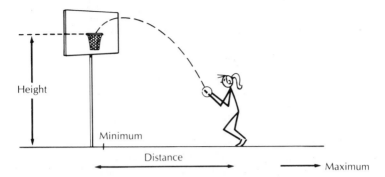

FIGURE 7–5   Factors affecting the degree of difficulty: Basketball

the hoop as the distance increases and less difficult as the distance de-creases. (There is also a limit of minimal distance—as we approach the position below the basket, the shot becomes increasingly more difficult.) The *range*, then, between the point of minimum and maximum distance offers many levels of difficulty to the learner in performing the task of shooting the ball into the basket.

These different options of distance can be marked on the floor to assist the learner in making a decision about a concrete entry point.

2. Factor 2—The height of the basket. Varying the height of the basket creates various degrees of difficulty that will serve as different entry points for dif-ferent learners.
3. Factor 3—The diameter of the hoop. Varying the diameter of the hoop creates different conditions for successful shooting of the ball into the bas-ket.
4. Factor 4—The size of the ball.
5. Factor 5—The weight of the ball.
6. Factor 6—The angle of the shot. The positions around the basket from which the shot may be taken offer different degrees of difficulty.
7. Factor 7—If you can think of any more factors, add them to the list.

All of these factors are part of the experience of shooting the ball through the hoop; some of the factors have been standardized (i.e., height, diameter of hoop, etc.) to provide fair competition during a game. The purpose here, however, is to illustrate that changes or adjustments in some factors provide a greater variety for learners who cannot readily participate in standardized ep-isodes developed for exclusion. In this style, we are focusing on episodes de-signed for *inclusion*. Remember that the Spectrum of Teaching Styles is based on the nonversus notion. Each style has its place in education as long as the objective is clearly defined and reachable. Any standardized activity (with the styles that accomplish it) is appropriate if the objective is to reach standards. When the objective is to discover if masses of students can reach a particular standard, then the activity must be designed accordingly (the horizontal rope principle) and the appropriate styles must be employed. Styles A, B, C, and D do just that—they require the learner to learn the single standard, despite the risk of exclusion.

Keeping the nonversus notion in mind, we must learn to design episodes for inclusion when inclusion is the educational objective. The multilevel design of the task in style E will accomplish this objective.

In physical education classes, an unusual opportunity exists to demonstrate the principle of education by including episodes of both kinds in the units for the week or the month. When students are excluded, they not only feel a sense of failure in that activity, they begin to resent the entire experience of physical education. Frequent episodes in style E invite the learner to begin successfully. The legitimate opportunity to succeed at the entry point and at subsequent levels of performance ensures continuous participation. *No one has ever learned an activity by not doing it!* Exclusion breeds rejection; inclusion invites involvement.

Identifying the Factor that Determines the Degree of Difficulty

The major questions confronting the teacher who wishes to arrange a style E task are: How do I identify the factors in the selected task? What do I need to know about the task? The Factor Grid chart (Figure 7-6) is a tool to guide you in answering these questions. It offers a way of thinking about both the intrinsic and external factors affecting the design of physical tasks. (Other disciplines have their own intrinsic Factor Grids.)

The following points explain the structure and use of this Grid:

1. After you select the task, the question you must keep in mind throughout planning is: Within this task, how do I provide for inclusion?
2. The Grid suggests two kinds of factors: intrinsic and external. The intrinsic factors are a part of the given task's structure. Some tasks may have all of these factors; others may have only some. The external factors are superimposed on the performance of the task. Both kinds of factors affect the degree of difficulty of the given task; any one of the factors can be changed (or manipulated) to vary the degree of difficulty.
3. Once you select the task, your next step is to decide which intrinsic factor can be manipulated to provide for inclusion in the ensuing episode. (In the example of the slanted rope, the key factor is height.) Sometimes tasks are affected by two or more factors. For example, throwing a ball at a target with an overhead throw readily suggests "size of the target" and "distance from the target" as possible key factors. Decide which one will serve as the key factor in planning and which one will be the supporting factor for the given episode. This choice is related to the task's objective. Indicate the rank order by writing the numbers (1, 2, . . .) on the line to the left of the factor.
4. Next, identify the range of possibilities in the key factor from which the learner will select his or her entry level. For example, in the case of the

FIGURE 7–6 The factor grid

External Factors	Range
_____ Number of Repetitions:	
_____ Time:	

Name of the task:

- Identify the rank order for the key and the supporting factor(s)
- Indicate the range

External Factors	**Range**
_____ Number of Repetitions:	
_____ Time:	
Intrinsic Factors	
_____ Distance	
_____ Height	
_____ Weight of Implements	
_____ Size of Implements	
_____ Size of Target	
_____ Speed	
_____ ?	
_____ ?	
_____ Posture	

size of the target, the range may include targets with varying diameters: small, medium, large; or 10″, 20″, 30″; or 15 cm, 30 cm, 45 cm. Also identify the range for the supporting factors.

5. If you select one of the external factors as the key factor (for example: the choices in the number of repetitions of a given task will be 5, 10, 15, 20, etc.), indicate it in the range. If not, indicate a specific quantity next to the external factor.

6. The speed factor. This factor can be placed on a range from slow to fast, controlled by a metronome, the music, or the pitching machine as in tennis or baseball.

7. The posture factor. This factor involves the position(s) of the body required to perform a static and/or a dynamic task. (It is also referred to as "form," "basic skill," or the "technique" of a given sport or dance.) If a learner cannot do the task, then manipulating the factors of distance, time, or size of target will not help. The entry point here is a modified posture such as changing the angle between body parts, adding further extension, and so on. For example, if a learner cannot do the T-scale, you can introduce (on a range) a modification in the angle of the lifted leg or the position of the upper body. This will be the entry point that includes all learners. Later on, factors such as repetition, time, and so on can be added. Knowing what is "less difficult" or "more difficult" in the posture factor is derived from biomechanical analyses of the task.

FIGURE 7–7   Factors affecting the degree of difficulty: Golf

Name of the Task: Chip Shot

External Factors	**Range**
____ Number of Repetitions: 10	
____ Time:	

Intrinsic Factors	
_2_ Distance	Lines A, B, C [3 yards, 5 yds, 7 yds]
____ Height	
____ Weight of Implements	
____ Size of Implements	
_1_ Size of Target	Small target 10'; Large target 30'
____ Speed	
____ ?	
____ Posture	

8. Let us examine the Factor Grid for the golf chip shot. Note the two intrinsic factors selected for inclusion by designation of the range in size of target and distance. The external factor involves the number of repetitions. From this grid (Figure 7-7), the teacher designs the individual program for practicing the chip shot (Figure 7-8).

Let us now examine the part of the Factor Grid dealing with the manipulation of the posture factor. If the objective of the episode is to develop strength in the shoulders and arms by using the push-up movement for example, then different *positions* of the body (such as starting positions or positions to be maintained during the movement of the push-up) will offer a range in the levels of difficulty. (See Figure 7-9.)

In Figure 7-10, position B, in which the hands are placed forward in front of the shoulders, is more difficult to assume and maintain than position A. Performing the push-up movement from this position is also more difficult than performing the movement from position A. The same is true for position C, in which the arms are extended further. The push-up movement from position C is more difficult than either A or B.[2]

In the individual program (Figure 7-11), a cluster of developmental movements are designed to strengthen various regions of the body. The task itself is the same for any learner using this program. The differentiation for each movement occurs by identifying the different levels. In each level, the task is to be performed from a *different* starting position, each more difficult than the last. The degree of difficulty was determined by the appropriate factor for each task.

---

[2]For a fuller kinesiological analysis concerning this issue, see Mosston, Muska. *Developmental Movement,* Copyright © 1992 by Muska Mosston.

FIGURE 7–8 Factors affecting the degree of difficulty: Golf

Name _____   Style B C D Ⓔ
Class _____   Individual Program # ___
Date _____

Golf—the chip shot

To the student:

1. Select an initial level and circle the number you expect to do.
2. Do the task and blacken out the number of the actual performance.
3. Compare your execution of the task with the performance criteria.
4. Decide whether to repeat the task at the same level or at a different level.

Criteria:

1. Stand with your feet close together.
2. Bend your knees slightly, as though starting to sit.
3. Contact the ball off your left heel.
4. Follow through along the path of the ball, keeping the left wrist firm at contact.
5. Refrain from letting the club pass the left hand.
6. Keep the flight of the ball low.
7. Hit to a predetermined spot and have the ball roll to the cup.

The task: Choose a distance (either line A, B, or C), and a target area (either the large or the small). Take 10 chip shots, and record the number of times you hit the target area.

Line A ____ ____ ____
Line B ____ ____ ____
Line C ____ ____ ____

Distance	LARGE TARGET										
A	0	1	2	3	4	5	6	7	8	9	10
B	0	1	2	3	4	5	6	7	8	9	10
C	0	1	2	3	4	5	6	7	8	9	10

Distance	SMALL TARGET										
A	0	1	2	3	4	5	6	7	8	9	10
B	0	1	2	3	4	5	6	7	8	9	10
C	0	1	2	3	4	5	6	7	8	9	10

FIGURE 7–9   The Factor Grid—push up

The Factor Grid will look like this:

Name of the Task: Push-Up

| **External Factors**   **Range** |
| ___ Number of Repetitions: 3 |
| ___ Time: |

Intrinsic Factors
___ Distance
___ Height
___ Weight of Implements
___ Size of Implements
___ Size of Target
___ Speed
_1_ Posture—angle between the arms and
        the body.

From   to

The *same* factor, then, can serve several tasks (as in the case of hitting the target), or a *different* factor can be identified for each task in the program (as in the last example).

The kinesiological analysis does not only apply to developmental movements or exercises. In many sports, it may be useful to reduce the degree of difficulty in the starting position, the swing, the lift, the stretch, the arc, the spin, the bend, or whatever else is involved in the sport. This is only a temporary compromise to provide an entry point. Don't let the desire for purity of form cause exclusion. A person who is excluded will never participate in the activity; a teacher must always be ready to offer the learner an opportunity to participate using another entry point.

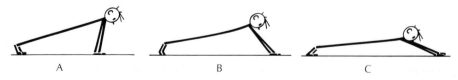

                A   B   C

FIGURE 7–10   Position of the body: A factor in the degree of difficulty

FIGURE 7–11 Individual program

Name _____   Style B C D Ⓔ
Class _____   Individual Program # ___
Date _____

Task Description	Factor	Level 1	Level 2	Level 3
1. Perform the push-up from the described starting position. Do it 3 times.	Angle between the arms and the body		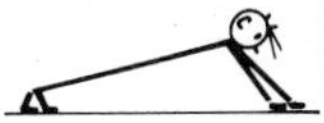	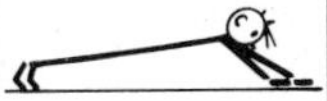
2. Perform the push-up from the described starting position. Do it 3 times.	Width of the base	 (Front view)		
3. In the described position, move each straight leg up or down 25 times (scissors motion).	Angle between the legs and the floor			
4. In the described position, hold the upper body for 20 counts. Repeat 5 times, with 10 count intervals	Length of lever			
5. Other?				

STYLE-SPECIFIC COMMENTS

1. Since one of the goals of Style E is continuous participation and development, pay attention to learners who stay at their initially chosen level. Be aware that while trying to reduce the gap between aspiration and reality, at times the aspiration may be high and the reality is low; sometimes it is the reverse—the aspiration is low but the reality (the ability to perform) is high. Often this gap is emotionally based rather than physically based, and it is the role of the teacher to lead the learner toward understanding this gap and working to close it. Ths is a delicate issue and must be dealt with using appropriate verbal behavior. Usually commands will not accomplish your purpose. Allow time to develop dialogues with the student so that he or she will understand the gap and be willing to reduce it.

2. Style E produces an interesting phenomenon that did not surface in styles A through D. There are good performers who have difficulty with style E episodes. They seem to function well in conditions where they are told what to do and where they know the "pecking order." Their goal is to be the best and their arena must facilitate those needs. Their emotional structure requires the kind of feedback that frequently singles them out as being "the best." Shifting to style E sometimes disturbs them. Since each learner is "OK" in his or her level, sometimes accepting that all learners are equal in such episodes is quite difficult. Learning to be oneself and make all the decisions of this style is demanding, as is breaking the emotional dependency on the teacher. This can often be a painful and delicate process.

3. Students who have frequently been excluded often react quite the opposite. They love this style. For many, it is the first time they have been included over a longer period of time. These students identify with this style because:
    a. They have an entry point that allows them to participate and succeed in the task.
    b. They see a chance for continuous progress and development.

Although this style is inviting to most learners, for students in special education it is perhaps mandatory. Style E is an excellent one to start with, and then expand to others. Perhaps all students need to experience the nonversus realities.

4. Operationally, this style offers the teacher and the learners longer periods for independent practice. The individual program should be designed for a series of episodes—quite a number of tasks and levels can be included in a single individual program. Infrequent, single episodes in this style do not create the opportunity to reap the full benefits of this style. Learning to be more independent takes time, and the design of the individual program can accommodate this objective.

5. Perhaps the single most important thing that can be said about this style is its power of inclusion. The stigma caused by exclusion in physical education classes can be reduced by different arrangements in the gymnasium and by different teaching behaviors. The invitation to participate offered by the slanted rope is so powerful, that sooner or later all learners who had previously been excluded (regardless of reason) join in. It is as if the learner says, "I have a place, too. I belong!"

THE DEVELOPMENTAL CHANNELS

Let us now examine the relationship between the reality of style E and the developmental channels (see Figure 7-12). Where would the individual be placed on each channel?

On the physical channel, the position moves toward maximum because the learner becomes very independent in making decisions about his or her physical development. Style E episodes are designed for this purpose because learners decide about their relationship to the options in the subject matter.

Since this style is designed to increase the individualization of each learner as he or she privately pursues decisions and choices in the individual program, the position on the social channel is toward minimum. The learner must not make a decision to socialize during episodes because this would then interfere with other people's decisions. Style E is a highly private style.

As in Style D, the position on the emotional channel is toward maximum because making decisions about one's success in task performance brings about a sense of self-confidence. Pressure and anxiety are reduced, success in performance is more frequent, and the feeling about oneself is more positive.

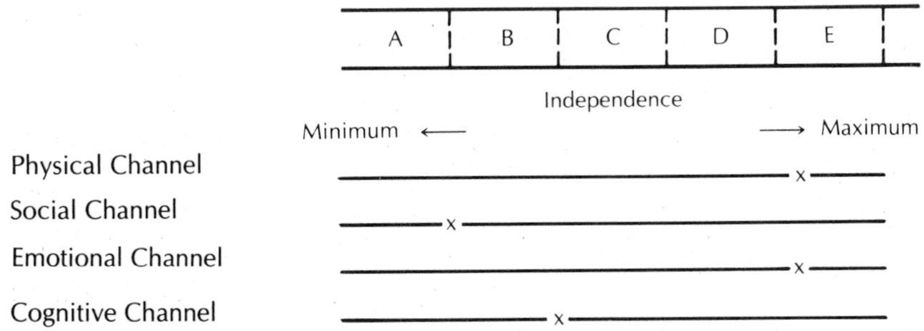

FIGURE 7–12 The inclusion style and the developmental channels

The position on the cognitive channel perhaps moves a bit toward maximum because learners have to use their own criteria (ability and aspiration) rather than an external criteria (prepared by the teacher). This decision-making process may require greater cognitive involvement, and the learner is certainly more independent in this style to engage in such involvement.

EXAMPLE INDIVIDUAL PROGRAMS

Figures 7-13 through 7-23 include a variety of individual program examples in various physical activities. All of them have several characteristics in common:

1. They adhere to the theoretical structure of the style.
2. They contain general logistical information.
3. They identify the activity and the task(s).
4. Some identify the key factor.
5. They offer samples of levels designed by the principle of the slanted rope.
6. Although the general format is similar, they offer flexibility in some details.

FIGURE 7–13   Individual program: Developmental program

Name _____   Style   E
Class _____   Individual Program # ___
Date _____

Developmental Movement

To the student:

1. This program offers you two factors affecting the degree of difficulty: (a) position of the body (determined by kinesiological analysis); (b) number of repetitions.
2. Place a check (√) at the level which represents your entry point and circle the quantity you intend to do.
3. Perform the selected tasks.
4. If there is a difference between your intent and your actual performance, please mark the latter.

Tasks	Level 1	Level 2	Level 3	Level 4

Straddle Jump
 	
Quantity:
1. 2 consec.
   rest
   2 consec.
   rest
 	
2. 4 consec.
   rest
   2 consec.
	—leg bent
	—trunk reaching down to the feet
		—legs straight
		—trunk reaching down to the feet
			—legs straight
			—trunk slightly bent forward
				—legs straight
				—trunk straight
				—legs hip level

Touch the Ground
 	
Quantity:
  Slowly bob:
 	
1. 2 sets
   of 10
 	
2. 4 sets
   of 5
	—legs spread wider than shoulders
	—bent legs
	—fingertips touching ground
		—straddle stance, legs apart at shoulder width
		—bent legs
		—fingertips touching ground
			—straddle stance
			—straight legs
			—fingertips touching ground
				—legs together and straight
				—fingertips touching ground

Leg Lift a. Stand on right leg.	—right leg bent	—right leg straight	—right leg bent	—right leg straight

Tasks	Level 1	Level 2	Level 3	Level 4
b. Lift left leg. c. Keep trunk straight. d. Keep arms stretched to the sides. Quantity: Hold for seconds. 1, 2, 3, 4, 5, 6, 7, 8, 9, 10 Do 3 sets. (Repeat above task standing on left leg.)	—left leg slightly raised and bent	—left leg slightly raised and straight	—left leg raised straight to hip level	—left leg raised straight to hip level
Push-Up Touch nose to the ground. Quantity: 1, 2, 3, 4, 5, 6, 7, 8, 9, 10, 11, 12, 13, 14, 15, 16, 17, 18, 19, 20	—on knees —back straight —arms straight under shoulders	—on knees —back straight —arms extended ahead of shoulders	—on toes —waist slightly piked —arms straight under shoulders	—on toes —back straight —arms extended ahead of the shoulders
Scale —Stand on right leg. —Lift left leg. —Extend arms to the sides. —Arch back. —Keep head up.	—right leg bent —bent left leg raised hip high	—right leg bent —straight left leg raised hip high	—right leg straight —left leg straight, hip high	—right leg straight —left leg straight, above the hip level
"Inchworm" 				

Tasks	Level 1	Level 2	Level 3	Level 4
Quantity: 1. 10 yards 2. 20 yards	—arms extended under shoulders —body weight over the shoulders —slight pike	—arms extended under shoulders —body weight over shoulders —high pike	—arms extended beyond the shoulders —body weight shifted backward —low pike	—arms extended beyond the shoulders —body almost extended
V-Position	75°	60°	45°	30°
Rest on forearms. Quantity: Hold for the count of "a thousand"— 1, 2, 3, 4, 5, 6, 7, 8, 9, 10. 5 times	—Lift straight legs 75° in air.	—Lift bent legs 60° in the air.	—Lift straight legs 45° in the air.	—Lift straight legs 30° in the air.
Back Arch				
—Stand with your back to the wall. —Arch backwards. —Place hands over head against the wall. —"Walk down" with your hands to your level. —Hold for a count of 1, 2, 3, 4, 5. —Then "walk" back up. Do 3 times.	"Walk" hands down to the center of the back.	"Walk" hands down to waist level.	"Walk" hands down to knee level.	"Walk" hands to floor level.

FIGURE 7–14 Individual program: Developmental program

Name _____   Style   E

Class _____   Individual Program # __

Date _____

Developmental Movement
(Quantitative Differentiation)

To the student:

Complete this individual program in style E. Circle your anticipated level and quantity of performance. If there is a difference between your intent and your actual performance, indicate the difference with a slash mark.

Abbreviations under the numbers mean:

AG = Agility   Flex = Flexibility   ST = Strength

#	Task Description	Level 1	Level 2	Level 3
1. (AG)	Jump consecutively while raising knees to hip level.	1, 2, 3, 4, 5, 6, 7, 8	9, 10, 11, 12, 13, 14, 15, 16	17, 18, 19, 20, 21, 22, 23, 24, 25
2. (AG)	Jump consecutively, raising knees to the chest.	1, 2, 3, 4, 5, 6, 7, 8	9, 10, 11, 12, 13, 14, 15, 16	17, 18, 19, 20, 21, 22, 23, 24, 25
3. (AG)	Bounce off the ground to *maximum* height; keep the body straight and bounce from spot to spot. Get off the floor the second you touch it—"Touch & Go."	Along 1 width of the room. Do 2 widths (w/rest). *Remember—* Maximum height	3 widths w/rest between innings	2 widths 3 widths 4 widths 5 widths No rest!
4. (Flex)	In straddle position bend down and touch the _____ 10 consec. times each side by *slow* bobbing. Keep knees straight.	Ankles	Toes	Outside toes several inches wider
5. (Flex)	The same description as #4 in sitting straddle position	Ankles	Toes (pointed)	Outside heels

#	Task Description	Level 1	Level 2	Level 3
6. (Flex)	The same as #4 in a "standing on one knee position," the other leg extended at 45°	Ankle	Toes	Outside heel
7. (ST)	From _____ tilt back and hold! Keep trunk straight.	20 degrees. Hold 10 counts. Hold 15 counts.	45 degrees. 10 counts. 15 counts. 20 counts.	60 degrees. 10 counts, 20, 30, 35, 40, 45, 50, 55, 60!
8. (ST)	Push-up. st. position as drawn. Nose touches floor *between* the hands, legs remain *straight*. 	5' between hands and feet 1, 2, 3, 4, 5	4' 6, 7, 8, 9, 10, 11, 12	3' 5, 6, 7, 8, 9, 10
9. (ST)	From standing position lift one leg forward. *Bend* the supporting leg; Return to standing position (hands on hips).	Half way down 1, 2, 3, 4, 5	2/3 down 1, 2, 3, 4, 5	All the way down 1, 2, 3, 4, 5
10. (AG)	Start with 2–3 running steps. Jump in the air, turn _____ degrees, land in squat position, and *stay* for count of 5!	180 degrees 1, 2, 3, 4, 5	270 degrees 1, 2, 3, 4, 5	360 degrees 1, 2, 3, 4, 5

FIGURE 7–15 Individual program: Weightlifting

Name _____

Class _____

Date _____

Style E

Weightlifting

To the student:

Following the decisions of Style E, complete all of the five tasks below.

Task	Factor	Degree of Difficulty			
		1	2	3	4
1. To perform the *deadlift*, stand with feet //, shoulder width; mixed grip, shoulder width; back straight; head up; hips & knees bent; feet flat under bar; arms remain straight. Pick up bar from a bent to a straight body position, with bar always in front. Perform 5 repetitions using any wt. _____	1. Weight increments: 8 barbells are arranged in a series of progressive resistances from 20 lb. (bar) to 400 lb.	0–100 lbs. wt. _____	105–200 lbs. wt. _____	205–300 lbs. wt. _____	305–400 lbs. wt. _____
2. To perform the *squat*, stand with feet //, slightly wider than shoulder width; support barbell across back of shoulders; wide grip; back straight; bend knees & hips until thighs are parallel to floor; return to standing position.	1. Weight increments: 2 barbells, may be adjusted to any resistance the lifter desires from bar wt. (30 lb.) to 100 lb. over body weight.	30–½ BWT wt. _____	¾BWT–BWT wt. _____	BWT + 20–BTW + 50 wt. _____	BWT + 60–BWT + 100 wt. _____

#	Instruction				
3.	To perform the *Big Four* exercise, assume a deadlift position; grasp handles; pull to a standing position (a); pull handle up to chin, elbows up (b); press handle full arm extension over head (c); raise up on toes (d).	1. Resistance levels; lifter may adjust resistance level on apparatus from 0 to 89 lb. by rotating dial clockwise.	1 rev. 0–10 lb. ___	2 rev. 11–29 lbs. ___	3 rev. 30–59 lbs. ___	4 rev. 61–89 lb. ___
4.	To perform 25 *incline situps*, assume bent knee position, feet supported; grasp hands in back of head; curl up trunk & head until elbows extend beyond knees; return to position.	1. Angle of incline board can be adjusted by the performer from 5°–45°.	5° ___	15° ___	25° ___	45° ___
5.	To perform the *bench press*, lie in supine position on bench, with feet on floor; support barbell in straight arm position using wider than shoulder width grip. Lower barbell to chest, push straight up to extended arm position. Return barbell to support.	1. Weight increments; may be adjusted by lifter from barbell weight (30 lb.) to resistance level exceeding body weight of lifter.	Bar Wt. ___	½ BWT ___	¾ BWT ___	BWT ___

FIGURE 7–16 Individual program: Golf

Name _____   Style B C D Ⓔ

Class _____   Individual Program # ___

Date _____

Golf—chip shot and putting

To the student:

1. Select an initial level and circle the number you expect to do.
2. Do the task and blacken out the number of the actual performance.
3. Compare your execution of the task with the performance criteria.
4. Decide whether to repeat the task at the same level or at a different level.

Chip shot
Criteria:

1. Stand with your feet close together.
2. Bend your knees slightly, as though starting to sit.
3. Contact the ball off your left heel.
4. Follow through along the path of the ball, keeping the left wrist firm at contact.
5. Refrain from letting the club head pass the left hand.
6. Keep the flight of the ball low.
7. Hit to a predetermined spot and have the ball roll to the cup.

The Task: Choose a distance (either line A, B, or C), and a target area (either the large or the small). Take 10 chip shots, and record the number of times you hit the target area.

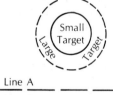

Line A ___ ___ ___

Line B ___ ___ ___

Line C ___ ___ ___

Distance	LARGE TARGET										
A	0	1	2	3	4	5	6	7	8	9	10
B	0	1	2	3	4	5	6	7	8	9	10
C	0	1	2	3	4	5	6	7	8	9	10

Distance	SMALL TARGET										
A	0	1	2	3	4	5	6	7	8	9	10
B	0	1	2	3	4	5	6	7	8	9	10
C	0	1	2	3	4	5	6	7	8	9	10

Putting
Criteria:

1. Use a comfortable stance that limits your body movement.
2. Hold your head directly over the ball.
3. Keep the club face square to the line of the putt.
4. Bring the club back smoothly and keep it low, close to the green.
5. Putt with the wrist and arm stroke only.
6. Follow through with a smooth, forward sweeping movement, keeping the clubhead on the line of the putt.

The Task: Choose a distance (either line A, B, or C) and a target (either the small can or the large can). Take 10 putts, and record the number of times you put the ball in the hole.

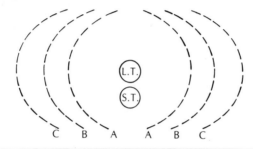

Distance	LARGE TARGET										
A	0	1	2	3	4	5	6	7	8	9	10
B	0	1	2	3	4	5	6	7	8	9	10
C	0	1	2	3	4	5	6	7	8	9	10

Distance	SMALL TARGET										
A	0	1	2	3	4	5	6	7	8	9	10
B	0	1	2	3	4	5	6	7	8	9	10
C	0	1	2	3	4	5	6	7	8	9	10

FIGURE 7–17 Individual program: Badminton

Name _____	Style A B C D Ⓔ
Class _____	Individual Program # ___
Date _____	

Badminton Skills

To the student:

The following tasks are designed to provide you with the opportunity to practice and develop at your level of performance. Your role is to:

1. Decide which task to do first.
2. Select an initial level and circle the number you *expect* to do.
3. *Do* the task and blacken out the number of the actual performance.
4. Compare your execution of the task with the performance criteria.
5. Decide to repeat the task at the same level, a different level, or to move on to another task.

Task: The forehand overhead clear (from a self-throw):

a. Select a distance (1, 2, or 3) and a target (large or small).
b. Record the number of times you hit the target area in 10 attempts.

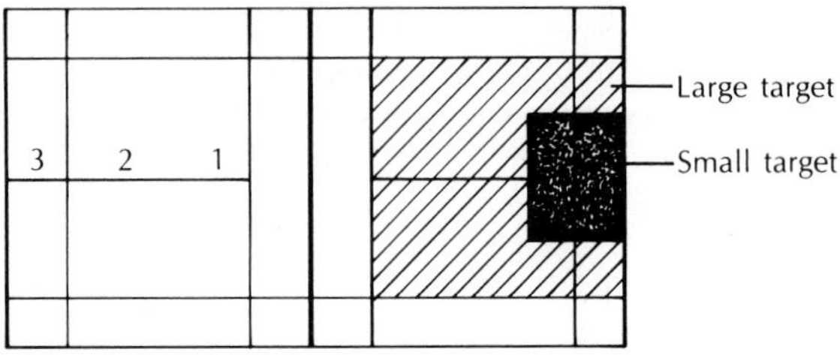

—Large target

—Small target

distance _____
target _____
anticipated # of hits _____
actual # of hits _____

Criteria: acc.   n.t.

1. Backswing racquet as if to throw it.   1.
2. Turn left side of body (if right-handed) to the net and   2.
   shift weight to back leg.
3. Strike shuttle overhead but in front of body, with arm   3.
   fully extended. Racquet head contacts bird from
   below.
4. As weight shifts onto front leg, put body weight into   4.
   shot. Use strong wrist action.
5. Follow through in direction of intended flight of bird.   5.

FIGURE 7–18   Individual program: Balance beam

Name _____   Style   E
Class _____   Individual Program # ___
Date _____

**Gymnastics—balance beam:
turns, turns and one additional position**

To the student:

One important aspect of good performance of the balance beam is the ability to execute any turn at any place on the beam, following most movements and preceding most movements. It is also very important to be able to perform each turn in different body positions.

Turns in standing position:
Stand on the beam facing the length of the beam, arms raised sideways for improved balance. In this position turns can be done under the following conditions: (a) with the line of gravity remaining between the legs, (b) with the line of gravity moved to the rear leg, (c) with the line of gravity moved to the front leg, (d) combinations of a, b, and c.

Tasks	Level 1	Level 2
a. **Line of Gravity in the Center**		
1. Turn 180° in a regular standing position.	1, 2, 3, 4, 5, 6 consecutive times.	7, 8, 9, 10
2. Turn 180° in standing position.	With arms at the sides of the body: 1, 2, 3, 4, 5, 6, 7, 8, 9, 10.	With crossed arms: 3, 6, 9, 12, 15, 18.
3. Turn 180°, propelled by one-arm swing at shoulder level.	3, 5, 7, 9, 12 consecutive times.	With two raised arms for intentional momentum: 3, 5, 7, 9, 11, 13, 15.
4. Repeat No. 2.	Dropping your chin to your chest: 3, 5, 7, 9, 11, 13, 15 times.	Look upward! *Safety!* 3, 5, 7, 9, 11, 13, 15.
5. Repeat No. 3—use both arms for momentum.	Dropping your chin to your chest: 3, 5, 7, 9, 11, 13, 15 times.	Look upward! *Safety!*
6. Repeat No. 2 with closed eyes.	Arms at sides of the body: 1, 2, 3, 4, 5, 6.	With slight arm momentum: 1, 2, 3, 4, 5, 6.
7. Repeat the turn.	With arms raised upward: 2, 4, 6, 8, 10.	Raised arms with a ball: 2, 4, 6, 8, 10.
8. Turn with slightly bent knees.	Arms as in 4: 2, 4, 6, 8, 10.	Arms as in 4—increase speed of turns: 2, 4, 6, 8, 10.
9. Turn in half squat position.	As in 8: 2, 4, 6, 8, 10.	As in 8: 2, 4, 6, 8, 10.
10. Turn in full squat position.	Turning 90° at a time: 2, 4, 6, 8.	Turning 180°: 2, 4, 6, 8, 10.
11. Turn in full squat with use of both straight arms to gain momentum.	Eyes focusing ahead, 180° turns: 2, 4, 6, 8, 10.	Eyes raised above horizontal line—180° turns: 2, 4, 6, 8, 10.
12. Repeat No. 11 with different arm positions.	One arm raised upward, the other hanging down: 2, 4, 6, 8, 10.	Both arms raised upward: 2, 4, 6, 8, 10.
13. Start in standing position.	Turning 180° and getting down to squat position: 2, 4, 6, 8, 10.	Getting down and immediately getting up and turning 180°: 2, 4, 6, 8, 10.

Tasks	Level 1	Level 2
b. Line of Gravity shifts to the rear leg		
1. As you turn shift your weight to the rear leg.	In regular standing position: 2, 4, 6, 8, 10.	Turn 180° with arms raised above the head.
2. Repeat No. 1, bending the rear leg as much as you can.	2, 4, 6, 8, 10, 12.	Turn 180° and use both arms for momentum (increase speed of turn): 2, 4, 6, 8, 10, 12.
3. Repeat No. 2.	Lifting the front foot to a slight touch of beam as you turn: 2, 4, 6, 8, 10.	As you turn lift the front foot and keep it in the air: 2, 4, 6, 8, 10.
4. Repeat No. 3.	Bending your head forward as you turn: 2, 4, 6, 8, 10.	As you turn bend your trunk forward: 2, 4, 6, 8.

FIGURE 7–19 Individual program: Volleyball

Name _____   Style   E
Class _____   Individual Program # ___
Date _____

Competitive volleyball–skills warm-up

To the student:

1. The following tests are to be practiced in style E.
2. Circle the level and/or quantity you think you can do today.
3. Begin the task.
4. Place an X where you actually performed today.

Skills:

Category 1: Tasks with the ball in the air	Level 1	Level 2	Level 3
1. a. Set the ball with two hands.	0–5	16–20	over 30
b. Use only the fingertips.	6–10	21–25	
c. Use a rhythm ball (a very light ball).	11–15	26–30	
2. a. Set the ball with two hands.	0–5	16–20	over 30
b. Use only fingertips.	6–10	21–25	
c. Use a volleyball.	11–15	26–30	

	Level 1	Level 2	Level 3
3. a. Set the ball with two hands. b. Use only fingertips. c. Use a basketball.	0–5 6–10 11–15	16–20 21–25 26–30	over 30
4. a. Set the ball with only the left hand. b. Use only fingertips. c. Use a ____ ball. 1. Rhythm ball 2. Volleyball 3. Basketball	0–5 6–10	11–15 16–20	21–25 26–30
5. a. Set the ball with only the right hand. b. Use only fingertips. c. Use a ____ ball. 1. Rhythm ball 2. Volleyball 3. Basketball	0–5 6–10	11–15 16–20	21–25 26–30
6. a. Set the ball. b. Use the *dig* position. c. Remain in a stationary stance.	0–5 6–10 11–15	16–20 21–25 26–30	over 30
7. a. Set the ball. b. Use the *dig* position. c. Movement is permitted.	0–5 6–10 11–15	16–20; 21–25; 26–30	over 30
Category 2: Tasks with the ball against the wall In all tasks: —use the volleybal. —use two hands. —set with only fingertips. —record how many serves hit the line or the target on the line. 1. a. Stand on the line marked with an X. b. Set to the yellow tape line on the wall.	0–5 6–10 11–15 ————	16–20 21–25 26–30 ————	over 30 ————
2. a. Stand on the line marked with a Y. b. Set to the red tape line on the wall.	0–5 6–10 11–15 ————	16–20 21–25 26–30 ————	over 30 ————
3. a. Stand on the line marked with an S. b. Set to one of the squares ( ). 1. largest size square	0–5 6–10 11–15	16–20 21–25 26–30	over 30

	Level 1	Level 2	Level 3
2. medium-size square 3. smallest size square	——	——	——
Category 3: Serving Tasks 1. a. Use the under-hand serve. b. Stand on the line marked with an S (square size _____). c. Serve with the right hand.	0–5 6–10 11–15 ——	16–20 21–25 26–30 ——	over 30 ——
2. a. Repeat the task above. b. Serve with the left hand.	0–5 6–10 11–15 ——	16–20 21–25 26–30 ——	over 30 ——
3. a. Use the side-arm serve. b. Stand on the line marked with an S (square size _____). c. Serve with the right hand.	0–5 6–10 11–15 ——	16–20 21–25 26–30 ——	over 30 ——
4. a. Repeat the task above. b. Serve with the left hand.	0–5 6–10 11–15 ——	16–20 21–25 26–30 ——	over 30 ——

FIGURE 7–20   Individual program: Volleyball

Name _____   Style B C D Ⓔ
Class _____   Individual Program # __
Date _____

Volleyball skills

To the student:

The tasks are designed for your practice and development.
Your role is to:
1. Decide which task to do first.
2. Read the criteria.
3. Select an initial level and circle the number you *expect* to do.
4. Do the task and blacken out the number actually performed.
5. Compare your performance of the task with the criteria.

6. Decide either to repeat the task at the same level, at a different level, or to move on to another task.

	acc.	n.t.

The Underhand Serve (Criteria):
1. Assume a crouched position with the left foot in front of the right, the ball held at waist height in the fingertips of the left hand.
2. Bring the right arm straight back with a clenched fist, while tossing the ball about 4 inches in the air.
3. Swing the right arm straight ahead like a pendulum, contacting the ball on the flat part of the wrist.

The task: Decide on both a distance (X_1 or X_2) and a target (the whole court or *one* of the corners). Perform 10 serves and record the result.

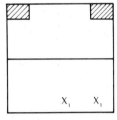

Distance	SMALL TARGET										
X_1	0	1	2	3	4	5	6	7	8	9	10
X_2	0	1	2	3	4	5	6	7	8	9	10

Distance	LARGE TARGET										
X_1	0	1	2	3	4	5	6	7	8	9	10
X_2	0	1	2	3	4	5	6	7	8	9	10

	acc.	n.t.

The Bump (Criteria):
1. Assume a crouched position with the knees bent, one foot slightly in front of the other, and the weight on the balls of the feet.
2. Interlock the hands with the thumbs parallel to form a flat surface between the wrists and the forearms.
3. Contact the ball just above the wrists, with the arms completely straight, and the ball directly in front of the body.
4. Follow through by extending (straightening) the legs without swinging the arms upward.

The task: Choose both a distance (5', 10', or 15') and a target size (large or small). With an underhand two-hand release, toss the ball in the air and bump it to the target. Do ten and record the results.

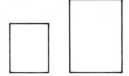

△ 5'

△ 10'

△ 15'

Distance	SMALL TARGET										
5'	0	1	2	3	4	5	6	7	8	9	10
10'	0	1	2	3	4	5	6	7	8	9	10
15'	0	1	2	3	4	5	6	7	8	9	10

Distance	LARGE TARGET										
5'	0	1	2	3	4	5	6	7	8	9	10
10'	0	1	2	3	4	5	6	7	8	9	10
15'	0	1	2	3	4	5	6	7	8	9	10

FIGURE 7–21   Individual program: Lacrosse

Name _____   Style B   C   D Ⓔ
Class _____   Individual Program # ___
Date _____

Lacrosse skills

To the student:

These lacrosse tasks are designed for your practice and improvement of performance.

Your role is to:

1. Decide which task to do first.
2. Select an initial level and circle the number you *expect* to do.
3. Do the task and blacken out the actual performance.
4. Compare the actual performance of the task with the criteria.
5. Decide either to repeat the task at the same level, a different level, or to move on to another task.

1. Lacrosse Overhand Pass (Criteria):

a. Place bottom hand on the butt (lower part of the stick), top hand 8–10 inches above.

b. Slant stick 45 degrees over the shoulder.

c. Point stick in the direction of the target.

d. Step forward with the leg on the same side as the hand that is on the butt of the stick. Flex knees and begin to move stick.

e. Push with the top hand and pull with the bottom hand, while always keeping your eyes on the target.

f. During the following-through point the stick in the direction of the target.

	acc.	n.t.
	___	___
	___	___
	___	___
	___	___
	___	___
	___	___

The task: Decide to which target you are going to throw (large or small), and from which distance to pass the overhand throw. Take 10 shots from the distance you decide and record the results.

Small Target

Large Target

Distance	SMALL TARGET										
1	0	1	2	3	4	5	6	7	8	9	10
2	0	1	2	3	4	5	6	7	8	9	10

Distance	LARGE TARGET										
1	0	1	2	3	4	5	6	7	8	9	10
2	0	1	2	3	4	5	6	7	8	9	10

DISTANCE 1 IS 20 FEET.

DISTANCE 2 IS 30 FEET.

2. Sidearm Shot (Criteria):

a. Hold the stick in the same position as in the overhand pass.

b. Sweep stick back and step forward.

c. Slant stick 90 degrees from the body.

d. Whip the left arm forward and pull back on the right arm (left hand shot).

	acc.	n.t.
	___	___
	___	___
	___	___
	___	___

The task: Follow the same procedure as in the overhand pass. Choose a distance and target size. Use the sidearm shot. Record your results after taking 10 shots.

Distance	SMALL TARGET										
1	0	1	2	3	4	5	6	7	8	9	10
2	0	1	2	3	4	5	6	7	8	9	10

Distance	LARGE TARGET										
1	0	1	2	3	4	5	6	7	8	9	10
2	0	1	2	3	4	5	6	7	8	9	10

acc.   n.t.

3. Underhand Shot (Criteria):
a. Sweep stick back in a large circle over the shoulder.
b. When the stick is almost at the floor, bring it forward rapidly.
c. Use both arms, as it is a difficult shot to control.

The task: Follow the same procedure as above but use the underhand shot. Be sure to record your results after taking 10 shots.

Distance	SMALL TARGET										
1	0	1	2	3	4	5	6	7	8	9	10
2	0	1	2	3	4	5	6	7	8	9	10

Distance	LARGE TARGET										
1	0	1	2	3	4	5	6	7	8	9	10
2	0	1	2	3	4	5	6	7	8	9	10

acc.   n.t.

4. Shuttle Run—Pick-ups and Stick Handling (Criteria):
a. Pick up the ball using either the trap and scoop pick-up (the stick is placed on top of the ball to stop any movement and then pulled back over the ball causing it to roll into the pocket) or the Indian pick-up (the stick is first inverted, putting the pocket downwards, and then with a quick motion the ball is hit with the wood of the stick causing it to bounce; then the stick is twisted with a half circular movement to capture the ball in the pocket).
b. Cradle the ball back and forth in the pocket while running by moving the stick from side to side.
c. Use the top hand to bring about the cradling action while using the bottom hand as a pivot point for the stick.
d. Cradle the stick close to the body.

The task: Decide on task 1 or task 2. You have the choice of pick-up technique for either task.

Task 1

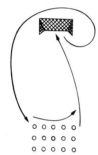

Start at a line 30′ from the goal. Have a series of balls on this line. Pick up a ball using whichever technique you prefer, run straight to the goal and place the ball in the goal. Then, run around the net, return to the line to pick up another ball, and repeat. Repeat this action for 60 seconds and record the number of balls that you can place in the net.

Task 2
a. Use the above criteria.
b. Handle the stick through a maze before you place the ball in the goal.

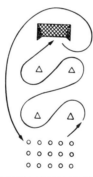

TASK 1				RESULTS												
0	1	2	3	4	5	6	7	8	9	10	11	12	13	14	15	more-

TASK 2				RESULTS												
0	1	2	3	4	5	6	7	8	9	10	11	12	13	14	15	more-

5. Standing and Running Accuracy Shooting (Criteria):
(Shots are described for a shooter shooting over the left shoulder. Right-shouldered shooters, do the reverse.)

acc.   n.t.

a. Start with both hands on the stick several inches apart—the right hand at the bottom of the stick handle, the left hand higher.
b. Start with the stick on an angle over the left shoulder and with the pocket above and behind the shoulder.

    c. Aim the face of the stick at the target. To shoot, push the left hand forward, and, at the same time, pull the right hand back towards the body. Shoot the ball straight over the shoulder.

    d. Step forward with the right foot and bend the body forwards as the shot is being made.

    e. Follow through by extending the left arm fully and pointing the stick directly at the target as the ball leaves the stick.

The task: Decide on task 1 or task 2 and decide on whether to shoot from distance 1 or distance 2.

Task #1 From a standing position, take 10 shots at the goal. Record the number of times that you put the lacrosse ball into the goal. Shoot from either distance 1—20 feet—or distance 2—40 feet.

Task #2 From a run take 10 shots at the goal. Record the number of times that you put the lacrosse ball into the goal. Shoot from either distance 1—20 feet—or distance 2—40 feet.

↑ Distance 1

↑ Distance 2

Distance	FROM STANDING POSITION										
1	0	1	2	3	4	5	6	7	8	9	10
2	0	1	2	3	4	5	6	7	8	9	10

Distance	FROM A RUN										
1	0	1	2	3	4	5	6	7	8	9	10
2	0	1	2	3	4	5	6	7	8	9	10

FIGURE 7–22 Individual program: Football

Name _____

Class _____

Date _____

Style A B C D Ⓔ

Individual Program # ___

Football skills

To the student:

The football tasks outlined below will help you determine your present level of performance in various skills. Your role is to follow this program at your own pace. If you have any questions about the program, ask your teacher.

Your role:
1. Decide which task to do first.
2. Read the performance criteria.
3. Select an initial level and circle the number you *expect* to do.
4. Do the task and blacken out the number actually performed.
5. Compare your performance of the task with the performance criteria.
6. Decide either to repeat the task at the same level, a different level, or to move on to another task.

Field Goal Kicking—The Straight On Kick (Criteria):

	acc.	n.t.
1. Take two steps. The last one, with the non-kicking foot, should be a long, lunging step. Plant the foot slightly behind and to the side of the ball.		
2. Swing the kicking leg forward with the knee bent and the ankle locked.		
3. Straighten the knee and contact the ball just below center with the toe area of the foot.		
4. Keep your head down and your body weight slightly over the ball.		
5. Follow through with a high straight leg kick.		

The task: Decide on a distance (10, 15, 20, or 25 yards) and decide between an angle from the hash marks or straight on. Take 10 kicks and record the result.

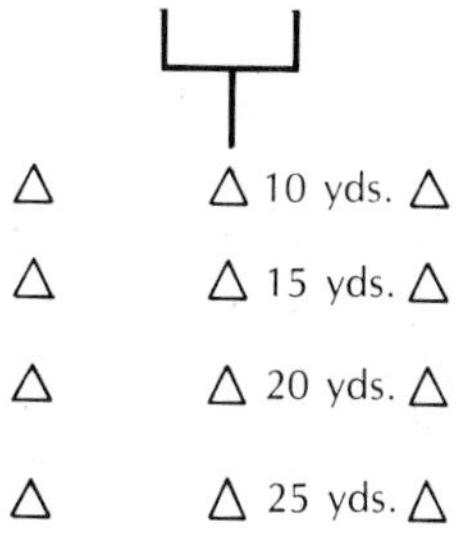

```
      └┘
       T
  △      △ 10 yds. △

  △      △ 15 yds. △

  △      △ 20 yds. △

  △      △ 25 yds. △
```

Distance	HASH MARK										
10 yds.	0	1	2	3	4	5	6	7	8	9	10
15 yds.	0	1	2	3	4	5	6	7	8	9	10
20 yds.	0	1	2	3	4	5	6	7	8	9	10
25 yds.	0	1	2	3	4	5	6	7	8	9	10

Distance	STRAIGHT ON										
10 yds.	0	1	2	3	4	5	6	7	8	9	10
15 yds.	0	1	2	3	4	5	6	7	8	9	10
20 yds.	0	1	2	3	4	5	6	7	8	9	10
25 yds.	0	1	2	3	4	5	6	7	8	9	10

                                                                       acc.   n.t.

Punt Centering (Criteria):
1. Assume a bent or crouched position with the feet apart at shoulder width.
2. Grip the ball as you would for a forward pass, the throwing hand on top of the ball. Use the other hand as a guide.
3. Keep the head down and look between your legs for the target.
4. Snap the ball with a backward jerk of the arms and a snap of the throwing wrist.

The task: Find a partner and choose a distance from which to center (15, 20, 25, or 30 ft.). Snap directly to your partner so that he/she can touch the ball with both hands without *moving either foot.* Complete 10 snaps and record the results.

                         P   — 0

                         △   15'

                         △   20'

                         △   25'

                         △   30'.

Distance	PARTNER AS TARGET										
15'	0	1	2	3	4	5	6	7	8	9	10
20'	0	1	2	3	4	5	6	7	8	9	10
25'	0	1	2	3	4	5	6	7	8	9	10
30'	0	1	2	3	4	5	6	7	8	9	10

                                                                       acc.   n.t.

The Forward Pass (Criteria):
1. Grip the ball with the fingers spread so that the 4th and 5th fingers cross the laces.
2. Plant the feet shoulder width apart, the back foot perpendicular, and the front foot on a 45 degree angle to the direction of the pass.

3. "Cock" the ball behind the head, guiding it back with the opposite hand. Then point the opposite arm forward in the direction of the pass to provide body balance.
4. Release the ball by extending the arm into a high overhead motion. Make a small step forward with the front foot to transfer the body weight forward during the throw.
5. Follow through with the throwing arm in the direction of the pass.

The task: Find a partner and choose both a distance from which to throw (10, 15, 20, or 25 yds.) and the type of passing action (from a standing position or while rolling out). Pass so that your partner can touch the ball with both hands without moving either foot. Complete 10 passes and record the results.

Distance	STATIONARY THROW										
10 yds.	0	1	2	3	4	5	6	7	8	9	10
15 yds.	0	1	2	3	4	5	6	7	8	9	10
20 yds.	0	1	2	3	4	5	6	7	8	9	10
25 yds.	0	1	2	3	4	5	6	7	8	9	10

Distance	ROLL OUT										
10 yds.	0	1	2	3	4	5	6	7	8	9	10
15 yds.	0	1	2	3	4	5	6	7	8	9	10
20 yds.	0	1	2	3	4	5	6	7	8	9	10
25 yds.	0	1	2	3	4	5	6	7	8	9	10

FIGURE 7–23   *Inappropriate* task design

The following examples of a task design is not appropriate for the individual program in style E because

1. Some of the activities are, indeed, sequential in terms of degree of difficulty; other are arbitrarily placed in this list. Can you identify which ones?
2. What is more important for our analysis here is that the stunts listed diagonally on the slanted rope represent different activities, *different* tasks. The principle of designing the individual program calls for using the slanted rope concept for the *same* task.

This illustration is an example of how *not* to design the individual program.

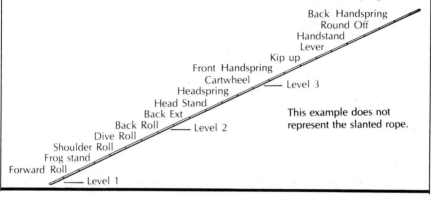

FIGURE 7–24 Style E classroom chart

THE INCLUSION STYLE

The purposes of this style are:

- To learn to select a level of a task you can perform

- To check your own work

ROLE OF LEARNER

- To make the 9 decisions of style B

- To examine the different levels of the task

- To select the level appropriate for you

- To perform the task

- To check your own work against criteria prepared by the teacher

- To ask the teacher questions for clarification

ROLE OF TEACHER

- To prepare the task and the levels within the task

- To prepare the criteria for the levels in the task

- To answer questions by the learner

- To initiate communication with the learner

This, then, is style E. What would the next style look like? What decisions will be shifted now to elicit still different teaching and learning behavior?

Before we move on to other styles, two major issues need to be discussed that apply to styles A–E as a cluster:

1. Organizational options
2. The demonstration

The next two sections discuss the relationship of these issues to this cluster of styles. It is imperative to realize that neither issue is style specific; rather, each is a part of styles A–E.

ORGANIZATIONAL OPTIONS

One of the problems in physical education is that of efficient learning, which is dependent on an appropriate ratio between the quantity of an activity and the unit of time. To learn any physical task and reach a reasonable level of performance, the learner must repeat the task! The learner must perform, receive frequent feedback, and perform some more. How, then, can the teacher organize the class to use time efficiently?

During the last decade, the issue of time-on-task, or academic learning time, has become prominent as a focal point in educational research for improving teaching.

In physical education, the issue is organizing the learners, the equipment, the space, and the time in particular relationships to create conditions for efficient learning.

Professional literature provides many studies that verify the need to improve this aspect of the teaching-learning process. Our purpose is to highlight this problem and offer some solutions. The suggestions that follow are not style specific—they apply to all styles. Since reasonable efficiency is important in education, any style should operate within organizational conditions that promote efficient learning.

The Issue of Efficiency

The following pages include a variety of charts depicting *inefficient* organizational patterns that still exist in schools; other charts suggest options for improvement. The organization of space, equipment, and people shown in Figure 8-1 is common in many schools. Note in particular the considerable amount of unused space and the number of learners per basket. This is an inappropriate arrangement of people, space, and equipment—it infringes on the time each learner has for practice.

FIGURE 8–1   Basketball—common equipment and space organization (four baskets in the gymnasium)

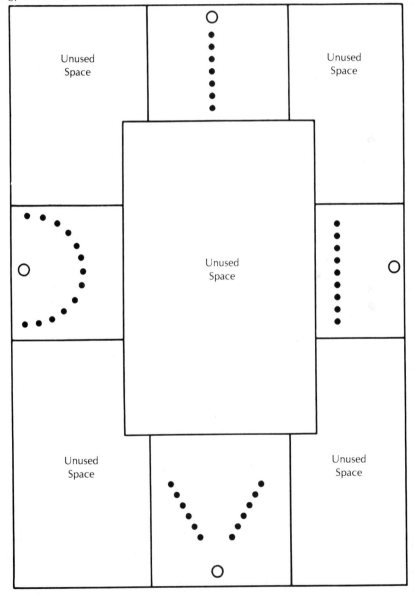

Examine the alternative organization suggested in Figure 8-2. This arrangement provides *frequent* opportunities for all learners to practice specific skills—all within the same activity, in this case, basketball. The nine assigned tasks represent various aspects of shooting, and the small groups rotate from task to task at designated time intervals. The ratio of participation per learner per unit of time will increase considerably with this arrangement, and so will learning and development.

To play basketball well, one must learn to shoot, dribble, pass the ball in various ways, move around the opponent, and so on. Each of these skills constitutes a particular task to practice. Figure 8-3 offers an example of space organization to accommodate all these tasks at the same time, increasing the efficiency of learning. This procedure and organization are successfully used in "circuit training," in physical fitness tests, and during coaching sessions; using them during physical education classes allows more people to benefit from the activity. Similar arrangements can be adapted to baseball, soccer, hockey, or any other ball games.

Before a similar organizational analysis and alternatives are offered for gymnastics, it is necessary to identify the physical prerequisites of gymnastics for working on the apparatus. One needs to develop agility, balance, flexibility, strength, and other abilities before and during the work on the apparatus. This certainly applies to the novice gymnast. Instead of sitting and waiting for their turn on an apparatus, students *can* and *should* be learning developmental movements that will help them progress in areas needing improvement.

This is an excellent opportunity for developing multiple tasks. For example, some students may need extensive work in push-up exercises to develop the strength needed to support the body in a simple parallel bar sequence. These students should be involved in this development instead of sitting near the parallel bars doing nothing.

It might be very revealing for the teacher to measure the actual waste of time that occurs in the traditional gymnastics unit for a large class. Select two or three students and follow them through the lesson; record the actual time spent both passively and actively using the apparatus. You will discover that most of a student's time is spent sitting and waiting for his or her turn. Obviously, this calls for an alternative arrangement.

In many schools with large classes, you will find unused spaces in the gymnasium, such as in Figure 8-4, because students are grouped according to the number of pieces of gymnastics equipment. With large numbers of students and few pieces of equipment, the frequency of experience is low, and development of agility, balance, strength, and so on is insignificant. Because students rarely get to use the apparatus, many students not only are poor performers in gymnastics techniques but also lack the physical abilities for such activities—they lack the strength, flexibility, and endurance to pursue a successful gymnastics program. In addition, when development is insignificant and learning does not take place, the student's attitude toward the activity may be negative, or at best, neutral.

By using the empty floor and wall spaces, you actually add equipment to your program. Present activities to the class that are relevant to the gymnastics

FIGURE 8–2   Sample organization of space

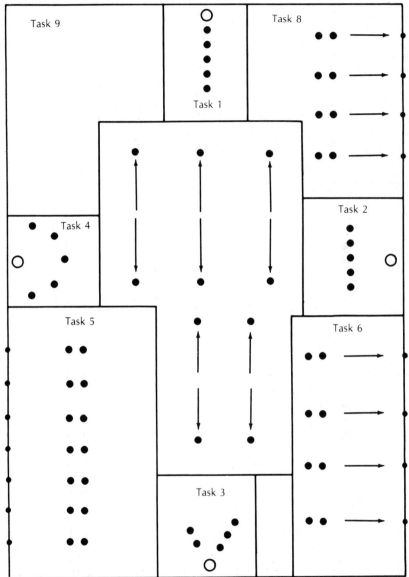

Dots on sidelines: Marked targets on walls for practicing accuracy

unit and your students will develop the required qualities and techniques for gymnastics. It is important, though, to explain to your students the connection between the variety of floor tasks, the development of the body, and the application to better performance on the apparatus. It is helpful, for example, for the student to realize that doing various push-ups and other support activities (there are many games in the support position that could serve this purpose)

FIGURE 8–3   Basketball: Space organization for multiple tasks

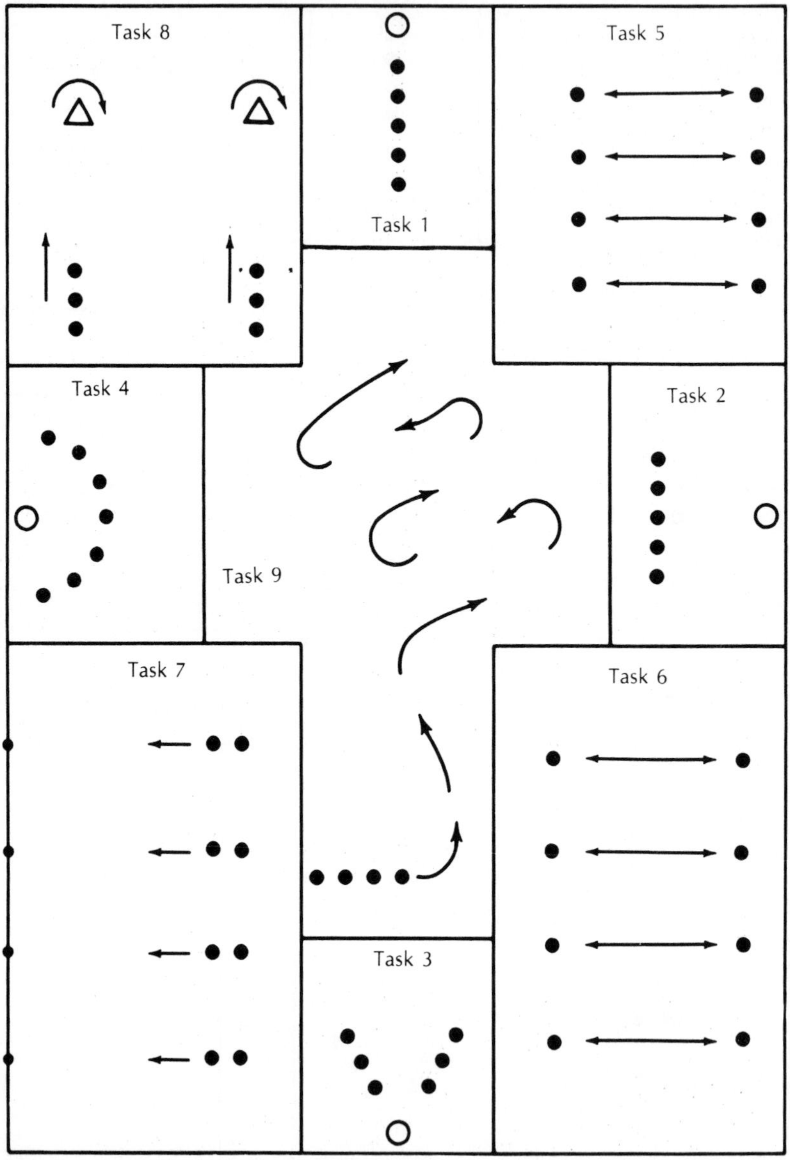

Tasks 1–4: Shooting tasks, either different shots or different tasks within the same shot

Tasks 5–6: Passing tasks (with a partner)

Task 7: Passing practice against a wall (and use of targets)

Task 8: Dribbling practice

Task 9: A dribbling course (changing direction)

FIGURE 8–4 Gymnastics—common equipment-space organization showing unused space

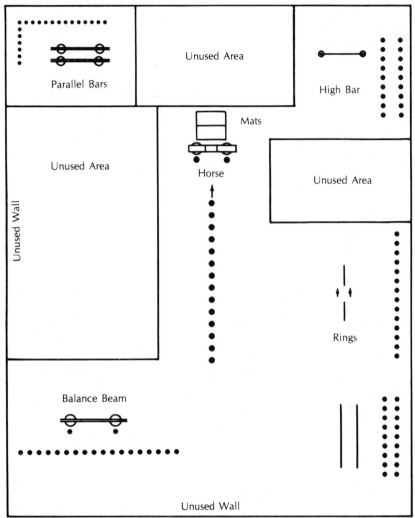

are absolutely necessary to develop shoulder, arm, and chest muscles. Explain that this development is vital in parallel bars performance because most movements and sequences of movement are performed while the body is constantly supported by the arms. (The bulk of the body weight is usually above the base of support in parallel bars sequences.) However, the rings and high bar shift the center of gravity below and above the base of support; therefore, the muscles involved in hanging must be developed so that the performer can hang in comfort and without effort for some time.

All these supplementary activities can be done in any regular class by using the alternative floor plan and time-activity sequence. The advantage of such an arrangement is impressive because even the weakest student can show significant progress.

Figure 8-5 shows a sample alternative arrangement of an equipment–space relationship. You may xerox the floor plan, with the tasks written in the various spaces, so that each student has a guide for the tasks. This saves a great deal of time and eliminates the need for repeated explanations. The teacher is then free to move about, observe, and offer feedback.

FIGURE 8–5   Gymnastics—an alternative equipment-space organization

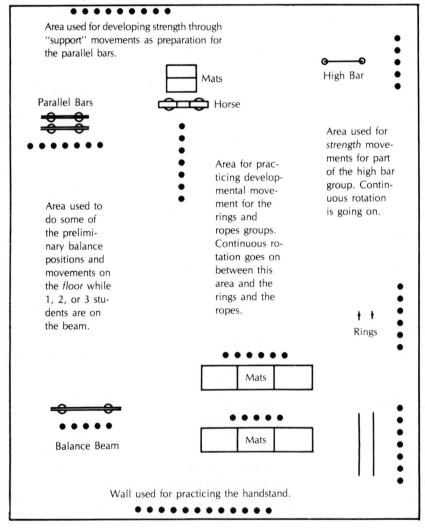

The unused space in Figure 8-4 is organized as shown in Figure 8-5 for *relevant* gymnastic activities. The principle of maximum activity per student per unit of time is observed here. More frequent experiences for each student helps learning, development, and enjoyment.

Let's examine the use of time in the arrangement shown in Figure 8-4. If 15 students gather around the parallel bars for a 30-minute lesson and we allow 30 seconds for a short sequence, it will take 7.5 minutes to conclude one "inning." During the entire lesson, each member of the group will be on the parallel bars four times for a total of 2 minutes. For each student, therefore, there will be 28 minutes of inactivity. Suppose we cut the time on the parallel bars in half (15 seconds); each participant will then be on the bar eight times—a rather unconvincing argument for the contribution of gymnastics to the development of each individual. This calculation applies to any activity or unit that employs this kind of equipment-space-time relationship. Those lost 28 minutes can be used more efficiently.

Organizational Options

The analysis of the relationship between number of learners, time, and space offers us four organizational options:

1. Single Station—Single Task (S.S./S.T.)
2. Single Station—Multiple Tasks (S.S./M.T.)
3. Multiple Stations—Single Task (M.S./S.T.)
4. Multiple Stations—Multiple Tasks (M.S./M.T.)

Single Station—Single Task   This arrangement allows each learner to make a decision about his or her location (one location) and perform one task at that location. After the teacher demonstrates and explains a particular task to the gathered learners, they go to their locations in the gymnasium and perform the task the number of times designated by the teacher (quantity decision).

Single Station—Multiple Tasks   This arrangement calls for more than one task to be performed in succession at the same location. The teacher demonstrates and explains two or more tasks, and the learners perform these tasks one after the other.

For example:

Task 1.   Dribble the ball in one spot, as demonstrated, 50 times with the right hand.

Task 2.   Dribble the ball in one spot, as demonstrated, 50 times with the left hand.

Task 3.   Dribble the ball in one spot, as demonstrated, 60 times; change hands every 10 dribbles.

In this case, each learner will have the opportunity to practice and develop the skill of dribbling in three consecutive tasks using one location. (If there are not enough basketballs, use volleyballs or any other type of ball—the purpose here is to dribble!)

Multiple Stations—Single Task   This arrangement provides each learner the opportunity to perform a task at a given location (station) and, when that task is done, move to another station and perform one task at the new location. This rotation can continue, depending on the number of stations and tasks designated.

This arrangement is very efficient when there is not enough equipment for everyone. (See the examples for basketball in Figure 8-3 and gymnastics in Figure 8-5.) It is a popular arrangement in weight-training sessions. Different weights and other pieces of equipment are distributed in different stations and the learner performs a task at each station and then moves to the next one.

Multiple Stations—Multiple Tasks   This is the same as the previous arrangement, except that at each station the learner performs more than one task.

For example:

At Station No. 1
Task 1.   Twenty set shots
Task 2.   Twenty hook shots
At Station No. 2
Task 1.   Twenty-five consecutive chest passes to a target on the wall
Task 2.   Twenty-five consecutive bounce passes against the wall
At Station No. 3
Task 1.   Dribbling the ball forward along the designated distance on the blue line
Task 2.   Dribbling the ball backward along the designated distance on the blue line
Task 3.   Dribbling as above, sideways
You can have as many stations as the area permits so that no square foot remains unused. Several clusters of variations in these three stations will bring about impressive results.

These four organizational arrangements accommodate all styles. They provide each learner with the time, equipment, and space to practice the task. While the learners are engaged in the task, the teacher has the time to move from station to station and offer the appropriate feedback.

Other options include: (1) Have different groups participate in different levels of the same task within the same style (Figure 8-6). (2) Have the teacher present several tasks from which each learner will select a certain number of tasks (four out of six, for example). The learner makes the decision about which four to select. (These tasks can be done in the same style, or in different ones.) (3) Have learners participate in concurrent styles. Once the learners are famil-

FIGURE 8–6 Different levels of a task within the same style

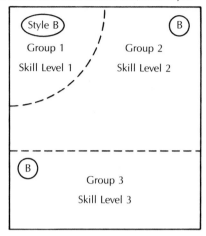

iar with several styles, it is possible to conduct the class by *concurrent styles* (Figure 8-7).

In this arrangement, the class is divided into three groups, each engaged in a different style. The subject matter, however, is the same. (In Figure 8-7, the subject matter is volleyball.) Both the task and the objectives in each style are different.

THE DEMONSTRATION

The demonstration merits a special discussion because of its importance in teaching physical activities. A demonstration by the teacher (or by a surrogate

FIGURE 8–7 Concurrent styles

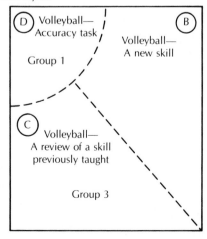

performer) has enormous impact on the observing learner. A demonstration has the following characteristics:

1. It presents an image or model of the activity (the quality of the movement).
2. This model establishes the performance standard for the learner.
3. It is rapid (unless shown on video in slow motion).
4. It can present the entire activity, parts of it, or any combination of the parts.
5. It saves time. Verbal explanation is sometimes too long and tedious. A demonstration tells the whole story quickly, and the visual impact is very powerful.
6. It can be integrated with a precise verbal explanation of the task and/or its parts.
7. Any other?

The demonstration can be presented to the learners by a person or by various technologies:

1. The teacher
2. A student who can perform the task
3. A film
4. Videotape
5. Photographs (in books, on task sheets, on wall posters, etc.)
6. Slides
7. Film loops
8. Computer
9. Other?

The Role of the Teacher

Since the impact of a visual demonstration is so powerful and effective in learning a physical task, the teacher must be rather careful, or precise, when he or she demonstrates the task. That demonstration becomes the model for the learner. If the teacher erroneously or sloppily demonstrates a task, that is the model for the learner in that episode. If a teacher delegates the demonstration to other people or technologies, the same principle prevails. The teacher must be certain that the demonstration will depict the desired model.

The Role of the Learner

The learner's role is to observe, to listen, to ask questions, and then to practice the task. As the learner practices, he or she must keep in mind the goal of approximating the model.

The Demonstration in Styles A–E

Each style from A to E includes presenting the task(s) in the impact set; therefore, the demonstration can be a part of styles A–E. The demonstration is necessary whenever a visual image is needed to deliver the task. To suggest that the demonstration is synonymous with style A is erroneous. The learners in styles B–E also need to know specifically what to do and how to do it.

9 | On Discovery

When we design tasks that invite the discovery of solutions to problems, what are we asking the learners to do? What is the nature of a task (the structure of the task) that actually motivates the learner to engage in discovering new movements, new ideas? What is the structure of the discovery process itself?

In styles A–E, the learner has been mobile along three developmental channels—physical, social, and emotional. The mobility along the fourth one, the *cognitive* channel, has been limited. This is because the learner has essentially been asked to perform and practice as told. The learner has primarily been engaged in the *reproduction* (replication) cluster of styles. In these styles the learner is invited to engage primarily in the cognitive operations of memory and recall.

Each one of these styles (A–E) has its own set of objectives for the accomplishment of tasks, and each style involves the learner in different roles (with their corresponding decisions). However, the common thread that runs through all the styles in the reproduction (replication) cluster is the engagement of memory and recall. These cognitive operations are essential for the practice of any physical task. Practice and replication are necessary for learning any task and for reaching a reasonable level of competency in performance.

When the objective of the episodes shifts to the *discovery* process, the teacher and the learner participate in a different cluster of styles: the *production* styles (F–K). These styles seek to engage the learner in cognitive operations other than memory and recall. These styles have different sets of objectives, which invite the learner to participate in the discovery of new movements by engaging in:

Problem solving
Inventing
Creating
Comparing
Contrasting
Categorizing
Hypothesizing
Synthesizing
Extrapolating
Critical thinking

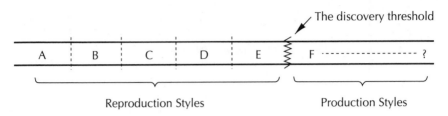

FIGURE 9–1 The discovery threshold

How can the teacher create conditions for engaging in any of these operations? Which tasks in sports, games, dance, gymnastics, and adventure activities are conducive to the *discovery process?* What are the new relationships between the teacher and the learner that must exist in order to initiate and maintain this process? How does the teacher do it *deliberately?* What are the new learning behaviors?

From the theoretical and practical standpoints, we are seeking a *transition* from one set of conditions to another, from reproduction of known facts, rules, and models to production of new ideas and new movements—new to the learner and, often, new to the teacher.

At this transition point on the Spectrum there is an invisible, yet real line called the *Discovery Threshold.* (See Figure 9-1.) This line of demarcation falls between one set of conditions and relationships (styles A–E) and another (styles F–?).

CROSSING THE DISCOVERY THRESHOLD

Thinking occurs when something or somebody triggers the brain to engage in memory, discovery, or creativity. The trigger is always in a form of a particular *stimulus* (S) that induces a state of unrest in the brain and evokes the need to know. The stimulus moves the person into a state of *cognitive dissonance* (D). The need to know motivates the brain to start a search for an answer, a solution, a response that will reduce the dissonance. The search, regardless of how long it takes, engages the memory process, the discovery process, the creative process, or any combination of these. This phase in the flow of thinking is designated as *mediation* (M).

When the search is completed, a *response* (R) is produced in a form of an answer, a solution, a new idea, or a new movement. The phases and sequence in the flow of thinking are:

S = The stimulus (the trigger)
D = The state of cognitive dissonance (the need to know)
M = Mediation (the search)
R = The response (the answer or solution)
Schematically, this general model looks like this:

$$S \rightarrow D \rightarrow M \rightarrow R$$

In the context of physical activities, the role of the teacher (and, subsequently, the role of the learner) is to design a problem (or a series of problems) that will serve as the *stimulus* (S) and an invitation to the learner to engage in discovery. For example: What are three possible movements that can follow a forward roll? In strength development of the abdominal region, what would be a rational sequence of positions (or movements) arranged by degree of difficulty? In soccer, what are two options for one player to overtake two defensive players?

When faced with such questions (problems to solve), the learner moves momentarily into the state of *cognitive dissonance* (D) and then, when the search of a solution or solutions begins to occur, into the *mediation* (M) phase. This process culminates in the production of the *response* (R) in the form of movements that, indeed, solve the problem.

This discovery process can follow two paths:

1. Convergent thinking
2. Divergent thinking

The convergent thinking process is described and illustrated in Chapter 10, "The Guided Discovery style (style F)" and Chapter 11, "The Convergent Discovery style (style G)."

The divergent thinking process is described and illustrated in Chapter 12, "The Divergent Production style (style H)," Chapter 13, "The Individual Program—Learner's Design style (style I)," Chapter 14, "The Learner-Initiated style (style J),"and Chapter 15, "The Self-Teaching style (style K)."

The challenge for the teacher initiating the discovery process is threefold:

1. To design tasks that are conducive to the discovery process
2. To learn the deliberate teaching behavior that is appropriate for this process
3. To monitor the learning behavior that is unique to this process

Together, teacher and learner can reach new levels of motivation, excitement, and achievement.

10 | The Guided Discovery Style (Style F)

The first style that engages the learner in discovery is called *guided discovery*.[1] The essence of this style is a particular teacher–learner relationship in which the teacher's sequence of questions brings about a corresponding set of responses by the learner. Each question by the teacher elicits a single correct response discovered by the learner. The cumulative effect of this sequence—a converging process—leads the learner to discover the sought concept, principle, or idea.

THE OBJECTIVES OF THIS STYLE

This specific process has the following set of objectives:

1. To engage the learner in a particular process of discovery—the converging process
2. To develop a precise relationship between the learner's discovered response and the stimulus (question) presented by the teacher
3. To develop sequential discovery skills that logically lead to the discovery of a concept
4. To develop the patience in both the teacher and learner that is required for the discovery process

THE ANATOMY OF THIS STYLE

The teacher makes all the decisions in the preimpact set (see Figure 10-1). The main decisions are the objectives, the target of the episode, and the design of the sequence of questions that will guide the learner to the discovery of the target.

In this style, more decisions are shifted to the learner in the impact set. The act of discovering the answers means that the learner makes decisions about parts of the subject matter within the topic selected by the teacher. The impact

---

[1]Katona, George. *Organizing and Memorizing.* New York: Columbia University Press, 1949.

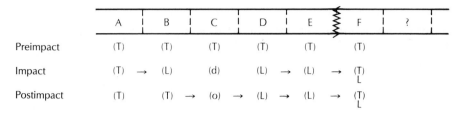

	A	B	C	D	E	F	?
Preimpact	(T)	(T)	(T)	(T)	(T)	(T)	
Impact	(T) →	(L)	(d)	(L) →	(L) →	(T) L	
Postimpact	(T)	(T) →	(o) →	(L) →	(L) →	(T) L	

FIGURE 10–1　The anatomy of the guided discovery style

set is a sequence of corresponding decisions made by the teacher and the learner.

In the postimpact set, the teacher verifies the learner's response to each question (or clue). In some tasks, the learners can verify the response for themselves. The roles of continuous, corresponding decisions in the impact and postimpact sets are unique to this style.

IMPLEMENTATION OF THE GUIDED DISCOVERY STYLE

Perhaps the best way for you to get an idea of a guided discovery episode is to read the following sections that describe the preimpact set and then study the first two or three examples of how to design the sequences. Ask one of your learners to volunteer for a short experimental session. During this one-to-one episode, your role is to:

1. Deliver each question as designed
2. Wait for the learner's response
3. Offer feedback (a combination of neutral and value feedback)
4. Move on to the next question

When the episode is over, review the results of the experiment. Were you able to follow the sequence? Were you able to wait for every response? Did you stay with the appropriate forms of feedback? Was the sequence of questions appropriate? Did you need to add questions? Once you've answered these questions, you are ready to practice this process with another learner. This process is new to most people; it takes time to learn to behave in this style. Let's review the roles of the teacher and the learner in each set of decisions.

The Preimpact Set

Preimpact decisions in guided discovery concern the specific subject matter to be taught and learned. After you have determined the subject matter, the next, and most important, step in guided discovery is to determine the *sequence* of steps. These steps consist of questions or clues that will slowly, gradually, and securely lead the student to discover the end result (i.e., a concept, a particular movement, etc.). *Each step is based on the response given in the previous step.*

Each step, then, must be carefully weighed, judged, tested, and then established at each particular location in the sequence. This also means that there will be an internal connection between steps that is related to the *structure* of the subject matter. To design related steps the teacher needs to anticipate possible student responses to a given stimulus (step). If these possible responses seem too diverse or tangential, then the teacher needs to design another step, perhaps smaller and closer to the previous step, to narrow down the number of diverse responses. In fact, the ideal form of guided discovery is structured to elicit only one response per clue. Whenever more than one response is possible, the teacher must be ready with another clue that guides the student to select only one possibility (the most appropriate for the present end) and abandon the others. This digression understandably happens in guided discovery. People's minds are different and do not always respond to the same clue (however carefully selected) in the same expected way. Often the learner will approximate the correct response, but you must guide him or her to the desired response with an additional clue or question.

The following two diagrams (Figures 10-2 and 10-3) represent the sequence structure of guided discovery. The first one describes the relationship between each stimulus (the question) and its corresponding response. The second diagram represents the size of the step and the need to design steps within the grasp of most (if not all) learners.

The process of guided discovery embodies the S→D→M→R relationship at every step. The first stimulus (S_1) is designed to move the learner to dissonance and mediation (M) in which the learner searches for the answer, and when the learner is ready, he or she will produce the response (R_1). The teacher continues by presenting the second stimulus (S_2), which again moves the learner to mediation, resulting in the production of the second discovered response (R_2), and so on until the last stimulus (S_n) elicits the response (R_n) that is the actual discovery of the target. This last response can be expressed by stating the discovered concept or by showing it through movement.

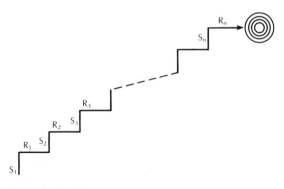

FIGURE 10–2   Steps of guided discovery

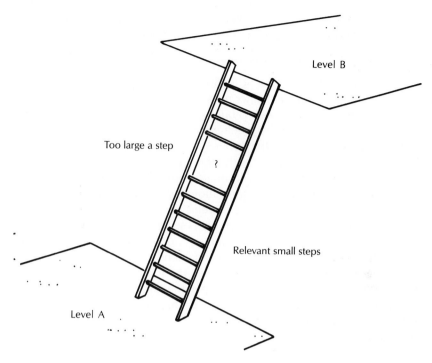

FIGURE 10–3　The ladder of guided discovery

The Impact Set

The impact set in guided discovery tests the sequence design. A sequence carefully designed and then tested by individual learners, then redesigned and retested, may become the prototype for the given target. When this level is reached, the same sequence can be used in many episodes with a high probability of success.

Any serious failure to respond by the student indicates inadequate design of the individual step or the sequence as a whole.

In addition to needing a carefully designed sequence, the teacher must follow several "rules" of this process:

1. Never tell the answer.
2. Always wait for the learner's response.
3. Offer frequent feedback.
4. Maintain a climate of acceptance and patience.

These behaviors may seem very demanding, but they are necessary for a successful episode in this style. The first rule is mandatory—if you tell the answer, you will abort the entire process of connecting one small discovery to another. The second rule, to wait for the answer, is necessary to provide the learner time to engage in mediation. Usually, the time the learner needs for a response is relatively short—perhaps a few seconds for each answer. The teacher must learn not to intervene during this time. (Research literature offers a number of studies on wait-time that reveals some teachers are unable to wait more than 2 seconds.)[2]

The third rule calls for frequent feedback to the learner. A short "Yes," a nod, or "Correct!" are sufficient after responses in the initial experiences in this style. In tasks where the feedback is built in, the learner will already know the results of some responses. The teacher's role is to continue the questions, which indicates to the learner that he or she is on the correct path.

The fourth rule calls for an affective awareness. The teacher must exhibit patience and acceptance. These will maintain the flow of the process. Reprimands and impatience will trigger frustration and discomfort in the learner and will eventually stop the process. The emotional and cognitive streams are visibly intertwined during the learning process by guided discovery.

The impact phase in guided discovery is a delicate interplay of cognitive and emotional dimensions between teacher and student, both bound intimately and intricately to the subject matter. The tension and anticipation that develops at each step are relieved only when the final discovery has occurred. The student, without being given the answer, has accomplished the purpose, has found the unknown, has learned!

In the impact set, then, the teacher must be aware of the following factors:

1. The objective or the target
2. The direction of the sequence of steps
3. The size of each step
4. The interrelationship of the steps
5. The speed of the sequence
6. The emotions of the learner

The Postimpact Set

The nature of feedback in guided discovery is unique. In a sense the feedback is built into every step of the process. The reinforcing behavior that indicates the student's success at each step is positive feedback about his or her learning and accomplishments. A total evaluation is obtained by the very fact that the process is completed, the purpose is achieved, and the subject matter is learned.

An approving response at each step constitutes an immediate, precise, and personal evaluation. In turn, the immediacy of positive feedback and reinforcement serves as a continuous motivating force to seek solutions, to investigate more, and to learn more.

---

[2]*Note:* Waiting is a part of all the styles that engage the learner in discovery. In the styles that deal with memory, waiting beyond a reasonable amount of time will not produce the answer. Instead, it will produce frustration.

This kind of feedback, consisting of the teacher's accepting behavior and approval of correct responses, has a potent social effect in a group situation. When this process develops in a class, the willingness to participate and offer overt responses (verbal or physical) becomes contagious. More and more students seem to feel secure and are less afraid to respond. Although this process is more efficient and promising in classes of regular size, the teacher's experience and energy make it possible with large classes. With large classes it is difficult to ascertain that each individual student is at or near the current step; nevertheless, the general excitement of learning seems to permeate even a large group and helps learners actively participate in the cognitive and physical processes.

Sometimes a response may be incorrect or tangential to the direction of the process of guided discovery. The teacher should do the following:

1. Repeat the question or clue that preceded the incorrect response. If the response is correct, proceed with the next question. If an incorrect response is again given, introduce another question that represents a smaller step for the learner.
2. The verbal behavior available to the teacher include: "Have you checked your answer?" or "Would you like to think some more?" These indicate to the learner that the teacher is patient and considers the learner to be the focus of the relationship.

IMPLICATIONS OF THIS STYLE

The use of this style implies that:

1. The teacher is willing to cross the discovery threshold.
2. The teacher is willing to invest the time in studying the activity's structure and in designing the appropriate sequence of questions (clues).
3. The teacher is willing to *take a chance* by experimenting with the *unknown*. Indeed, styles A–E are safe styles for the teacher; the tasks are designed and presented to the learner in different ways, and the learner's role is to follow through. The responsibility of performance is mostly on the learner. In guided discovery, however, the responsibility is the teacher's. The teacher is the one who designs the questions that will elicit the correct response; *the performance of the learner is closely related to the performance of the teacher!*
4. The teacher trusts the cognitive capacity of the student.
5. The teacher is willing to wait for the response and will wait as long as the learner needs to discover the answer.
6. The learner is capable of making small discoveries leading to the discovery of a concept.

SELECTING AND DESIGNING THE SUBJECT MATTER

Before you study the examples illustrating guided discovery in different subject matter areas, consider the following three points:

1. Learners can discover many different things, such as
   a. Concepts
   b. Principles (governing rules)
   c. Relationships among entities
   d. Order or system
   e. How
   f. Why
   g. The reason for something
   h. Limits (the dimensions of "how much," for example)
   i. How to discover
   j. Others
2. The topic and the target to be discovered must be unknown to the learner. One cannot discover what one already knows.
3. When selecting topics you must consider (or reconsider) the choice of targets in sensitive areas. Some religious, sexual, or political topics may not be appropriate for this style. Since guided discovery prompts learners to see and say things that are selected by the teacher (the target), it might conflict with the learner's background or personal preferences. Conflict and embarrassment are not the purpose of the episode and will not enhance the relationship between the teacher and the learner. These topics can be discussed when an exchange of views takes place; style F, however, is not designed for this process.

STYLE-SPECIFIC COMMENTS

1. Often teachers say, "We usually use this style; we often ask questions." Merely asking questions does not mean that you are using style F. To reiterate, the questions are designed in a logical sequence related to the structure of the episode's subject matter. Random questions are not a part of this style.
2. If learners fail to reach the target, usually it is because the sequence of questions allowed them to digress. Recheck the sequence, correct it, and test it again.
3. Short episodes in guided discovery can be used within episodes of other styles (except A) to clarify the task. Style F can be used with individual learners when the teacher offers individual feedback. Obviously, the teacher must be skilled in this process to use it when needed.
4. Style F is very useful as an introduction to a new topic. It immediately engages the learner and creates curiosity to know the specifics of the topic.

5. It is difficult to suggest a reasonable length of time for an episode in this style; however, short episodes are easier to conduct and helpful in maintaining the learners' concentration.

THE DEVELOPMENTAL CHANNELS

Once again, let's examine the learner's position on the developmental channels in this new relationship among the teacher, the learner, and the subject matter (see Figure 10-4).

On the physical channel, the learner is dependent on the specific stimuli from the teacher. Independence is the criterion for placement on the developmental channels; in this case, the learner will be placed toward minimum.

The same applies to the social channel—since the learner is so closely connected with the teacher, minimal social contact occurs with other learners.

Placement on the emotional channel moves toward maximum. Because the learner is successful in each step of discovery, this creates a positive sense of accomplishment.

A significant change occurs on the cognitive channel. Engaging in the particular cognitive operation and crossing the discovery threshold place the learner toward maximum on this channel.

Since the command style, you have come a long way in providing learners with several alternative realities. You have seen that *each* style has its place in the physical education program. Remember that the Spectrum is based on the *nonversus* notion: the realization that each style of teaching can accomplish a particular set of objectives that another style cannot. Your reason for selecting a particular style for a given episode is the *specific* objective(s) that you wish to reach.

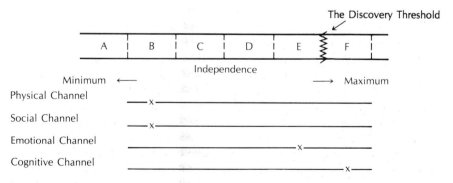

FIGURE 10–4 The guided discovery style and the developmental channels

EXAMPLES OF GUIDED DISCOVERY IN PHYSICAL EDUCATION AND RELATED AREAS

Example 1

Subject matter: Soccer

Specific purpose: To discover the use of the toe-kick in long and high-flying kicks.

Question 1: "What kind of kick is needed when you want to pass the ball to a player who is far from you?"

Anticipated response: "A long kick!" (Response: "Correct!")

Question 2: "Suppose there is a player from the opposing team between you and your teammate. How can you safely get the ball to your teammate?"

Anticipated response: "Kick the ball so that it flies high!" ("Correct!")

Question 3: "Where should the force be applied on the ball to raise it off the ground?"

Anticipated response: "As low as possible!" ("Yes!")

Question 4: "Which part of the foot can comfortably get to the lowest part of the ball while you are running?"

Anticipated response: "The toes!" ("Very good! Let's try it!")

Let us analyze this short process of interaction between the questions and the inevitable responses produced. This process will always work because there is an intrinsic (logical, if you wish) relationship between the question and the answer in terms of the stated purpose—the high toe-kick. Sometimes it might be necessary to inject an additional question depending on the age of the learner, the level of word comprehension, and similar variables. The basic structure of the sequence, however, remains the same. After several experiences using a given sequence, the process becomes quite refined and successful.

One can see why the two behavioral adjustments proposed at the beginning of this chapter are needed to achieve this cognition-motion bond. The same *physical objective* of using the toes for the high flying kick could have been accomplished by *showing* or *telling*. The student would have learned the high kick as demonstrated by the teacher by observing and repeating the action. The comprehension of relationships, the understanding of "why," which is essential to high-quality learning, would be missing from the whole experience.

Let us try to understand the technical aspect of the sequence design. How do you decide which question comes first? Second? As a rule of thumb, proceed from the *general to the specific,* relating each question to the *specific purpose* of the movement. The purpose of the long high kick is to get the ball to a faraway player. By presenting the learner with the situation of two players far apart, the need for a long kick is made obvious. Since there are two kinds of long kicks—one rolling on the ground and the other high flying—the teacher introduces the condition of an opponent in question 2, which suggests the need to raise the ball into the air. Now move to simple mechanics (which are within the realm of every child's experience); if you want to raise the ball into the air, you must, in most cases, apply force to the bottom of the ball in an upward direction. Question 3 leads to this appropriate, inevitable answer. The next question practically follows by itself; you need to apply a particular art of the foot to meet the conditions established in the previous response.

The following benefits are derived from this process:

1. The student has learned the physical response for the soccer lesson planned by the teacher.
2. The student has learned the relationship between the flight of the ball and the foot—both the rudimentary mechanics involved and the place of this kick in soccer tactics.
3. The student has learned that he or she can discover these things by himself or herself.
4. Psychologists believe that when this process is employed frequently and purposefully, the learner will begin to ask the questions by himself or herself whenever a new situation arises; the learner will be able to transfer this thinking and discovery process.

The beauty of guided discovery is most evident when teaching novice students. It is most interesting to use this style with students who do not know anything about the subject matter at hand. They respond almost uninterruptedly to the sequence of clues and are not pulled astray by partial knowledge or dim memories of some movement detail. Learning is fresh, clear, and flowing.

Example 2

Subject matter: Shot put
Specific purpose: To discover the stance for putting the shot.
Question 1: "What is the main purpose of putting the shot in competition?"
Anticipated response: "To put it as far as possible."
Question 2: "What is needed to achieve distance?"
Anticipated response: "Strength, power!"
(Teacher's response: "Correct!")
Question 3: "What else?"
Anticipated response: "Speed!" ("Good.")
Question 4: "In the total motion of putting the shot, where should the power and speed reach their maximum?"
Anticipated response: "At the point of release!" ("Correct!")
Question 5: "Where is the point of minimum strength and speed?"
Anticipated response: "At the stationary starting position!" ("Very good.")
Question 6: "To achieve the maximum strength and speed at the point of release, how far from this point should the starting position be?"
Anticipated response: "As far as possible!" ("Correct!")
This is the rationale behind the starting position used by the top shot putters. If the answer to question 6 is not readily given, an additional step must be

taken: "To gain maximum momentum, should the body and the shot travel a short or a long distance?" Then ask, "How long?" From this point on, physical responses are called for.

Question 7: "If the point of release is at this line in front of your body, what would be *your* starting position that fulfills the requirements of response 6?"

Anticipated response: Here some students might stand in a wide stance with the shot resting someplace on the shoulder. (The balance requirement becomes clear immediately, and some sort of straddle position is usually offered. If this is not apparent you may ask, "Are you well-balanced?" and wait for the new physical response.) However, others may take the concept of "maximum distance from the point of release" quite literally and attempt to stretch out the arm holding the shot; here you intervene with another question.

Question 8: "Since the shot is quite heavy, can the arm do the job alone, or could the body help?"

Anticipated response: "The body could help!" (The student has already felt the weight of the shot and the awkwardness of holding it in the outstretched hand.)

Question 9: "Where could you place the shot to get maximum push from the body?"

Anticipated response: "On the shoulder!" ("Correct!")

Question 10: "To gain maximum momentum, do you place your body weight equally on both legs?"

Anticipated response: "No. On the rear leg!" ("Correct!")

Question 11: "What should the position of this leg be to gain maximum thrust from the ground?"

Anticipated response: "Slightly bent!" ("Yes!")

Question 12: "Now, what would be the position of the trunk to fulfill the conditions we've just discovered?"

Anticipated response: "Slightly bent and twisted toward the rear leg!" ("True!")

Teacher: "Good! Does this position seem to be the starting one we were looking for?"

This painstaking procedure may frighten the uninitiated teacher, but one gets used to it. Since the learning accomplishments outweigh by far the initial difficulties and apprehension, the teacher will be motivated to try this style whenever the situation merits.

The sequence developed here follows the same principles as in the previous example. As always, the biggest obstacle is deciding which question to ask first. Once the purpose of putting the shot becomes clear, the interrelated steps toward accomplishing this purpose become clearer. In fact, the *intrinsic structure* of the shot put becomes clearer to the student and teacher alike. We have progressed in the teaching-learning process by moving backward, by retracing the movements and positions from the end result (the put) to the starting position (the stance). It is the same technique used for discovering the road between point A and point B in a maze. Often one starts from point B and traces the road back to point A.

Together we have discovered the technique of structuring the process of guided discovery. Polya sums it up in the following way:

> There is certainly something in the method that is not superficial. There is a certain psychological difficulty in turning around, in going away from the goal, in working backwards, in not following the direct path to the desired end. When we discover the sequence of appropriate operations, our mind has to proceed in an order which is exactly the reverse of the actual performance. There is a sort of psychological repugnance to this reverse order which may prevent a quite able student from understanding the method if it is not presented carefully.
>
> Yet it does not take a genius to solve a concrete problem working backward; anybody can do it with a little common sense. We concentrate upon the desired end, we visualize the final position in which we would like to be. From what foregoing position could we get there? It is natural to ask this question, and in so asking we work backwards.[3]

Example 3

Subject matter: Developmental movement, dance, gymnastics

Specific purpose: To discover the effect of the base of support and center of gravity on balance. (This lesson has been taught successfully many times in grades 3–5.)

Question 1: "Do you know what balance is?"

Anticipated response: Answer is given in motion; there is no need here for a verbal response. Some children will place themselves in a variety of balance *positions,* and some will *move* sideways, which requires a degree of balance other than "normal." Chances are that *all* children will have a response that illustrates balance.

Question 2: "Could you *be* in maximum balance?" (Sometimes it is necessary to use the word *most* instead of maximum.)

Anticipated response: Usually the responses here vary. Some will assume a variety of erect positions, and some will assume lower positions they have seen in football, wrestling, or various gymnastics stunts. It may be necessary to repeat this question.

Question 3: "Is this your most balanced position?" (Check the solutions by pushing each child slightly and, thus, upsetting the position of balance.) Within a short period of time, several children will get close to the ground in very low balance positions. Some may

---

[3]Polya, György. *How to Solve It*. Garden City, NY: Doubleday & Company, Inc., 1957).

even lie flat on the floor. (These will be the hardest positions to upset by a slight push.)

Question 4: "Could you, now, be in a position that is a little bit *less* balanced?"

Anticipated response: Most or all children will assume a new position by reducing the size of the base. This is often accomplished by removing a supporting hand, raising the head in supine position, or rolling over to one side from a supine position.

Question 5: "Now, could you move to a new position that is still *less* balanced?"

Anticipated response: Now the process is in motion. All children will assume a position that has less area of contact between the body and the floor. Some will start rising off the floor. Within two or three more steps to reduce the balance, most of the class will be in rather high positions with close to the minimum point of contact between the body and the floor (Questions 6, 7, and 8).

Question 6: "Could you be now in the *least* balanced position?"

Anticipated response: Most children stand on the toes of one foot; some raise their arms. Occasionally somebody will suggest standing on one hand or even on one finger.

In a sense, by use of motion the students offered the correct answers and discovered some factors affecting balance. They discovered that a low, wide-based position is more balanced than a high, small-based position.

This is sufficient—the concept is understood through the use of motion. Verbalizing the principles is unnecessary. However, if the teacher feels that a verbal summation is needed, he or she can ask, "What is the difference between the most balanced and least balanced position?" and "What made it so?" The correct answers will be readily available to the children. Children can learn to discover not only new movements, but also the principle that organizes them into a concept.

Example 4

A classic lesson in guided discovery is teaching students to discover the three classes of levers, and the roles of the axis, the force arm, and the resistance arm in the operation of the lever in each class.

This lesson has been used many times in kinesiology classes. To understand the relationship between the three classes of levers and muscular action, the student must see clearly the components of each lever class and their integration into a system of levers. The rote method and sheer memory rarely produce insight into a new condition and the ability to apply to it the proper level analysis. The use of guided discovery has proven successful with most students in both understanding and application.

The equipment for this lesson are the standard meter stick and a balancing stand used in physics classes. Two equal weights (50–100 grams), two weight hangers, and a string will complete the set.

Step 1: Place the meter stick on the balancing stand in a balanced position.

Step 2: Ask, "How can we upset the equilibrium?"

Anticipated response: "Push one side down or up!" ("Correct!")

Step 3: Ask, "Can we do the same by using weight?" One of the students usually places one of the weights on one side of the meter stick. ("Good!")

Step 4: Ask, "Can you balance the seesaw now?"

Anticipated response: Another student will place the other weight on the other side of the meter stick, moving it around until it balances.

Step 5: Ask, "What factors are involved in the maintenance of equilibrium?"

Anticipated response: "Equal weights at equal distances from axis A."

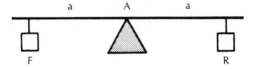

Step 6: Ask, "Which factor can we change now to upset the balance?"

Anticipated response: "The distance of either weight from the axis." (One of the students is asked to do it by moving one of the weights.)

Step 7: Ask, "How far can you move it?"

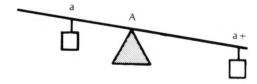

Anticipated response: "To the end of the meter stick."

Step 8: Ask, "Is this the maximum distance possible between the weight on the end of the stick and axis A?"

Anticipated response: "No. It is possible to move the axis farther."

Step 9: Ask, "Would you do it, please?"

Anticipated response: Action:

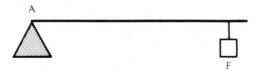

Step 10: "Now, could you do anything, using the present equipment, to balance the stick?"

Anticipated response: More often than not students discover the following solution: Put the string around the stick between the weight (F) and the axis (A) and slowly pull the stick up until it is balanced in the horizontal position.

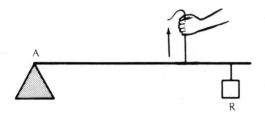

Step 11: "In terms of A, F, and R, what kind of balanced arrangement have we had thus far?"

Anticipated response:

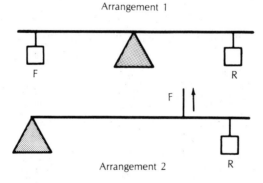

Arrangement 1

Arrangement 2

Step 12: "Look at the second arrangement. Is it possible to change any factors and have a new balanced arrangement?"

Anticipated response: After a possible short pause the following will be offered:

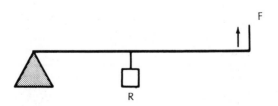

Step 13: "These are the only three possible arrangements of levers. They are called:

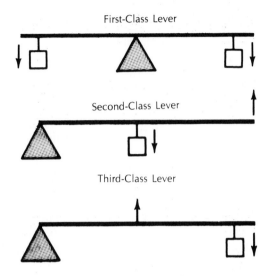

The next step is to relate this to muscular action by identifying the skeletal joint as the axis (A), the weight of the limb as the resistance (R), and the pulling muscle as the force (F); this makes it relatively easy for the student to relate the lever principle to a particular part of the body that is involved in a particular movement. This, too, is taught by guided discovery.

Bruner, in analyzing the assets of the discovery process, proposes that memory is greatly enhanced when the student discovers things by himself or herself.[4] Learning the lever by guided discovery commits this phenomenon to memory for a long period of time.

In fact, this lesson has been taught to 8-year-old children, who, after understanding the required relationships, were able to reproduce the accurate three arrangements discovered in the seesaw game a year earlier.

Before we conclude this chapter on guided discovery, let us list some topics or phases in various activities that may be taught by guided discovery. Select one topic at a time and develop a lesson in guided discovery. It does not have to be a long lesson, or even one that will occupy a complete period. When comprehension is crucial for successfully learning a physical activity, 15 minutes of guided discovery (if done with some frequency) will develop a new learning climate in the class—a cognitive climate!

As suggested earlier in the chapter, to invoke full learning participation you must move the student from the state of cognitive acquiescence to the state of

---

[4]Bruner, Jerome S. "The Act of Discovery," *Harvard Educational Review* 31 (1961): 21–32.

cognitive dissonance in order to cross the Discovery Threshold. This will precipitate the process of inquiry and lead to discovery.

After you have taught the lesson, try to identify and isolate the obstacles that came up during the lesson. If you can identify these awkward moments, you can go back to your sequence of clues or questions and make adjustments. Check to see whether each step is relevant to the development of the subject matter at hand. Try to analyze the response or responses you received from the class to that particular clue; try to discover *why* the students did not produce the anticipated response. Was the step unclear? Did your clue lead to two or more choices other than the correct one? Was the step too large? Did you need to give too many additional clues?

After answering all these questions, you will be able to introduce the necessary modification in the sequence.

Now go back to the gymnasium and try again by teaching another individual or small group. Experiences and observations by teachers who use guided discovery have indicated that after several attempts and analyses of the process, one can become quite proficient using style F. Start small. First succeed in one short episode in one phase of one activity. Then you can go on to teach another episode by guided discovery. Eventually, you may find yourself quite adept at this style.

SUGGESTED TOPICS TO BE TAUGHT BY GUIDED DISCOVERY

Gymnastics

1. The role of the center of gravity in performing turns on the balance beam
2. The role of momentum in maintaining balance on the balance beam
3. The relationship between the trunk and the appendages in developing balance
4. The factors affecting stability in positions on the balance beam
5. The factors affecting stability in motion on the balance beam
6. The factors affecting the smoothness of connecting elements in a continuous sequence of movements on the balance beam
7. Suggest a phase concerning the mounts on the balance beam that you would like to teach by guided discovery
8. Suggest a phase concerning the dismounts
9. Suggest any topic in any phase of teaching balance that could be taught by guided discovery

All these topics involve more than just learning a particular movement; they involve a principle, a *concept*. Principles and concepts are the building blocks of any activity and have been developed over the years by master teachers, coaches, and supreme performers. Discovering these principles and concepts by the learner creates a more complete understanding of the activity, and this understanding provides the learner with the tools and motivation for further search, for broader learning, and for better performance.

This level of insight and comprehension can be reached only through cognitive involvement, and a fuller cognitive involvement can be invoked only by styles of teaching that by their structure and operational procedures evoke the heuristic process. Do not allow the learner's cognitive faculties to take even a small nap during an episode!

Let us continue with some more examples in gymnastics:

10. The categories that exist in the variety of rolls in tumbling
11. The principles that relate the variety of rolls to one another

The novice teacher in guided discovery and other discovery styles will be amazed to find a new wealth of subject matter materials suggested by the students as the discovery process develops and blooms. Use your students as a resource.

12. The relationship between directions and postures in tumbling movements
13. The relationship between the length of the lever produced by the legs and success in performing the kip
14. The relationship between the kip principle learned on the mat and the kip used for various mounts on the parallel bars
15. The role of the lever (the whole body) in producing various degrees of momentum when swinging on the parallel bars
16. Suggest other aspects of performance on the parallel bars.
17. Can your suggestions for the parallel bars lead to discovering the application to other apparatus?
18. In vaulting, the various phases involved in a vault
19. The assets and liabilities in each phase of a vault, and discovery of a generalization
20. Application of the generalization to a specific vault
21. The variables affecting changes in the form of a given vault
22. Suggest another aspect of vaulting.
23. Suggest two consecutive aspects to be taught by guided discovery.
24. Three consecutive aspects?
25. Any other proposals?

In gymnastics, with all its variety, there are dozens of phases that can be taught by guided discovery, creating a deeper understanding of gymnastics.

Developmental Movement

An area in physical education that is most readily taught by guided discovery is developmental movement. Examples for specific episodes include:

1. The physical attributes that exist as prerequisites for movement (agility, balance, flexibility, strength, endurance, and so on)
2. The kind of movements that contribute to developing a specific attribute
3. Specific movements that contribute to developing a specific attribute
4. Movement that overlaps two physical attributes

5. Movements that develop a particular attribute by using a specific part or region of the body
6. The involvement of a particular part or region of the body in a specific movement
7. The *limits* of involvement of a particular part or region of the body in a specific movement
8. The variable affecting the degree of difficulty in an exercise of strength development (i.e., amount of resistance, duration of resistance, repetition of resistance, intervals of resistance)
9. Specific movements and patterns that will cause the change in degree of difficulty in strength development by manipulating one or more of the mentioned variables
10. Can you suggest similar topics for discovery in the areas of flexibility, agility, balance, and others?

The guided discovery lessons in developmental movement can be integrated with kinesiology in a most satisfying and contributory way. Can you think of some ties?

11. The relationship between a particular physical attribute, a phase of a given sport, and a specific developmental movement
12. The relationship between the need for flexibility of the shoulder for a javelin thrower and specific developmental movements
13. The relationship between the need for flexibility at the hip joint for a hurdler and specific developmental movements
14. The relationship between the need for leg strength in the shot put and specific developmental movements
15. The relationship between the need for abdominal strength in a performer on the uneven parallel bars and specific developmental movements
16. Can you suggest other aspects of developmental movement that can be taught by guided discovery?

Basketball

1. The need for a variety of passes
2. The relationship between various game situations and the variety of passes available
3. The possible *connection* between two consecutive passes, three passes, a series of passes
4. The logic (or reason) behind a particular arrangement of players on the court
5. The feasibility of this arrangement in a *variety* of situations
6. The best positioning in zone defense against a given strategy of offense
7. The efficiency factors of a given offense strategy against a particular defense arrangement
8. Can you teach by guided discovery *all* the techniques of basketball? Some? In which ones would you prefer not to use guided discovery? Why?

9. Can you teach all aspects of strategy in basketball by guided discovery? Would it be helpful if your players gained a good understanding of each aspect of the strategy by this style?
10. Can you suggest other aspects and topics in basketball to be taught by guided discovery?

Swimming

1. The buoyancy principles
2. Specific postures for specific purposes (i.e., "dead man's" posture for best floating)
3. The principle of propulsion in the water
4. The role of breathing during propulsion
5. The role of each specific part of the body in propulsion
6. The role of each specific part of the body in propulsion in a specific direction
7. The relationship between a particular phase in a stroke and the physical attribute needed
8. Can you teach other technical aspects of swimming by guided discovery?
9. Can you discover which are the preferred aspects of swimming to be taught by this style?

Other Sports

1. Think of any phases in football, hockey, volleyball, archery, wrestling, soccer, modern dance, or track and field that can be taught by guided discovery.
2. Can you discover which aspects of the *techniques* of these sports will be desirable to teach by this style?
3. Can you discover which aspects of the *strategy* of these sports will be desirable to teach by guided discovery?

Now that you have crossed the discovery threshold, what is the next style?

FIGURE 10–5   Style F classroom chart

GUIDED DISCOVERY

The purpose of this style is to discover a concept answering a sequence of questions presented by the teacher.

ROLE OF LEARNER

- To listen to the teacher's question or clue

- To discover the answer for each question in the sequence

- To discover the final answer, which constitutes the concept sought

ROLE OF TEACHER

- To design the sequence of questions, each designed for a small discovery by the learner

- To present the questions to the learner, in a sequence

- To provide periodic feedbeck to learner

- To acknowledge the learner's discovery of the concept

11 | The Convergent Discovery Style (Style G)

The convergent discovery style (style G) is the second style past the Discovery Threshold. In this style the learner is engaged in reasoning, using the rules of logic, critical thinking, and "trial and error" in order to discover the *one* correct answer to a question or the *one* solution to a problem.

The difference between this style and the previous one (guided discovery) is that now the learner proceeds through the discovery process without any guiding clues from the teacher. Indeed, the learner makes more decisions about:

1. The discovery process itself
2. The use of the cognitive operations needed to solve the problem at hand
3. The *one* correct solution
4. The verification of the appropriateness of the solution

Take a few minutes to solve the following problems.

Problem A

Place yourself close to the floor in the following balance positions (stay in each position for a few seconds):

1. With six points of contact between the body and the floor
2. With four points of contact with the floor
3. With two points of contact

Notice what happens to your balance! Now, place yourself in a vertical balance position with two points of contact, as high as you can. Also, place yourself with one point of contact, in a nonvertical position.

The Question   What is the rule that governs balance positions? This rule consists of three interacting principles that always govern the ability to maintain a balance position.

In order to solve this problem, the learner must engage in trial and error (actually trying these balance positions). These experiences provide the learner with information needed to discover the solution. The discovery process itself involves the activation of several cognitive operations: (1) comparing the data derived from "doing" these balance positions, (2) organizing the compared data into categories, (3) drawing conclusions about each category, and (4) identifying the relationship among the three (and only three) principles involved in the sought, single rule.

In relating this experience to the steps in the discovery process described in Chapter 9, we can see the flow of S → D → M → R.

The problem served as the stimulus. When the learner gets involved with the problem, he or she enters the state of cognitive dissonance, then moves on to the phase of mediation—searching for the solution. When the learner is ready to produce the solution, the response emerges.

Since this problem has only one solution—one rule that governs balance— the road traveled by the learner illustrates the process of convergent discovery. (*Note:* Since this rule is based on the laws of physics, it is a universal rule. All participants will discover the same rule.)

Problem B

Design and perform a smooth, flowing "movement sentence" by combining three of the following words: grow, spin, creep, pounce, explode, shrink, or gallop. The key in the design of this problem is that single letter "a." Design and perform *a* smooth . . . .

At first glance, it may appear that there are many alternative solutions to this problem. However, the wording of the problem asks the learner to design *a* sentence. It means that *each* learner is invited to design only *one* sentence.

Each individual learner must make decisions about which three words to choose, the order of the words in the sentence, the movement that will represent each word, and the way of performing the movements, thus, each will discover his or her own single solution to the problem. Again, each learner is engaged in convergent discovery. (*Note:* The same problem with a subtle, yet significant change in wording will invite the learner to participate in divergent production (see Chapter 12).

Can you see the relationship between Problem B and the S → D → M → R? Can you identify the cognitive operations that are activated by the learner during the process of discovering the solution? Are you ready to suggest (design) "problems" that will invite your students to engage in convergent discovery?

THE OBJECTIVES OF THIS STYLE

As with previous styles, style G has its own specific objectives, objectives that only this style can accomplish. Here, too, they fall into two categories: subject matter objective, and role objectives.

Subject Matter Objective

To discover the single correct answer to a question or the single correct solution to a problem

Role Objectives

To cross the discovery threshold by discovering the one correct response

To engage in a specific sequence of cognitive operations that lead to the solution

To become aware of one's engagement in problem solving, reasoning, and critical thinking

THE ANATOMY OF THIS STYLE

The shift of decisions occurs in the impact set (see Figure 11-1). The learner makes the decision about engaging in the cognitive operations that lead (or might lead) to the discovery of the solution. The learner asks himself or herself questions concerning the problem to be solved. This process distinguishes this style from guided discovery, in which the teacher made the decision about each step toward the discovery of the solution. In style G, the learner is significantly more autonomous during the search for the solution and in the construction of the solution itself.

The role of the learner in postimpact set is to verify the solution by rechecking the reasoning process, by rechecking the trial and error and, at times, by simply seeing that the solution did indeed solve the problem.

The role of the teacher in the preimpact set is to design the problem(s). In the impact set, after presenting the problem(s) to the learner(s), the role of the teacher is to observe the learners as they proceed through the discovery process. This role requires patience. At times there is a tendency to "jump in" and intervene. Physical performances are visual and quite apparent. Not all movement attempts are appropriate in leading to the solution of the given problem. It is *imperative* for the teacher to wait! Thinking takes time. Discovery takes time. It is the learner's time to evolve ideas, to examine them, to sift through the ideas, and to *decide* about the appropriate solution. This process is a very private one—don't intervene! In the postimpact set, however, after the learner has spent time in inquiry, in trial and error, and in examining the solution, the teacher may participate—by asking questions—in verifying the solution.

	A	B	C	D	E	F	G
Preimpact	(T)	(T)	(T)	(T)	(T)	(T)	(T)
Impact	(T) → (L)		(L_d)	(L) → (L)		→ (T_L)	→ (L)
Postimpact	(T)	(T) → (L_o)		→ (L)	(L)	→ (T_L)	→ (L_T)

FIGURE 11–1   The shift from style F to style G

SELECTING AND DESIGNING THE PROBLEMS

As a general guideline for selecting tasks (problems) for this teaching style, use the following criteria:

1. Does the task have only one correct response?
2. Does the task invite convergent thinking? (This depends on the structure of the task and on the verbal behavior used to introduce the task.)
3. Is the discovery process evident?
4. Does the task represent the area of mechanical analysis of the movement? (Most, if not all, "problems" in this area do have one correct solution; for example, the discovery of the lever principle that governs a particular movement.)
5. Does the task invite the discovery of a specific sequence of movements?
6. Does the task require the learner to discover his or her limits in performing the task? (This kind of problem will be initiated with the words *How long . . . ?, How high . . . ?, How far . . . ?*—see the examples that follow.

SOME EXAMPLES

Problem 1 (Absorbing Force)

When learning about absorbing force, catch balls of different sizes thrown from varying distances and at varying speeds.

The problem: What relationships exist between absorbing the force of objects and

1. the size of objects?
2. the weight of objects?
3. the speed of the traveling object?

Problem 2 (Creating Force)

Experiment with striking various objects with your hand(s) and striking and throwing various objects with implements. Vary the distance over which you propel the objects, the distance you move the implements before striking the objects and the speed at which the implement moves.

The problem: What relationships exist between creating the force and

1. the size of the object?
2. the weight of the objects?
3. the length of the implements?
4. the distance?
5. the speed?

Problem 3 (Creating Force)

Jumping to cover distance. Measure the distance you can jump when you start from the following positions:

1. Bending ankles *only,* _____ ft. _____ in.
2. Bending ankles and knees *only,* _____ ft. _____ in.
3. Bending ankles, knees, and trunk, _____ ft. _____ in.
4. Same as (c), and swinging arms forward from the shoulders, _____ ft. _____ in.

The problem: With which jump were you able to create the most force? Why?

Problem 4

Design a sequence of movements that include a hop, a skip, a jump, and a change in speed. Note that in a class of a number of students, the designs (the situations) will vary, but each individual learner will produce one solution (one sequence), and that is the result of convergent discovery. The key to this process, as previously explained, is the wording of the task—the use of the article "a."

Problem 5

What is the highest number of consecutive times you can volley a tennis ball against the wall with a paddle?

Problem 6

Throw the hoop up and away from you. What is the farthest distance the hoop can travel while you run and catch it before it falls flat on the ground?

Problem 7

How long can you balance on one foot with the body in a nonvertical position on the 4-inch-high beam?

Although the solutions (answers) to problems 1, 2, and 3 are *universal* and the solutions to problems 4, 5, 6, and 7 are *personal,* the process in reaching the solutions to all these problems is convergent discovery.

THE DEVELOPMENTAL CHANNELS

As with previous styles, we will use the criterion of *independence* to place the learner on the developmental channels when style G is used (Figure 11-2).

The Physical Channel   Any student who is successfully functioning in style G is demonstrating a high degree of independence about his or her engagement

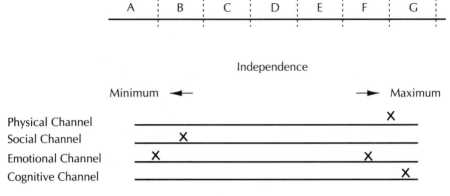

FIGURE 11–2 The convergent discovery style and the developmental channels

in physical tasks. The placement on the physical developmental channel is therefore close to "maximum."

The Social Channel   Engaging in thought processes and discovering single solutions is a very private experience. Social contact is minimal, except for occasional exchange with another learner. The placement on the social developmental channel is therefore toward "minimum" in style G.

The Emotional Channel   The placement on the emotional developmental channel is dual. For those learners who can deal with the emotional stress of doing cognitive tasks, the placement is toward "maximum." For others, the placement is toward "minimum."

The Cognitive Channel   By definition, a learner who is able to function in style G is placed toward "maximum" on the cognitive developmental channel.

The Moral Channel   The placement of a learner on the moral developmental channel is a matter of conjecture. The learner might ask the question: "What is the value of thinking?" The answer to this question depends on the learner's values, as well as his or her degree of independence using the various thought processes. We shall leave to you the decision about the placement of the learner on this channel.

As we have seen, style G engages the learner in learner-initiated thought processes that converge on the discovery of a single correct solution expressed in a movement or a sequence of movements. (See Figure 11-3 for an overview.)

The emphasis, the purpose of this style is to create conditions for the learner to *initiate* a reasonably organized and systematic thought process that leads to the discovery of the sought solution. It is a unique process, an intriguing and an interesting process. Are you ready to design convergent discovery episodes for your students?

FIGURE 11–3   Style G classroom chart

THE CONVERGENT DISCOVERY STYLE

The purpose of this style is to discover the solution to a problem, clarify an issue, or arrive at a conclusion by employing logical procedures, reasoning, and critical thinking.

ROLE OF LEARNER

- To examine the problem or issue

- To evolve his or her own procedure toward a solution or conclusion

- To use the minihierarchy that will lead to the solution or conclusion

- To verify the process and the solution by checking them against criteria appropriate for the subject matter at hand

ROLE OF TEACHER

- To present the problem or issue

- To follow the learner's process of thinking

- To offer feedback or clues (if necessary) without providing the solution

The divergent production style (style H) occupies a unique place on the Spectrum. For the first time the learner is engaged in discovering and producing options within the subject matter. Until now, the teacher has made the decisions about the specific tasks in the subject matter—the role of the learner has been either to replicate and perform or to discover the specific target. In style H, within certain parameters the learner makes the decisions about the specific tasks in the chosen subject matter. This style involves the learner in the human capacity for diversity; it invites the learner to go beyond the known.

The fields of physical education, sports, and dance are rich in opportunities to discover, design, and invent. There is always another possible movement or another combination of movements, another way of passing the ball, another strategy, another dance choreography. The variety of human movement is infinite—the possibilities for episodes in style H are endless. What, then, is the change in teaching behavior that will invite the learner to participate in divergent production? What are the new O–T–L–O relationships? When and for what purpose should this style be used?

THE STRUCTURE OF THIS STYLE

The structure of style H represents general steps similar to the previous style: stimulus → cognitive dissonance → mediation → discovery. The significant difference is that the specifics of these steps lead to the discovery of alternatives. The following diagram represents the process that takes place in this style.

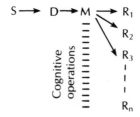

The Stimulus (S) and Cognitive Dissonance (D)

The stimulus, in the form of a question, a problem, or a situation, moves the learner into a state of cognitive dissonance. The need to seek solutions is created. The stimulus is designed and worded to trigger the search for multiple and divergent responses.

The Mediation (M)

During this time the learner searches for the variety of solutions that will solve the problem. This engagement focuses on one dominant cognitive operation aided by the necessary supporting ones. The stimulus is designed to engage the brain in divergent production in that particular cognitive operation. It is possible, for example, to conduct episodes that elicit from the learner divergent ideas in a specific cognitive operation such as categorizing, hypothesizing, solving, and so on.

The Responses (R)

The search in the mediation phase results in the discovery and production of multiple and divergent ideas. These ideas, the responses, may be expressed in different forms that are unique and intrinsic to the subject matter area. In poetry, the responses may be expressed in words; in music they are expressed through melodies; in physical education—through human movements. The process is the same even though the means of expression are varied.

THE OBJECTIVES OF THIS STYLE

The objectives of this style are:

1. To invite the cognitive capacities of the teacher in designing problems for a given subject matter area
2. To invite the cognitive capacities of the learner in discovering multiple solutions to any given problem in physical education
3. To develop insight into the structure of the activity and discover the possible variations within this structure
4. To reach the level of affective security that permits the teacher and the learner to go beyond accepted, conventional responses
5. To develop the ability to verify solutions and organize them for specific purposes

THE ANATOMY OF THIS STYLE

To design episodes in this style, an additional shift of decisions takes place. The roles of the teacher and the learner change again—new realities are experienced and new objectives are reached (see Figure 12-1).

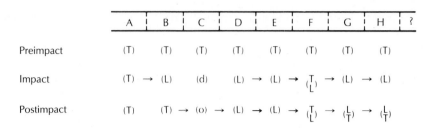

	A	B	C	D	E	F	G	H	?
Preimpact	(T)	(T)	(T)	(T)	(T)	(T)	(T)	(T)	
Impact	(T) → (L)		(d)	(L) → (L) → (T/L) → (L) → (L)					
Postimpact	(T)	(T) → (o) → (L) → (L) → (T/L) → (L/T) → (L/T)							

FIGURE 12–1   The anatomy of the divergent production style

The Preimpact Set

In the *preimpact set,* the teacher makes the three major decisions about the subject matter:

1.   A decision about the general subject matter for the ensuing episode (i.e., tumbling, golf, modern dance, etc.)
2.   A decision about the specific topic that will be the *focus* of the episode (i.e., back handspring, the putt, spinning, etc.)
3.   A decision about the design of the specific problem or series of problems that will elicit multiple and divergent *solutions*

This decision about designing the problems is the crux of the episode for the teacher. It is also the teacher's most demanding cognitive task. The teacher must first have insights into the specific elements of the activity, the sequence of the activity, and the structure of the activity.

The Impact Set

In the *impact set* the learner decides which multiple and divergent solutions are applicable to the problem. The learner discovers the alternative answers that solve the problem. These solutions constitute the *specific subject matter* discovered by the learner in this episode. In the preimpact set, then, the teacher makes the decision about the general subject matter; in the impact set, the learner makes the decision about the *specifics* of the subject matter. The solutions discovered by the learner *become* the subject matter, the content of the episode.

The decisions about designing the solutions are the crux of the episode for the learner. The learner enters the state of cognitive dissonance, gets involved in finding solutions to the problems, tests them in actual movements, and makes the decisions about the final product.

The Postimpact Set

In the *postimpact set,* the learner makes evaluation decisions about the discovered solutions. The learner asks himself or herself, "Is my solution answering the question? Did my response solve the problem?" If the answer is yes, then the learner knows that the solution is another *possible* solution to the problem. If the answer is no, the learner knows the solution is invalid.

Whenever the learner can see the solution, there is no need for verification by somebody else. For example, in examining alternative solutions to a problem in kicking a soccer ball, the learner can see the result of the kick by watching the path of the ball. The learner can verify the solution. On the other hand, in some activities the learner may not be able to see some aspects of the solutions. In this instance, the verification must be done with the aid of videotape or by the teacher. The more the learner is engaged in the postimpact phase, the more the objectives of this style are reached.

IMPLEMENTATION OF THIS STYLE

A general description of a style H episode should help you visualize the process and the sequence of events that take place in this style. Initially, the teacher sets the scene by telling the learners about divergent production and about the legitimacy of seeking and producing alternatives. The teacher reassures the learners that their ideas and solutions to problems will be accepted within the parameters of the situation. This assurance in the first few episodes is necessary to establish a reasonable level of affective comfort in taking a risk. Learners who are used to producing single, correct responses often hesitate when asked to design and develop alternative movements. (After several episodes in this style, you will no longer need to talk about the acceptance of solutions. The process of the episode and the teaching behavior serve as assurance for the learners.)

The next step in the episode is presenting the question or the problem to the learners. The learners disperse and begin to design and examine solutions to the problem. The time allotted provides each learner with the opportunity to inquire, explore, design, move, and assess the alternatives that he or she has produced. The teacher will actually see the involvement of each learner in the process of dissonance → mediation → production of solutions. It is a very special and private time for each learner to engage in the particular cognitive operation, to produce one's own movements, and to examine their validity in reference to the problem.

The teacher's role during this time is to wait and watch the process evolving. The teacher moves about and observes each learner (initially from some distance) to get the flavor of the produced solutions and to observe the degree of involvement by each learner. After a while, the teacher begins giving feedback. The teacher has two options. One option is to offer neutral or value feedback to the entire group, acknowledging that the process of discovery and divergent production is going well. The teacher does not focus on any particular solution by any individual learner. The other option is to make one-to-one contact with each learner, again offering neutral or value feedback about the divergent production process without singling out any one solution. The teacher who is a novice in the style may find it difficult to refrain from responding to a certain solution (it is very tempting to say, "I like this movement"), but keep in mind that the purpose of this style is to develop the learner's capacity to produce his or her movements independently of the teacher's standards or values.

At times, there will be learners who momentarily stop producing solutions. There is a need for periodical pauses in cognitive production. Ideas do not always flow without interruptions. The teacher must wait for the process to continue. At other times, however, a learner might have difficulty producing alternatives. This is not always due to physical limitations in performance or cognitive interruption. Instead, it is the affective uncertainty that holds the learner back from continuing the process. It is the role of the teacher, then, to reiterate the purpose of this process and to reassure the learner that what is sought in this episode is the search. Make certain the learner knows it is all right to produce individual ideas and movements. This teacher–learner relationship may require several episodes and does require patience by both teacher and learner. It also requires more frequent contact between the teacher and a particular learner. It takes time to cross the discovery threshold. Styles A–E demand an almost immediate response from the learner. Style F provides for some thinking time and a delayed response. In style H, the time needed for discovering each solution depends solely on the individual learner. The individualizing process is manifested in the pace and rhythm of the individual—first, in the cognitive process, and second, in the physical performance. With time and practice, both develop in quantity and quality.

At the end of the episode, the teacher assembles the group for closure. The closure can take the form of questions by the learner about the style or process. It can also take the form of feedback to the entire group about their participation in the process of divergent production; reassure the learners and invite them to participate in this unique style where their cognitive capacity is the focus.

COGNITIVE PRODUCTION AND PHYSICAL PERFORMANCE

The process described thus far deals with the theoretical and operational relationships between cognitive production and physical responses. Sometimes the reality in the gymnasium and in the playing field imposes limitations on this process. There are two kinds of limitations involved.

Physical Limitations

At times, a learner can design alternative solutions to a problem but cannot perform them. We have a situation in which the cognitive processes are functioning and are productive, but the physical capacities have boundaries—the performance has limits. This is a reality that must be accepted by both the learner and the teacher. It is necessary to recognize the gap between the two.

One way of handling this potential dilemma is to ask the learner to identify two sets of solutions. One set will include solutions that are the product of the learner's cognitive capacities. The second set will include solutions selected from the first set that the learner can actually *perform*.

As a variation, the learner can ask a skilled peer to perform and verify the solutions that he or she could not perform. This is identified as the *reduction process*. It is a reduction from the *possible* cognitive solutions to the acceptable *performance* solutions.

Cultural Limitations

Cultural limitations are those imposed by *agreement* among people. They are often called the rules of the game. Rules always define the "do's" and the "don'ts"; they define the limits for conduct within a particular activity. In physical education, then, it is necessary to distinguish between two *conditions:*

1. The condition in which the structure of the activity depends on the agreed-upon rules. There are many examples—any game played according to national or international rules, any track and field event in national or international competition, or any dance performance that claims to reflect a particular "school" represent this category.

    Any problems designed in this set of activities must accommodate the rules that govern the activity. This means that although many alternatives are *possible,* only some are *acceptable.* Again, this is the *reduction process* from the possible cognitive solutions to acceptable performance solutions.
2. The condition in which the purpose of the activity is not to compete against each other within a set of rules, but to compete against the present limits of knowledge. The purpose of discovery is to develop into the unknown, to push beyond established boundaries. This sense of inquiry and expansion can be the domain of every learner in physical education. Keeping within the notion of the nonversus, the physical education teacher should plan activities in both conditions—the condition to practice and perfect the known, and the condition to discover and experience the unknown.

IMPLICATIONS OF THIS STYLE

When this style is in use, it implies that:

1. The teacher is ready to move beyond the Discovery Threshold.
2. The teacher is ready to design relevant problems in one or more subject matter areas.
3. The teacher can accept the possibility of new designs within subject matter that was previously (in previous styles) conceived of as fixed.
4. The teacher is ready to provide students with the time needed for the process of discovery.
5. The teacher values the process of discovery and can accept divergent solutions presented by the learners.

6. The teacher is secure enough to accept solutions that are not his or her own.
7. The teacher accepts the notion that developing the ability of divergent cognitive production is one of the goals of physical education.
8. The students are capable of producing divergent ideas when presented with relevant problems.
9. The students can learn the relationship between cognitive production and physical performance.
10. The students are capable of producing novel ideas that expand the horizons of the subject matter.
11. The students are capable of accepting other people's divergent responses.
12. Are there any other possible implications?

DESIGNING THE SUBJECT MATTER

As previously mentioned, cognition or thinking involves particular cognitive operations such as comparing, contrasting, categorizing, problem solving, hypothesizing, extrapolating, and so on. In physical education, it is possible to conduct episodes that engage the learner in each of these operations; however, it seems that problem solving is most conducive to this field when divergent production in movement design is the goal of the episode(s).

This section focuses on the following aspects:

1. The design of a single problem and its consequences
2. The design of a sequence of problems
3. Guidelines for designing problems in various activities

The Design of a Single Problem

The crux of the problem-solving process in problem design is identifying the specific question that will trigger the process. Using the paradigm $S \rightarrow D \rightarrow M \rightarrow R$, let us examine the familiar area of tumbling, focusing on the concept of rolling. It is obvious that this particular subject matter is intrinsically composed of many options. Theoretically, there are endless possibilities in rolling such as different directions, different postures, different rhythms, and different combinations. The designed problem should elicit some of the possible movements in these aspects of rolling. Experiences in single-problem episodes serve as a warm-up in problem solving.

The purposes of an episode based on a single problem are:

1. To experience problem solving
2. To learn to relax affectively and experience the capacity to produce ideas
3. To do this within a particular activity
4. To experience the connection between cognitive production and physical performance

In focusing on the concept of rolling, the initial experience can be triggered by asking, "What are four possibilities for rolling the body?" Practically everyone has done some rolling in the gymnasium; most learners will roll quite readily. Each learner, in response to this question, will produce four different rolls. Some learners will do this in rapid succession; others will need more time between rolls. The important aspect is that this question (problem) invited the learner to decide which four rolls to perform.

Chances are high that many of the performed rolls will repeat what the learners already knew from past experiences. It is always safe to do this in the initial phase of such episodes. The teacher should accept this and move on with the episode. Feedback is given to the entire group, acknowledging the initial production of alternatives, followed by, "Your task is to design and do five more rolls." The teacher stays with the original problem and so do the learners. During this second attempt at discovering alternatives, some learners will go beyond their remembered experiences and will actually start designing and performing rolls that are new to them. Often, it may be necessary to ask the learner to make several attempts before going beyond memory. When this occurs, the learner is beginning to participate in divergent production in the cognitive operation of problem solving. The teacher may actually observe some learners in the state of cognitive dissonance. They will pause, search for a new roll, and then try it out. As this process continues, the purposes of this episode are realized.

In subsequent lessons, the teacher can design episodes in other activities, always keeping in mind the purposes of a single problem design. Schematically, this process looks like this:

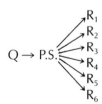

$$Q \rightarrow P.S. \begin{cases} R_1 \\ R_2 \\ R_3 \\ R_4 \\ R_5 \\ R_6 \end{cases}$$

The question about possibilities in rolling activates the mediation phase, resulting in the production of multiple and different rolls by each learner.

It is necessary to realize that the purpose of such episodes is not "anything goes"; the verbal behavior of the teacher must not include the phrase "do whatever you like." This phrase produces exactly what it asks for—learners will do whatever they wish. Often the responses have nothing to do with the task at hand.

Single-problem episodes do not necessarily have to focus on large concepts with infinite solutions; rather, they can focus on the discovery of alternatives in a part of the activity. For example, if you say, "Your task is to design and perform six different rolls in a forward direction," the specific designation of the direction puts parameters on the *scope* of the discovery but not on the *process*. These kinds of episodes can serve as the initial steps in this style because they accomplish the purposes previously cited.

The Design of a Sequence of Problems

Once the teacher and learners go beyond the initial stage of single-problem episodes, they are often confronted with the question of "What's next?" Scattered episodes in problem solving that deal with different activities each time often produce a sense of restlessness and a lack of direction and closure. Such episodes do not develop the skill of problem solving. To alleviate these liabilities, a more systematic plan is needed. Episodes must occur with some frequency and the problems must have some connection to one another. The teacher has at least two options in designing such problems:

Option 1   The teacher identifies several aspects of the activity and then designs a problem within each aspect. For example, within the concept of rolling, it is possible to focus on discovering alternatives in rolling forward, then in rolling backward, and then in rolling sideways. The discovery of alternatives in each aspect is elicited by a problem designed for that particular objective.

Problems can be presented to learners one at a time or announced as cluster of consecutive tasks for the ensuing episode. The learners, in turn, pursue the alternative solution for each problem at their own cognitive and physical pace. Solving these consecutive problems will allow learners to engage in problem solving for a longer period of time, and to see the relationships among the various aspects of rolling. Schematically these episodes will look like this:

$$\left[Q_1 \rightarrow \text{P.S.} \rightarrow \text{R} \lessgtr \right] + \left[Q_2 \rightarrow \text{P.S.} \rightarrow \text{R} \lessgtr \right] + \left[Q_3 \rightarrow \text{P.S.} \rightarrow \text{R} \lessgtr \right]$$

Each statement in brackets represents one episode composed of a question, time for solving the problem, and time for performing and validating the multiple solutions. A lesson can be planned for one, two, or more episodes in problem solving. Each episode should have a purpose and a reasonably clear objective in mind.

The result of such episodes will be an accumulation of movements in a particular area of physical education—all discovered by learners. The total of these discoveries is the "body of knowledge" in a given area; in the previous example, the total of the discoveries will constitute some of the movements possible within the concept of rolling.

Anyone who has experienced style H has discovered that many of the movements go beyond the teacher's movement vocabulary. The teacher must develop an attitude of acceptance, welcoming these new possibilities. A projection of other feelings about the process and the discovered movements will abort the divergent production within a very short time. Before selecting the subject matter for this style, the teacher must examine his or her values about that area. If the teacher's connection with the subject matter compels him or her to stay within the realm of the "known," styles A–E should be used. However, if the teacher is ready to cross the discovery threshold with the learners and risk the unknown, style H is most appropriate.

Option 2   The second option for designing episodes with multiple problems may be called *branching off*. To trigger the process, ask, "What are the possibilities in rolling the body?" After a while the teacher stops the episode, selects one kind of solution (one variable), and presents the next problem within this variable; the learners move on with the discoveries. For example, ask, "Within the forward direction (one variable within the concept of rolling), what are some possibilities of rolling?" The second problem focuses the learner on one variable, but within this variable the learner discovers and performs the multiple solutions. At this point the learner has accumulated a number of different rolls by moving forward:

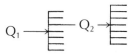

Episode 1   Episode 2

Next, the teacher stops the group again and presents the third problem: "In a forward direction, what are several possibilities in rolling with different leg positions?" The learners, staying within the general area of rolling and the one variable of forward direction, will now discover and examine the next variable—posture during rolling; in this case, the posture involved is the multiple possibilities for varying positions of the legs. Schematically:

Episode 3

This process can continue for a period of several episodes. The teacher continues to present problems that focus on additional variables all connected with the previous ones. The result is that each learner has discovered and performed multiple movements within the particular subject matter and has begun to see the connection that exists among the variables of the given subject matter.

Guidelines for Designing Problems in Various Activities

The next question is: How does the teacher design problems for specific activities in ball games, gymnastics, dance, outdoor pursuits, and so on? How does one know where to begin?

It is perhaps possible to design a problem (or a sequence of problems) for any activity; however, one must consider whether the experience is relevant and worthwhile. Episodes in style H must have some relationship to the structure of the activity, as well as to the meaning and the purpose. Some sports are quite fixed (nonvariable) in their movement design; the movements or techniques of the sport have been determined by experience and biomechanical principles. These exercises in style H will be quite futile. In crew, rowing movements are dictated by the design of the shell. The posture and goal of the sport are such that designing problems to elicit alternatives simply does not make sense. Alternatives are not useful for the performance of the sport. They are irrelevant. (We are not talking about stopping the search for better rowing techniques but the inappropriateness of style H for those learning to row.) Another example is throwing the discus. General and specific techniques have evolved that determine the performance of this event. These techniques are quite fixed (despite the slight variations that occur due to individual idiosyncrasies), and anyone who wishes to reach the goal of this event (distance) must adhere to the model.

In contrast, there are activities and sports that do provide variability and alternatives. In fact, variety is the essence of the activity. Examples abound in the development of strategies for any ball game. The search for options is continuous. Gymnastics is rich with opportunities for discovering new movements and new combinations. Beyond the basic movements, the very structure of this sport is based on variability. With its variety of cultural origins and schools of choreography, dance offers infinite possibilities for discovering new ideas. In these areas it is not only worthwhile to develop episodes in style H, it is essential for their development and expansion.

The following schema are proposed guidelines for designing problems conducive to discovering options.

Each activity (sport) has several parts (variables) that must exist for that activity to be what it is. These variables define the general structure of the activity. For example, in gymnastics, the balance beam experiences are always composed of getting on the beam, moving along the beam, turning, and getting off. All the possibilities of movement occur within these variables. A learner can discover the variations in movements, postures, and combinations within these variables. (See Figure 12-2.)

The horizontal row identifies the variables within the activity. The variables suggested are only some of those possible. You are welcome to identify others that are a part of the balance beam experience. The vertical column identifies the things to be discovered—variations in movements, posture, and combinations within each variable. Each cell, then, becomes the objective of an episode, and the problem is designed to elicit options within this objective. (See Figure 12-3.)

Problem 1 is designed to elicit alternative ways of moving forward on the balance beam. That cell to which the arrow points clearly identifies the objective of the episode. The cell where "turns" and "posture" converge identifies the objective for that episode and guides the design of problem 2.

The teacher can use the problem-design grid for any activity in style H. Using the two options of single-problem design and sequence of problems, the

FIGURE 12–2 Problem-design grid

Gymnastics—balance beam							
Variables Variations	Mounts	Moving Forward	Moving Backward	?	Turns	?	Dismount
Movements							
Posture							
Combinations							
Other ?							

teacher has infinite possibilities for conducting episodes that will invite the learner's capacity for divergent production. In fact, designing such episodes will invite the teacher's capacity for divergent production.

Ball games provide a rich opportunity for episodes in problem solving, particularly the parts that deal with tactics and strategy. The purpose of such episodes is not a mere exercise in problem solving; rather, it is to engage the learner in the essence of the game—the thinking required to succeed in every

FIGURE 12–3 Problem-design grid: Balance beam

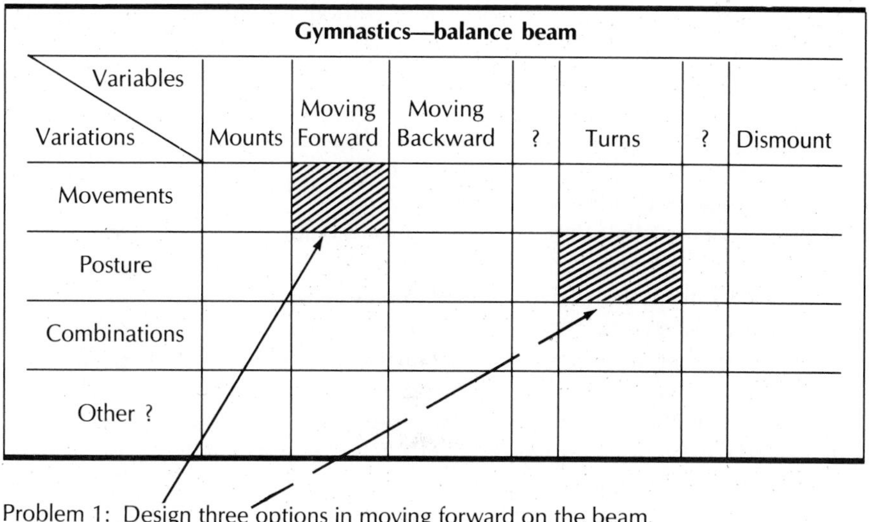

Gymnastics—balance beam							
Variables Variations	Mounts	Moving Forward	Moving Backward	?	Turns	?	Dismount
Movements		▨					
Posture					▨		
Combinations							
Other ?							

Problem 1: Design three options in moving forward on the beam.

Problem 2: Design four possibilities in turning while the body is in angular postures.

game. The existence of an opponent demands more than just performing the movements (skills) themselves; each participant must join with his or her teammates to find ways to outmaneuver the opponent. This requires thinking beyond the routine offense and defense patterns. This type of game thinking can be taught by episodes in style H.

Soccer provides some examples of problems that can serve as the focus for episodes in style H.

EXAMPLES IN VARIOUS SPORTS

Many tactical issues of soccer can be taught by discovery. The essence of a tactical issue is that it is a problem. By analyzing the structure of soccer, one can conceive of many tactical situations that call for alternative solutions to the same problems. A fundamental example of this is the following situation: Player A is in possession of the ball, moving toward the opponent's territory; opponent B appears in front of player A. What can player A do? Obviously, player A has many options; each answer depends on the specific circumstances. The focus is on the relationship between A and B within a set of possible circumstances as they relate to the rest of the team and to the purpose of manipulating the ball. Let us examine the kinds of relationships that could exist, which, in turn, determine the nature of the problems to be designed.

The first relationship to consider is the *distance* between players A and B. This prompts the following problem (assume that player A has the ball and that player B is 2 or 3 feet away):

1. Design two ways player A can avoid (without touching) player B and still have possession of the ball.
2. Design two ways of accomplishing this by touching player B within the limitations of the rules.
3. Accomplish 1 and 2 facing player B.
4. Accomplish it with your side to player B.
5. Accomplish it with your back to player B.
6. Can you use other directions in relation to player B?
7. Accomplish it moving slowly. Quickly. Which speed is preferable? Why?
8. Which one of the above solutions is preferred if player A remained stationary? Why?
9. Which solution is preferred if player B indicated by his body position the intention to move to the left? To the right? Forward? Backward? Do you know why these solutions are preferred?
10. What can be done if player B charges at player A?
11. How else can player B move against player A?
     a. _____
     b. _____
     c. _____

12. What can player A do if player B does 11a and still remains in possession of the ball? If player B does 11b? 11c?
13. Repeat 1–12 when the distance between A and B is different.

These are *real* game problems faced by players during a game. The problems focus on specific phases; being able to solve them efficiently, accurately, and frequently will help a player adjust better to the sequence of game events, become more imaginative, and become a better player!

Another kind of relationship between A and B could result from the *size* of the players:

1. What can be done if player B is much taller?
2. What can be done if player B is much faster?
3. What are two things that can be done if player B is as fast as A and as tall as A, but is considerably heavier?
4. How would you determine which of your solutions is best in 1–3?

The next kind of relationship concerns the *location* of players A and B.

1. B could be between A and the goal.
2. B could be between A and A's teammate, who is:
  a. Behind player B
  b. On either side of player B
  c. Other places?
3. B could be between A and B's teammate, who is:
  a. Behind player B
  b. On his or her side
  c. Other places?
4. Player B could be between A and two other players—one B's teammate and the other A's teammate.
5. B could be between A and two of his or her teammates.
6. B could be between A and two of A's teammates.
7. Where else could B be?
8. What can A do in each situation?
9. Which of the previous solutions will apply in each one of these situations?
10. Is there only one solution for each situation? Any alternatives?

Organizationally, this process of problem solving requires pairs and sometimes small groups of three or four. Divide the class accordingly; each group is either assigned to an area of the field or may select its own area. Each group receives a ball and a set of problems (cards or xeroxed sheets do the job quite efficiently). Special soccer balls are not necessary for this purpose; any ball (including rubber or plastic playground balls) will be adequate. The students are not actually playing the game. They are learning how to think and how to execute the variety of elements that constitute the structure of soccer. This, in turn, will lead to better performance during a full-scale game situation.

An interesting aspect of soccer that can serve as a focus for problem design is kicking to the goal. Here one can design sets of problems that will elicit discoveries in relationships, preferences, limitations, variations, or any other dimension.

Some goal situations that require a decision and a solution can involve one player against the goalie. Elements of this situation will be:

1. Distance between player and the goal
2. The angle between player's sagittal plane (a plane that follows the player's nose when the head and body face forward) and the goal
3. The location of the goalie in relation to 1 and 2
4. The relationship between the player's body postures and the goal
5. The relationship between the player's body and the ball
6. Any other?

If the teacher can identify several variations in each of these kinds of relationships, then he or she can convert them into problems. To design meaningful and relevant problems, one must know the subject matter rather well and be able to analyze its individual components and relationships. Only then can problems become sequential and purposeful. The solutions to these problems will synthesize scattered elements into one complete structure—the activity at hand.

Kicking to the goal can also serve as a focus for problems involving the goalie and a back. This new situation may have the following dimensions:

1. Distance between each two participants in the situation
2. Location of each participant (Example: What are two things that can be done when the goalie is close to the near corner of the goal and the back is farther away?)
3. Direction of motion of each participant in the given situation
4. Speed of motion of each participant
5. Posture of each participant at a given moment (Example: What can be done if the back is half bent in front of the center of the goal and the goalie is kneeling behind him?)
6. Any other dimensions?

Another game situation could involve a player, a teammate, one back, and the goalie. This lends itself to multiple problems.

A teacher can design problems in all these situations by following the formula—*if* so and so occurs, *then* what can you do? It is possible to continue this chain of additional players—each addition creates new circumstances with new problems that demand new solutions—until the entire team is on the field solving problems in action, problems relevant to soccer, relevant to them as individual members of a team, and relevant to the team's total purpose.

We have touched on some techniques and tactics of soccer. Now the teacher or coach is ready to tackle the big one—*strategy!* The same process applies. A teacher can analyze the components and requirements of a strategy and present them to the players in the form of problems. The players will inquire, try out, examine, and *learn* the strategy and eventually be able to execute it better mentally and physically.

The problem-design grid can be a useful planning tool for ball games. The top horizontal row identifies the variables involved in the game such as the particular tactical situation, the number of opponents, the particular area of the field or court, and so on. The vertical column designates the variations sought: variations in the options possible for the individual player, variations for two players, the role in offense, and so on.

The combination of styles B and H within the same individual program (designated as B/H) is very helpful for the learner who is a novice in style H. The combination is a comfortable way to move from the *known* to the new. Notice that this is for the "novice in style H" and not the "novice in soccer." This is because the *new behavior* is divergent production (style H) and not a particular exercise in soccer.

Let us examine the next example in the design of the individual program (Figure 12-4). The subject matter is vaulting, and the purpose is to engage the learner in discovering *variations* in the specific parts of the vault (see Figure 12-5). To accomplish this, the program designer tells the learner that there are three specific parts to every vault: (a) the approach (see Figure 12-6), (b) the posture over the obstacle, and (c) the landing. Specific conditions (parameters) are then prescribed for the design of each vault.

Vault 1 is to be designed with:

1. A 90° approach, but the approach is *not* specified. The learner's task is to discover and design the approach. There are many possible approaches to the apparatus within the parameters of a 90° approach.
2. A posture of two-hand contact with the body in round position. Again, these are parameters. The exact posture of the body was *not* specified. It is the learner's task to examine the conditions and design a posture that complies with these parameters. (It is obvious that different learners will discover *different* postures that are within these parameters—hence, divergent production occurs within the class. If the individual learner is asked to design more than one variation, *each* individual learner will then be engaged in divergent production.)

FIGURE 12–4   Problem design: Gymnastics

Name _____	Style B/H
Date _____	Individual Program
Section _____	_____ Accomplished
	_____ Needs more time

Gymnastics

To the student:
In past weeks, we have discussed the attributes of agility and balance. Last week you specifically assessed the role of agility and balance of the trampoline. This week's lab includes these attributes and introduces *flexibility*, which we define as

the ability to increase the range of motion at a given joint.

Instructions:
1. Perform the prescribed movement on the respective piece of apparatus three times.
2. Check off the *primary* attribute involved in the performance of that movement.
3. Now, design and perform three variations for each (use a separate sheet).

Apparatus	Prescribed Movement	*Primary* Attribute Involved (Check one)
Parallel Bars	1. Jump to front support.	_____ Balance _____ Agility _____ Flexibility
	2. Swing six times.	_____ Balance _____ Agility _____ Flexibility
	3. Straddle seat.	_____ Balance _____ Agility _____ Flexibility
	4. "Skin the cat."	_____ Balance _____ Agility _____ Flexibility
Uneven Parallel Bars	1. Sit sideways on lower bar, hands extended to side.	_____ Balance _____ Agility _____ Flexibility
	2. T scale on the lower bar, holding higher bar with one hand.	_____ Balance _____ Agility _____ Flexibility
	3. Perform forward swing, use rear dismount.	_____ Balance _____ Agility _____ Flexibility
Balance Beam	1. T Scale.	_____ Agility _____ Flexibility
	2. Jump to 180° turn, dismount.	_____ Agility _____ Flexibility
	3. Jump 90°, turn on the beam.	_____ Agility _____ Flexibility

Horizontal Bar	1. Jump to arm hang.	_____ Balance _____ Agility _____ Flexibility
	2. Swing.	_____ Balance _____ Agility _____ Flexibility
Horizontal Bar	3. "Skin the cat."	_____ Balance _____ Agility _____ Flexibility
	4. Swing to 180° turn, dismount.	_____ Balance _____ Agility _____ Flexibility

3. A landing on two feet, with no turn. Within these parameters, many variations for landing can be discovered and performed. One can vary the position of the feet in relation to each other, the position of the trunk, the arms, and combinations of all of these. This particular individual program calls for the design of five vaults.

Imagine what would happen if a class were asked to design two or three different vaults for each set of conditions (parameters).

The next example (Figure 12-7) involves discovering and designing movements on two pieces of apparatus selected by the learner. The learner first makes a decision about which apparatus to use and then designs movements for each within the prescribed parameters.

The intriguing aspect of this program is that the problem is designed so that the learner must discover movements (within the parameters) that fit the two selected pieces of apparatus.

This problem requires the learner to examine more possibilities because although sometimes a single solution will fit both pieces of apparatus, at other times two different solutions might be necessary.

The possibilities for divergent production in this program are quite evident and they trigger the imagination.

The next examples of the individual program in style H are in developmental movement.[1] This concept, as presented by Mosston, suggests a model for the structure of human movement. It shows the relationships among three di-

---

[1]Mosston, Muska. *Developmental Movement,* Copyright © 1992 by Muska Mosston.

FIGURE 12–5 Problem design: Vaulting

Name _____   Style H
Date _____   Individual Program
Section _____

Gymnastics
(Vaulting)

To the student:
There are three specific parts to every vault:
a. Approach
b. Posture over the obstacle
c. Landing

Each of these may be varied in a number of ways to increase or decrease the degree of difficulty of the vault.

Design two vaults that meet the prescribed conditions.
Perform each of your designed vaults 4 times.
Apparatus: Side Horse (no pommels)

Conditions

Vault 1
a. Approach: 90° approach to the apparatus
b. Posture: Two-hand contact, body in round position
c. Landing: Two feet, no turn
                              _____ Task accomplished
                              _____ Needs more time

Vault 2
a. Approach: Less than 90° approach
b. Posture: Two-hand contact, two foot contact, body in round position
c. Landing: Two feet together, 90° turn
                              _____ Task accomplished
                              _____ Needs more time

Vault 3
a. Approach: 45° running approach
b. Posture: Your choice
c. Landing: One leg
                              _____ Task accomplished
                              _____ Needs more time

Vault 4
a. Approach: Less than 45° running approach
b. Posture: A rotary movement
c. Landing: Two feet, body fully stretched
                              _____ Task accomplished
                              _____ Needs more time

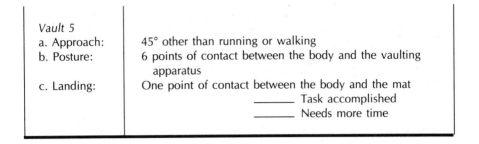

Vault 5
a. Approach: 45° other than running or walking
b. Posture: 6 points of contact between the body and the vaulting apparatus
c. Landing: One point of contact between the body and the mat
                     _____ Task accomplished
                     _____ Needs more time

mensions that *always* exist whenever any movement is performed. The three-dimensional model is composed of:

1. *The anatomical dimension*—this involves identification of the part(s) engaged in the given movement.
2. *The "kind" of movement* produced or performed by a given part of the body.
3. *The attribute* invoked and developed while the particular movement is performed.

These three dimensions are intrinsically connected. They always exist. Whenever we move a part of the body (arm, leg, trunk, etc.), we always produce a particular kind of movement (swing, lift, twist, bend, etc.). Whenever this kind of movement occurs, a specific attribute is called on and developed. This concept represents a universal model for the structure of all human movements. These relationships always exist. They transcend geographical location, culture, time, and the design of a particular sport. Any sport or physical activity bound by an apparatus, specific equipment, or a set of rules—elaborate as it may be—represents only a *selected portion* of the infinite variety of human movement.

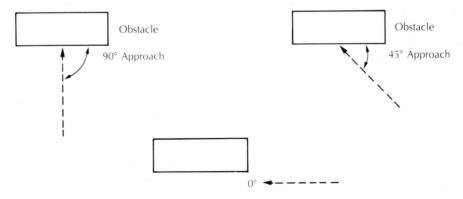

FIGURE 12–6 Angles of approach

FIGURE 12–7   Problem design: Developmental movement

Name _____   Style H
Date _____   Individual Program
Section _____

Gymnastics

To the student:
Using two pieces of apparatus of your choice, design one movement for each apparatus, according to the parameters in each attribute named below. Use written descriptions of each movement and use stick figure drawings.

Apparatus 1 _____
Apparatus 2 _____

Parameters	Designed Movement Apparatus 1	Designed Movement Apparatus 2
A. Strength movement involving upper arm strength		
B. Agility movement involving at least a 90° turn in the air		
C. Flexibility movement of the hips (not in standing position)		
D. Dynamic balance with two points of contact between the body and the apparatus throughout the exercise		

E. Static balance with two points of contact between the body and the apparatus (other than standing on two feet)		

This difference between *selected movements* (designed for the specific purpose and objectives of the given physical activity and sport) and *developmental movement* is reflected in the degree of freedom possible in the problem design. In sports (as we previously observed), problems can be designed to elicit multiple solutions, but the designs are always dictated by the structure, purpose, and rules of the particular activity or sport. In developmental movement (and in some branches of dance), these boundaries *do not* exist. The concept of developmental movement is an attempt to embrace all varieties of human movement. Hence, the possibilities of problem design are limitless.

In the following individual programs, the task of the learner is to begin to discover the possible relationships among the three dimensions—the parts of the body, the movements they produce, and the attribute that is being developed in each movement.

The first example is illustrated in Figure 12-8. The first column on the left identifies the attribute. The learner is asked to seek and discover movement(s) that *mainly* represent the given attribute. To enable learners to do this, they must know the definition (and description) of each attribute. The definition must be universal. It cannot be idiosyncratic, representing one individual's opinion. If developmental movement is a concept that represents a universal model, then each of its dimensions and their definitions must also be universal.

Before an individual program is given to the learners, then, definitions must be given and explained to them. This, of course, can be done by style B. Identify the attribute by name, define it, and give a few examples of movements that represent it. Select movements that clearly represent that attribute. For example, when you talk about strength as an attribute, you can lift a weight, climb a rope, and push a cart as examples for movements representing this attribute. (What *is* the definition of strength? Does physical education have definitions for some of these universals?) Even better, after you have defined the attribute, ask your students to offer you some examples (and demonstrate, if they can). Be sure your examples clearly focus on the main attribute. There are always secondary attributes that enter the picture, but for illustration stick to one example. It will be clear to the learners that the main attribute of the three examples just cited is strength.

The second column identifies the part(s) of the body to be used.

The third column is blank—the designed movement is recorded here. (A byproduct of this experience is that the learner knows the terminology, the correct spelling of terms, and the accurate phrases that describe the movement.)

FIGURE 12–8   Problem design: Developmental movement

Name _____   Style   H
Class _____   Individual Program
Date _____

Developmental movement

To the student:
1. The individual program (student's design) offers you the opportunity to make decisions about subject matter that affects your development.
2. Your task is to design movements that correspond to the *Physical Attribute* (left column). Write your idea (your design) in the *Designed Movement* column.
3. The design should be a *new* movement to you.
4. Identify your present level in the described task.
5. Identify your *expectations* of performance in this task, and estimate the *amount of time* you need to get there (time parameters).

AG = Agility; Flex = Flexibility; ST = Strength;
Bal = Balance; Acc = Accuracy

Physical Attribute	Part(s) of the Body	The Designed Movement	Present Level, Approximate Maximum Level	Developmental Expectations and Time Parameters
1. (AG)	The whole body			
2. (AG)	The whole body			
3. (AG)	The whole body			

4. (Flex)	The spine area			
5. (Flex)	The shoulders area			
6. (Flex)	The neck area (for relaxation)			
7. (Flex)	The hip area			
8. (ST)	The thigh muscles (quadriceps)			
9. (ST)	The abdominal muscles (other than sit-ups)			

10. (ST)	The arm muscles (either biceps or triceps—circle the selected group)			
11. (Bal)	With body in a low position			
12. (Bal)	With high center of gravity			
13. (Bal)	With the center of gravity touching or almost touching the base			
14. (Acc)	Using any other attributes, design a movement which will focus on the development of accuracy.			

The fourth column identifies how well the learner is performing his or her designed movements. After the learner designs the movement, he or she performs it to find this level.

The last column gives the learners the opportunity to project their aspirations. Columns four and five are suggested as practical and useful ways to use the ideas discovered and recorded in column three. This connects the cognitive production with the physical performance. The crux of this exercise is discovering movements for the part of the body in each attribute. However, the actual physical performance is the culmination of this exercise.

The program in Figure 12-8 contains 14 exercises in problem solving. When the learners complete the program, ask them to design and perform another movement for each of these conditions. Each learner will have 28 newly designed movements. (Remind them to establish a quantity for the performance of each movement. Doing it once is not sufficient when the objective is development!)

Imagine the rate and diversity of production that occurs when students are engaged in such a program!

In Figure 12-9 the learner is asked to use objects or a partner to design movements that represent various attributes. This added condition widens the possibilities for problem design even further. The learner must discover the possible relationship between his or her designed movement and the particular object or partner. This requires the learner to discover, experiment with, and select the appropriate movement and verify it by performing the idea.

The Theme

Another format for style H designs is the use of a *theme*. The individual program invites the learner to discover and design a variety of movements in various attributes, all of which focus on the particular theme.

FIGURE 12–9   Problem design: Developmental movement

Name _____   Style   H
Class _____   Individual Program
Date _____

Developmental movement

To the student:
The focus of this task is to design movements that you have not seen before. Based on your knowledge of strength, balance, flexibility, and agility, design *three different* movements that will fit each of the following conditions.
Perform each design several times until it works well.

 1. An "easy" movement for agility, using the wall
 2. An "easy" movement for strength of the arms, using a partner
 3. A "difficult" movement for strength of the legs, using a partner
 4. An "easy" mvovment for balance, using planks of wood
 5. A "difficult" movement for agility, using a rope
 6. A "difficult" movement for flexibility, using a partner
 7. A "difficult" movement for flexibility, using the wall
 8. An "easy" movement for flexibility of the hips, using a rope
 9. A movement for strength (of any part of the body), using a rope
10. A movement for accuracy, using a paper cup

Now, the theme in Figure 12-10 is "in pairs for mutual benefit." This means that:

1. Every discovered movement is designed to be performed in pairs.
2. The *focus* of this theme is "mutual benefit;" each learner in the pair will participate and benefit from the *same* attribute.
3. The parameters require the learners to be in constant physical contact during the performance of the movement.

The theme serves as a connecting thread through the entire program and organizes the discovered movements. It invites the learner to use his or her cognitive capabilities in a reasonably organized manner and to produce ideas within a particular context.

Let us examine some of the conditions that are set for the learner. Condition 1 presents the pair with the problem of designing a movement to develop agility when the center of gravity will be relatively high. It is quite a problem. The learners have to make the decision and *agree* on the particular jump, leap, or flight that will represent the condition of having a high center of gravity. Further, they have to discover the possible ways to keep in physical contact while they are in the air.

Condition 5 calls for the learners to discover a position (or positions) that will challenge the balance of both while they are in constant physical contact. The parameters state that the base must be other than the feet. This problem triggers many possible solutions.

Imagine the experimentation that will take place when they discover movements in problem 10.

Problem 13 can create a strong state of cognitive dissonance. What are three possible solutions to this problem? As you can see, each problem by itself rep-

FIGURE 12–10 Problem solving—in pairs

Name _____   Style H
Class _____   Individual Program
Date _____

Developmental movement
Theme: In pairs for mutual benefit

To the student:
A. The focus of this program is *novel movements!*
B. "In pairs for mutual benefit" means that the movement is designed for two people who are in *physical contact* during the performance and *both* are engaged in the *same* attribute.
C. Next to your design, indicate in writing the *duration* of the performance (i.e., time, no. of repetitions, distance, etc.).
D. Perform the *entire program* and check for detail and precision.

1. Agility—Relatively high center
   of gravity
   Duration: 1.

2. Agility—Low center of gravity   2.
   Duration:

3. Agility—Covering distance   3.
   Distance:

4. Balance—Base: one foot   4.
   Duration:

5. Balance—Base: other than feet   5.
   Duration:

6. Balance—Upside down   6.
   Duration:

7. Balance—Your choice of position   7.
   Duration:

8. Flexibility—Shoulder girdle   8.
   lying down
   Duration:

9. Flexibility—Spine, while   9.
   kneeling
   Duration:

10. Flexibility—Hip joint, while   10.
    the whole body is
    in motion
    (locomotion)
    Duration:

11. Strength—arms and shoulders—   11.
    a pushing movement,
    not in a standing
    position
    Duration

12. Strength—Abdomen, while the   12.
    body is in motion
    Duration:

13. Strength—Legs, in an upside-   13.
    down position
    Duration:

14. Your choice   14.

15. Your choice   15.

resents conditions for divergent production. All the problems in the program are bound together, interrelated by the theme of mutual benefit.

There are many themes that can be used similarly. Put yourself into style H for a while and see if you can discover other themes for problem design.

STYLE-SPECIFIC COMMENTS

The Affective Domain

Each style imposes demands on the learner in the various domains. Style H creates unique conditions that every learner must learn to deal with. These conditions are primarily expressed in the affective domain either through joy in the process of discovery or through stress (this is often produced in style H).

The expression of joy results from participating in evolving new ideas—one's own ideas. The sense of ownership pervades the climate of episodes in this style. A particular sense of intimacy between the learner and the subject matter develops. It is reasonable to suggest that every style produces a degree of intimacy with the subject matter; the difference, however, is that in the previous styles the learner develops a relationship with subject matter designed and presented by somebody else. In this style the subject matter belongs to the learner.

The other aspect is the stress that often evolves in style H episodes. This stress varies in intensity and frequency, but it exists whenever one faces the demands of divergent production. The main reason for this stress is having to face the unknown. Delving into the unknown involves risk taking—risk taking produces stress. In addition, the learner may experience feelings such as fear of failure, fear of being incorrect, fear of revealing one's cognitive limitations—all add to stress and, indeed, may stop the process of divergent production. The teacher must be constantly aware of these conditions and manifestations; this awareness must guide the conduct of the teacher during these episodes. These comments may not apply to all learners; some individuals operate very well under stress. The teacher, then, needs to develop the necessary insight to distinguish among the capacities of the different learners.

Entry Point

With novice performers, single-problem episodes may serve as an appropriate entry point to the experiences in style H. Short, single-problem episodes supported by neutral feedback help the novice overcome some of the stress previously discussed. A reasonable transition through early episodes motivates learners to continue. Advanced performers who do well with tasks designed by others (primarily in styles A and B) need to see the relevance of style H experiences to their goals as performers. The "branching off" approach may be more effective with these learners.

Familiarity with the Subject Matter

If the learners are familiar with the subject matter, episodes in style H are of no consequence. One cannot discover what one already knows. New, unknown areas of discovery are highly motivating to some learners and they will readily delve into the process.

H/B and H/D Combinations

To gain the full benefit from episodes in style H, they should be followed by episodes in B or D. In physical education, the act of discovery itself may not be sufficient to accomplish the objectives of various activities. Performing the discovered movements must follow the discoveries. The learner needs to repeat some (or all) of the discovered movements to both verify the solutions and to reach the developmental purposes of the given activities. Episodes in style H, then, should be followed by a series of episodes in B or D. These episodes are designated H/B or H/D combinations.

Verbal Behavior

In examining the verbal behavior involved in problem design and the implications of such verbal behavior, the following insights have emerged. One of the phrases preceding many problem designs in physical education books is: Can you . . . ? This kind of question gives the learner permission to say, "No, I cannot!" It permits the learner to stop.

The second prevalent phrase preceding problem designs is: How many ways . . . ? or, In how many ways can you . . . ? There are two problems with this kind of verbal behavior. First, it gives the learner permission to produce only one solution and then stop! When this occurs (and it has happened many times in problem-solving episodes), there is nothing the teacher can say. It is legitimate behavior on the part of the learner. The teacher asked, "How many . . .?" The learner responded, "One!" Obviously, this is not the purpose of this style. It conflicts with the intent of eliciting and developing the capacity for divergent production.

Another problem with this second phrase concerns the issue of *magnitude* of responses. When the problem is *initially* presented in this fashion, many learners block the flow of responses. Some freeze and cannot respond at all. The question, How many . . . ?, seems to connote a large number to many learners. It triggers an instant affective discomfort that inhibits a learner regardless of age. *Affective discomfort results in cognitive inhibition.* Consequently, very few or no responses come forth. There is no engagement in the process of discovery.

A chain of events occurs—affective discomfort leads to cognitive inhibition which, in turn, leads to either verbal expression ("I can't!") or the culmination

of physical responses. All of this can be triggered by inappropriate verbal behavior by the teacher.

What is the alternative verbal behavior that will avoid these reactions by the
learner? Consider this verbal behavior: "Design three possible ways to . . . ?"
First, it eliminates the potential hazard of the word *can*. Second, it eliminates
the pronoun *you*. The burden is off the individual. The focus is on the divergent
cognitive production—the possible. Third, the introduction of a limited number of solutions creates a manageable condition for the learner. Seeking three
or four initial solutions feels safer. It is manageable. When the solutions are
produced, the teacher must display an attitude of acceptance. The teacher
should not judge the solutions. *The feedback must be neutral!* This will indicate to the learner that all his or her responses were correct; they are accepted.

This initial sense of safety creates a reality of inclusion of one's cognitive
production. Inclusion ensures continued participation! When the learner is
asked to produce three more solutions, there will be less hesitation. If the
teacher follows with acceptance and neutral feedback, the learner will be motivated to continue and to produce even more. And, thus, the process of divergent cognitive production has begun!

The more we study teaching behavior, the more important the role of verbal
behavior becomes. The verbal behavior that the teacher uses affects the design
of the problems, the inclusion of the learner, the feedback offered to the
learner, and the continuous engagement in discovery.

There are a couple of verbal behavior patterns that one must avoid. The
phrase, "You can do better than that," tells the learner that his or her solutions
are not really valued by the teacher. It may also indicate to the learner that the
teacher has *particular* solutions in mind and therefore does not accept the
learner's solutions. This kind of climate is not only contrary to the process and
spirit of style H, it will abort the whole process! Learners will stop their involvement in divergent production.

Another rather common verbal behavior in the gymnasium is: "Hold it
everyone! Let's all look at Jane's solution!" And when the demonstration is
over, one often hears, "Excellent, Jane!" and so on. All this is seemingly an
innocent event. Many teachers have explained this behavior by saying, "I
wanted the class to see a good solution; I wanted to motivate them." Usually,
the exact *opposite* is accomplished. This kind of singling out of a learner and
his or her solution tells the learners what the teacher *prefers*. This style is not
designed for the teacher's preference of either a learner or his or her solution.
If this frequently occurs, it will abort the very process the style is designed to
develop. What usually happens is that learners will narrow their responses to
conform to the demonstrated and rewarded solutions; eventually they will
abandon divergent production.

The teacher's role is to observe and accept the solution offered by each
learner (provided the solution solves the problem). If a solution does not, the
teacher can merely say, "This solution is not valid because it does not solve
the problem at hand. Continue with your search for solutions."

The Group

Many of the problem-solving examples previously cited involve individual participation in this process. Style H, however, offers a unique opportunity for group interaction. When a group has a common purpose or common problem to solve, incredible dimensions and forces are recruited to produce a solution. Group participation in problem solving is the only condition that calls upon the social, emotional, and cognitive domains to interact with great intensity and balance. This process of interaction, to achieve the goal of finding a solution for the benefit of the group, involves balancing the following components:

1. Opportunity for everyone to suggest a solution
2. Opportunity to try anyone's solution
3. Negotiating and modifying solutions
4. Group reinforcement of the valid solution
5. Group tolerance of the invalid solution
6. A climate of inclusion
7. Other?

When these components interact, a social basis is created for producing a solution that, in the case of physical education, will be manifested through physical responses. These physical responses will in turn move the group towards its common goal. An excellent example occurs when a group of people are confronted with an obstacle to overcome in the woods or in the mountains and must use only the available, natural conditions of the environment. Getting a group over a rocky ledge, for example, calls for integrating all these components and domains. Failure in any of these will result in failing to attain the group goal. These components are recruited, in varying degrees of intensity, whenever a group of people are joined in solving problems as in ball games, dance, and other group activities. Designing style H episodes for group problem solving is a wonderful opportunity to bring together the social, affective, cognitive, and physical domains.

THE DEVELOPMENTAL CHANNELS

On the physical developmental channel, the placement of the learner is toward maximum (see Figure 12-11). Because the learner is responsible for making decisions about his or her physical responses and development, the learner becomes highly independent. (Independence is the criterion for placement on the channel.)

On the cognitive channel—the essence of this style—the learner is placed toward maximum. The very structure of this style calls on the learner to be independent in producing ideas. In fact, no other style on the Spectrum pro-

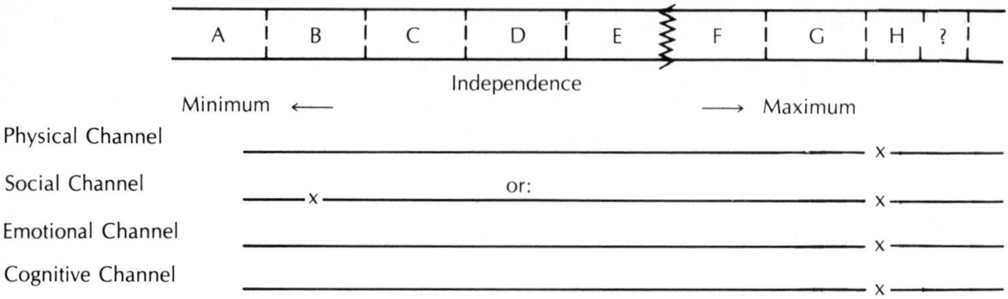

FIGURE 12–11   The divergent production style and the developmental channels

vides the learner with a legitimate opportunity to examine divergent ideas and to discover alternatives.

On the emotional channel, the learner is placed toward maximum. Only when a learner has been able to reduce the affective inhibition is he or she able to be more independent in producing divergent ideas.

On the social channel, there are two possible conditions: (1) if the learner is individually engaged in producing solutions, then the process of discovery is private; hence, socializing contact is minimum. (2) If, however, the process of discovery is accomplished with a partner (or partners), then the placement on this channel is toward maximum.

CLOSURE

Teaching and learning by problem solving creates a level of endurance that is self-motivated. Knowing that there is still another way keeps the cognitive process kindled and lead to inquiry, which in turn brings about discovery. This behavioral chain of cognitive dissonance → mediation → discovery as represented in the process of problem solving has a dimension that occurs *only* in problem solving in the Spectrum of Teaching Styles.

Problem solving is an open-ended process in two avenues: First, the subject matter itself is open-ended because there is always the possibility of another solution, movement, way to pass the ball, or way to break through the opponent's defense. Thus, the subject matter becomes dynamic; it is constantly renewed! Second, the process of discovery is self-perpetuating. The act of finding a new solution tests the validity of the discovery. The joy of discovery is so powerful that the act of discovery itself becomes the reinforcing, motivating agent propelling the student to seek more solutions, alternatives, and ideas.

All previous styles on the Spectrum are different in this respect. All have the dimension of *finality*. Their definitions, descriptions of their anatomies, and their implications for the emerging individual connote *finality*—finality in the structure and content of subject matter and finality in the learning process. This realization clarifies, in part, the *dependency* on the teacher for the subject matter in all previous styles as well as for external motivation and feedback, and involvement in the process of learning itself. The problem-solving process proposes to develop greater *independence* in both cognition and physical responses, and it is the *only* process so far on the Spectrum that actually demonstrates the cognitive-physical relationship in its various dimensions.

FIGURE 12–12   Style H classroom chart

DIVERGENT PRODUCTION STYLE

The purpose of this style is to engage in producing (discovering) multiple responses to a single question.

ROLE OF LEARNER

- To make the nine impact decisions of style B

- To produce divergent responses (multiple responses to the same question)

- To ascertain the validity of the responses

- To verify responses in some subject matter tasks

ROLE OF TEACHER

- To make the decision about the question to be asked

- To accept the responses

- To serve as source of verification in some subject matter tasks

---

Style I represents another step beyond the discovery threshold, which has been crossed thus far in styles F, G, and H. In style F, the guided discovery style, the specific response at each step of the process was discovered by the learner, but the learner's responses depended on the meticulous sequence of stimuli (questions, clues) presented by the teacher. Style G, the convergent discovery style, called for greater independence on the part of the learner in the process of discovering the one correct answer. The dependence on the teacher (or surrogate source) decreased because the learner did not require a separate stimulus from the teacher at each step. The structure and the reality of this style, though, still maintained a powerful bond between the learner and the teacher because the teacher designed the question or problem. In style H, the learner was even more independent in producing divergent ideas, but the teacher continued to make the decisions about the design of the specific problems.

In style I, the learner's independence becomes even more pronounced. In this style the teacher designates the general subject matter area (i.e., a particular period in history, a particular phase of physics, a particular aspect of shop, a particular aspect of physical education, etc.). The learner discovers and designs the questions or problems within the subject matter area *and* seeks the solutions.

It is imperative to understand that style I is not an "anything goes" or a "do whatever you want" style. On the contrary, this style is a *highly disciplined* approach to evoke and develop the creative capacities of the individual learner. It is a model for a systematic way to explore and examine an issue in order to discover its components, the relationships among the components, and a possible order or sequence for these components. In a word, style I enables the learner to discover the *structure* of the issue at hand. It requires the learner to know some facts, to be able to identify categories, to engage in analysis, and then to construct a schema. It requires an integration of the skills—cognitive and others—learned in all previous styles. Although style I is highly disciplined and focused on structure, it does not require that spontaneous ideas and random discoveries be excluded or rejected. These can always be woven into the rest of the structure and find their proper place in juxtaposition to other ideas.

This style is most fruitful with students who have successfully experienced styles A–H. It is for the student who is ready for this expansion of discovery but is also well-versed in the decisions and the processes learned in the other styles. Without the background of the previous styles, students may face difficulties in organizing both the questions and the answers into a reasonable, rational, and workable structure. Raising random questions and finding random answers is not enough. In order to understand an issue and the relationships of its components, one needs the skills learned in previous styles. Style I provides the learner with the opportunity to practice all of these skills and find ways of interrelating them over a *longer* period of time. This style cannot be done in one episode; it requires a *series* of interconnected episodes.

The very nature of style I is the development of an idea or ideas. Style I is a process of discovering and creating series and sequences of questions and problems that inquire into the very essence of the issue at hand. It is a process of discovering and creating multiple and alternative solutions to each of the problems, and developing a structure that binds them together.

THE OBJECTIVE OF THIS STYLE

The objective of this style is to provide the learner with the opportunity to develop a program for him- or herself based on cognitive and physical capacities in the particular topic. The knowledge and physical skills needed for participating in this style result from the cumulative experiences in styles A–H. Entering a series of style I episodes requires some knowledge of one's physical abilities as well as familiarity with the processes of discovery and divergent production (see Figure 13-1). The learner must also possess the affective capacity to endure the development and use of a long-range program.

THE ANATOMY OF THIS STYLE

Preimpact Set

1. The teacher decides about the selected, general subject matter area.

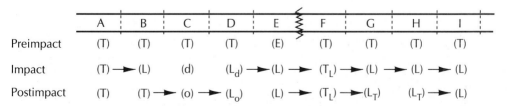

FIGURE 13–1 The shift from the divergent production style to the individual program—learner's design

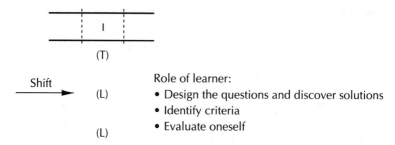

FIGURE 13–2   The shift of decisions

Impact Set

1. The shift of decisions occurs in the impact set (Figure 13-2). The learner decides how to design the questions and the multiple solutions within the general subject matter area.
2. The learner decides what will constitute a completed program. These guidelines will be used as criteria in the postimpact set.
3. The teacher's role is to be available when the learner initiates questions about the subject matter and/or the style.
4. The teacher also initiates contact with the learner to verify where the learner is and how he or she is progressing, to reexamine subject matter connections, and so on.

Postimpact Set

1. The role of the learner is to examine the solutions, validate them in relationship to the problems, establish connections, organize them into categories, and maintain the development of the individual program.
2. The teacher should conduct dialogues with the learner about the progress of the program, meeting the criteria, any existing discrepancies, and to answer questions by the learner.

IMPLEMENTATION OF THIS STYLE

1. In this context, the term *subject matter area* defines the broad parameters of the activity (i.e., ball games, gymnastics, developmental movement, and outdoor pursuits). A *topic* is defined as a part (or parts) of that subject matter (i.e., volleyball, vaulting, strength development, and rock climbing).
2. Perhaps the most important consideration for choosing style I is the readiness of the learner(s). Participation in style I requires prior experiences in styles A through H. Learners must be reasonably proficient in performing

some aspects of the chosen topic (usually a result of style A–E), and must feel comfortable in the discovery process (styles F–H). With these background experiences, the learners can be productive in style I. Productive participation in style I makes demands that a novice cannot handle; frustration and inability to proceed will result.

3. Introducing this style must be done patiently and in detail. The learners must clearly understand their role and your expectations.

4. Time is crucial in the evolvement of style I. Style I must be done in a series of episodes over a period of time. Learners need thinking time, experimenting time, performing time, and recording time. Style I cannot be rushed—time is always needed for ideas to come to fruition. The teacher needs time to observe the production and performance of individual learners, time to listen to learners, and time to conduct periodic individual conferences.

5. The process of style I is exciting for the participants. The constant challenge of developing and integrating ideas motivates those who endure the style. There are those who start with great enthusiasm and a variety of ideas but cannot endure the rigor of continuous experimentation and discovery. With these learners, change styles and wait for a more appropriate time. The teacher must not insist that all students participate in style I; it is a highly individualistic style that reflects a great deal of independence.

6. It is virtually impossible to give examples of style I episodes because they come from the individual learner's choices, imagination, and decisions. The preceding sections offer the spirit of this style and guidelines for the process.

Once more, it is important for you to realize that style I is not "anything goes" or "do whatever you want." On the contrary, this style is a *highly disciplined* approach for developing the capacities of the individual learner. It is a systematic model for exploring and examining an idea. It is a systematic way to discover the components of an issue, the relationships among the components, and the possible order and sequences. It is a way to discover the *structure* of the issue at hand. The learner must know some facts to be able to identify categories, to engage in analysis, and then to construct the schema. Cognitive and physical skills learned in all the previous styles are integrated in this style. Spontaneous ideas and random discoveries are not excluded or rejected—they can always be woven into the rest of the structure.

THE DEVELOPMENTAL CHANNELS

The position of the learner is toward maximum on the physical, emotional, and cognitive channels for style I if the criterion is being independent. It is also obvious that this highly individualistic style provides for choice of social development. The picture that emerges is seen in Figure 13-3.

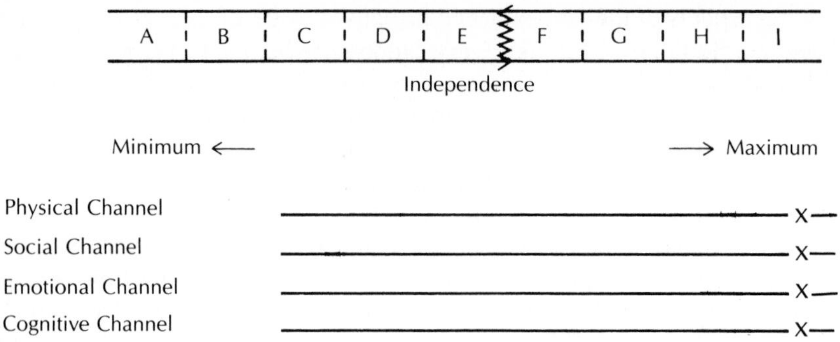

```
| A | B | C | D | E ≷ F | G | H | I |
```

Independence

Minimum ⟵   ⟶ Maximum

Physical Channel   ————————————————————— x—
Social Channel   ————————————————————— x—
Emotional Channel   ————————————————————— x—
Cognitive Channel   ————————————————————— x—

FIGURE 13–3 The individual program—learner's design style and the developmental channels

FIGURE 13–4 Style I classroom chart

THE INDIVIDUAL PROGRAM—LEARNER'S DESIGN STYLE

The purpose of this style is for the learner to design, develop, and perform a series of tasks organized into a personal program.

ROLE OF LEARNER

• To select the topic that will be focus of his or her study

• To identify questions and issues appropriate for the topic

• To organize the questions, organize the tasks, and design a personal program—a course of action

• To collect data about the topic, answer the questions, and organize the answers into a reasonable framework

• To verify his or her procedures and solutions based on criteria intrinsic to the subject matter at hand

ROLE OF TEACHER

• To select the general subject matter area from which the learner selects his or her topic

• To observe the learner's progress

• To listen to the learner's periodic presentation of questions and answers

14 The Learner-Initiated Style (Style J)

We have traveled a long way since the command style. We have identified a variety of styles, seen their place in the Spectrum, and examined their contributions to the learner's development.

We have reached the point where the individual learner is ready to make maximum decisions during teaching-learning episodes.

This style, although quite similar to style I in its structure and proceedings, represents a significant change. It is the first time that the individual learner *initiates* the style itself. The individual learner recognizes his or her readiness to move on, to inquire, to discover, to design a program and perform it for self-development.

The learner comes to the teacher and states the willingness to conduct a series of episodes in style J. This is quite a difference! The readiness and ability to initiate create a different reality for the learner and for the teacher—a reality in which the learner takes maximum responsibility for initiating and conducting the teaching-learning episodes.

THE ANATOMY OF THIS STYLE

Since the essence of this style is the individual's initiation of the process, the whole class cannot reach this point at the same time. Style J is always an individual style (see Figure 14-1).

For the first time in the Spectrum, the preimpact decisions shift from the teacher to the learner. Operationally, this means that:

1. The learner *initiates* participation in this style. "I want to be in style J. I am ready to design my own problem(s) and seek the solutions." This attitude reflects the individual student's readiness to engage in this style. (An entire class cannot be ready for this style at the same time.)
2. The learner makes *all* the decisions in the preimpact set.
3. In the impact set, the learner makes all the decisions about discovery and performing the movements according to the problems designed in the preimpact set. In this respect, the role of the learner here is the same as in the impact set of style I—discovering and examining solutions.

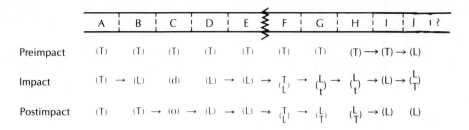

FIGURE 14–1 The anatomy of the learner-initiated style

In addition, the learner in the impact set "checks in" periodically with the teacher to share the decisions made in the preimpact set and the discoveries and performances that take place during the impact set.

The role of the teacher in the impact set is to listen, watch, ask questions, and alert the learner to decisions that were omitted. The teacher is, in effect, in a supportive role.

4. In the postimpact set, the learner makes all the decisions in assessing and evaluating the activities. This evaluation is done against the criteria according to the evaluative procedures decided on during the preimpact set. All this is done *by* and *for* the individual learner. The teacher's role, once again, is to be supportive, to listen to the learner, and to watch his or her solutions done through movement. If discrepancies are identified by the teacher, it is his or her role to ask questions that will enable the learner to also identify them. The teacher neither evaluates nor judges.

In physical education, the "final product" of the discoveries could be given as a presentation that might include a written document, a visual model, and an actual physical performance of parts or of the entire discovery.

Let us examine an example of a learner engaging in this style.

Preimpact Set

1. The learner decides about *selecting* the general subject matter area (aquatic activities, use of gymnastics apparatus, use of other apparatus, dance, snow activities, etc.).
2. The learner selects a particular topic within the subject matter area. For example, in the area of aquatic activities, the learner may decide to focus on "transportation and aquatic games."
3. The learner decides what environment to use for examining and discovering the possibilities of this topic. For example, the environment could be a little island in a pond reasonably close to the "mainland." The island is strewn with some rocks and half covered with tall trees. Rocks jut out from the water between the island and the "mainland," which is covered by bushes.
4. The learner decides what tools and equipment are necessary for dealing with the issues involved in this topic.

5. The learner now makes the decisions about the questions and the problem design for this topic. For example:
   a. What are the possible uses of the waterway between the island and the mainland? Is it conducive to swimming? Diving? Wading through? Floating objects around the rocks?
   b. What are possible land and water games that can be designed for the narrow part between the island and the mainland?
   c. There are many more questions that can be asked.
6. The learner makes the rest of the preimpact decisions, including a plan for evaluating the process and the solutions. The evaluation will take place in the postimpact set.

Impact Set

1. The learner responds to each problem by experimenting, examining, and discovering the multiple movements that will solve the problems. Some of the responses remain within the cognitive domain alone; others are products of the cognitive process and the physical performance.

   The responses to the questions designed in the preimpact might include instances of swimming activities, floating activities, games on the land, and so forth.

2. The learner organizes the discovered movements into categories required by the designed parameters. These categories might be:
   a. Transporting the body through and over the water without implements
   b. Transporting the body with implements (i.e., log for flotation, rope for swinging over the water, etc.)
   c. An obstacle course using the jutting rocks
   d. Propulsion under water (variations!)
   e. Games using small stones
   f. Games using rocks on the island's bank and a rock in the water
   g. Possibilities for shallow diving, deep diving
   h. Others?
3. During experimentation in the impact set, the learner adjusts the design of the problem, reorganizes the order and sequence, checks the validity of the intended categories, and slowly builds up the entire integrated program of possible movements suitable in this environment.

   Style J can only be done when time is allotted for a series of episodes. This kind of involvement requires several weeks or more so that one can immerse oneself in the process of discovery.

Postimpact Set

1. Decisions are made every time the learner verifies a response by performing the movement, checking its validity as a solution to the problem, and ascertaining its membership in a category.

2. During the entire process, the learner records the solutions in an organized way so that the total written product reflects the relationships between the problems and the categories of solutions.
3. At the conclusion of this process, the learner could perform parts or the entire program to the observing teacher or, at times, to an audience of peers or guests.

The same process and the same procedures can be used to discover and organize programs examining the relationships between body movements and other environments, various kinds of equipment, objects, and other people.

Omitting more examples in this style is deliberate. The intent is to invite *you* to participate in style I. If you are intrigued, follow the outlined steps. Immerse yourself in divergent cognitive production, discover ideas, and experience the frustrations and joys of going beyond!

THE DEVELOPMENTAL CHANNELS

When we use the criterion of *independence* to place the learner on the developmental channels, we find in style J, as in style I, the position of the learner is very close to "maximum" on all four channels (Figure 14-2). The learner is highly independent in making decisions *about* him- or herself in reference to all the developmental channels.

A	B	C	D	E	F	G	H	I	J

Independence

Minimum ◄—   —► Maximum

Physical Channel	X
Social Channel	X
Emotional Channel	X
Cognitive Channel	X

FIGURE 14–2   The learner-initiated style and the developmental channels

FIGURE 14–3 Style J classroom chart

THE LEARNER-INITIATED STYLE

The purpose of this style is to provide the learner with the opportunity to initiate his or her learning experience, design it, do it, and evaluate it.

ROLE OF LEARNER

- To initiate the style

- To design the program for him- or herself

- To do it

- To evaluate it

- To decide how to use the teacher

ROLE OF TEACHER

- To accept the learner's decision to initiate his or her own learning experience

- To provide the general conditions for the learner's plans

- To accept the learner's procedures and products

- To alert the learner to any discrepancies between the learner's intent and action

---

Only a little needs to be said about this style. Since the Spectrum identifies the shift of decisions from the teacher to the learner, style K exists. The internal logic of the Spectrum leads us to the realization that it is, indeed, possible for a person to make all the decisions—in the preimpact, impact, and post-impact—for oneself. This style does not exist in the classroom, but it does exist in situations when an individual is engaged in teaching him- or herself. In such situations, the same individual makes all the decisions that were previously made by the teacher and by the learner. This individual participates in the roles of both teacher and learner.

This interplay of roles occurs in the privacy of one's mind and one's experiences. It does not necessarily need an audience, an outside receiver, or an outside appreciator. If needed, it could move outside the individual's private domain. This style can occur anytime, anywhere and in any social context, environment, or political system. It is a testimony to the unfathomed human capacity to teach, to learn, and to grow.

THE ANATOMY OF THIS STYLE

Just for the fun of it, see Figure 15-1:

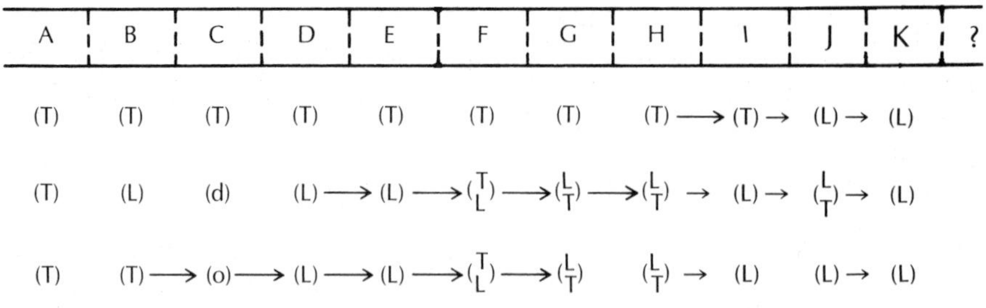

A	B	C	D	E	F	G	H	I	J	K	?
(T)	(T)	(T)	(T)	(T)	(T)	(T)	(T) $\longrightarrow$ (T) $\rightarrow$		(L) $\rightarrow$	(L)	
(T)	(L)	(d)	(L) $\longrightarrow$ (L) $\longrightarrow (\frac{T}{L}) \longrightarrow (\frac{L}{T}) \longrightarrow (\frac{L}{T})$				$\rightarrow$ (L) $\rightarrow$		$(\frac{L}{T}) \rightarrow$	(L)	
(T)	(T) $\longrightarrow$ (o) $\longrightarrow$ (L) $\longrightarrow$ (L) $\longrightarrow (\frac{T}{L}) \longrightarrow (\frac{L}{T})$						$(\frac{L}{T}) \rightarrow$		(L)	(L) $\rightarrow$ (L)	

FIGURE 15–1 The spectrum of teaching styles

16 | Some Thoughts About the Spectrum

This chapter's purpose is to offer some thoughts about the Spectrum's implications and relationships to a variety of educational aspects and issues. If the Spectrum is a framework proposing a shift of paradigm in the ways we can look at teaching, then it is imperative to view this structure from several broad perspectives that go beyond the structure and function of each individual style.

THE CLUSTERS A–E AND F–K

The entire Spectrum is organized into two clusters of styles, one on each side of the Discovery Threshold. These two clusters are fundamentally different from one another in terms of their objectives, the behaviors of the teacher, and the expectations of the learner's behavior. The Threshold serves as a significant line of demarcation between two fundamental human behaviors: reproduction of the known (A–E), and discovery and production of the unknown (F–K).

The styles in each cluster share common characteristics (or general objectives) that are the hallmark of the particular cluster. The table in Figure 16-1 presents some of these characteristics.

Remember that the entire Spectrum rests on the *nonversus* notion of education. Many of the philosophical conflicts about teaching methods occur because of anchorage to one side of the Threshold, to one cluster and, at times, to one style.

The Spectrum calls for a nonversus reality in our schools where deliberate mobility along the Spectrum, in both directions, is a daily occurrence. (See Figure 16-2.)

RELATIONSHIPS TO VARIOUS EDUCATIONAL ASPECTS

A number of statements have been made recently about a variety of educational aspects and variables. Investigations were made of class management, motivation, time-on-task (or Academic Learning Time-PE, ALT-PE), discipline, feedback, and so on. Ways of treating these variables have been proposed and techniques for improvement (when needed) have been devised.

These proposals, identified as teaching skills, teaching strategies, or teaching models, are all designed for improving teaching.

FIGURE 16–1   Characteristics of the clusters of teaching styles

Common characteristics (objectives) of styles A–E	Common characteristics (objectives) of styles F–J
1. Re-production of knowledge and skills (known to the teacher and/or the learner)	1. Production of knowledge and skills new to the learner and/or the teacher.
2. The subject matter is concrete, mainly containing facts, rules, and specific skills. (Basic knowledge, Fixed knowledge)	2. The subject matter is variable, mainly containing concepts, strategies, and principles.
3. There is one correct way to perform the task—by emulation of the presented model.	3. Alternatives in design and performance are called for. There is no single model to emulate.
4. Time is needed for practicing and learning to adhere to the model.	4. Time is needed for the cognitive processes involved.
5. The cognitive operations mainly engaged are memory and recall.	5. Time is needed to evolve an affective climate conducive to producing and accepting alternatives and options.
6. Feedback is specific and refers to the performance of the task and its approximation to the model.	6. The cognitive operations engaged are comparing, contrasting, categorizing, problem solving, inventing, and others.
7. Individual differences are accepted only within the learner's physical and emotional boundaries.	7. Discovery and creativity are manifested through these cognitive operations.
8. The class climate (the spirit of the learning environment) is one of performing the model, repetition, and reduction of errors.	8. Discovery by the learner is developed through covergent and divergent processes or a combination of both.
	9. Feedback refers to producing alternatives and not a single solution.
	10. Individual differences in the quantity, rate, and kind of production are essential to maintaining and continuing these styles.
	11. The class climate (the spirit of the learning environment) is one of searching, examining the validity of alternatives, and going beyond the known.

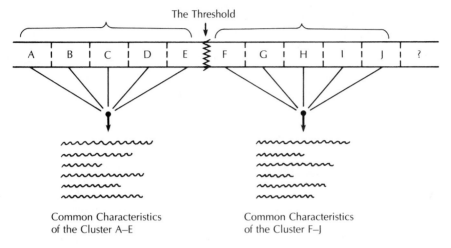

FIGURE 16–2   The nonversus reality

Experience in the Spectrum brings different and varied information about these educational variables. If we accept that in the face-to-face relationship the behavior of the teacher affects the behavior of the learner, then we must look at each of these educational variables in light of each style. When we experience the Spectrum this way we derive different meanings for these variables.

Since the Spectrum offers a schema for differentiated styles, each defined by its intrinsic T–L–O, the implications for the educational variables must also be differentiated. For example, feedback behavior *must* be different in style B than in style D, different in E than in H, and so on. Therefore, the study of feedback must be related to the particular style in use.

In the same fashion, discipline cannot be generalized as an educational variable. Discipline requirements and expectations vary from style to style. Definitions and treatments of discipline problems also vary and are always

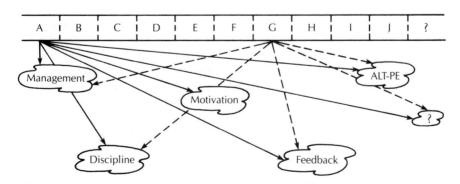

FIGURE 16–3   Implications network for each style

related to the particular style in use in a given episode. The same is true for ALT-PE, management procedures, and any other variable that has an impact on learning—they all stem from the particular style used at a given time.

These teaching skills, or models, are the result of previous decisions—perhaps primary decisions—embodied in the structure of each style.

Figure 16-3 represents the network of implications that are intrinsic and unique to each style.

THE PURPOSE AND THE ESSENCE OF EACH STYLE[1]

Since each style has a particular structure that defines the role of the teacher and the role of the learner, it also identifies the purpose (objective) of this relationship. The roles are defined by the decisions that the teacher makes and the decisions that the learner makes in the given episodes. When these decisions are made with reasonable authenticity, the purpose (objective) of the episode can be accomplished.

What follows for each style is a description of its purpose and a description of its essence. The "essence" of a style indicates that the implementation of a given style is reasonably flexible—flexible within the boundaries of what each style is supposed to accomplish. The essence of a style provides the picture of that style. Any further reduction will nullify the operation of the style and will not accomplish the intended purpose. Again, a deliberate behavior, a behavior that is authentic to the structure of the given style, will ensure a reasonable accomplishment of the purpose of the teaching-learning episode. When a teacher becomes skilled in using each style, he or she becomes more flexible and able to shift styles and, thus, accomplish more objectives and reach more students.

Style A: Command   The purpose of this style is to learn to do the task accurately and within a short period of time, following all decisions made by the teacher. The essence: Immediate response to a stimulus. Performance is accurate and immediate. A previous model is replicated.

Style B: Practice   This style offers the learner time to work individually and privately and provides the teacher with time to offer the learner individual and private feedback. The essence: Time is provided for the learner to do a task individually and privately and time is available for the teacher to give feedback to all learners, individually and privately.

Style C: Reciprocal   In this style learners work with a partner and offer feedback to the partner, based on criteria prepared by the teacher. The essence: Learners work in a partner relationship; receive immediate feedback; follow

[1]From: Mosston, Muska. "Tug-O-War, No More." *JOPERD,* January 1992.

criteria for performance designed by the teacher; and develop feedback and socialization skills.

Style D: Self-Check   The purposes of this style are to learn to do a task and to check one's own work. The essence: Learners do the task individually and privately and provide feedback for themselves by using criteria developed by the teacher.

Style E: Inclusion   The purposes of this style are to learn to select a level of a task one can perform and to offer a challenge to check one's own work. The essence: The same task is designed for different degrees of difficulty. Learners decide their entry point into the task and when to move to another level.

Style F: Guided Discovery   The purpose of this style is to discover a concept by answering a sequence of questions presented by the teacher. The essence: The teacher, by asking a specific sequence of questions, systematically leads the learner to discover a predetermined "target" previously unknown to the learner.

Style G: Convergent Discovery   Here learners discover the solution to a problem and learn to clarify an issue and arrive at a conclusion by employing logical procedures, reasoning, and critical thinking. The essence: Teachers present the question. The intrinsic structure of the task (question) requires a single correct answer. Learners engage in reasoning (or other cognitive operations) and seek to discover the single correct answer/solution.

Style H: Divergent Production   The purpose of this style is to engage in producing (discovering) multiple responses to a single question. The essence: Learners are engaged in producing divergent responses to a single question. The intrinsic structure of the task (question) provides possible multiple responses. The multiple responses are assessed by the Possible-Feasible-Desirable procedures, or by the verification "rules" of the given discipline.

Style I: Learner's Individual Designed Program   The purpose of this style is to design, develop, and perform a series of tasks organized into a personal program with consultation with the teacher. The essence: The learner designs, develops, and performs a series of tasks organized into a personal program. The learner selects the topic, identifies the questions, collects data, discovers answers, and organizes the information. The teacher selects the general subject matter area.

Style J: Learner-Initiated   The purpose of this style is for the learner to initiate a learning experience, design it, perform it, and evaluate it, together with the teacher based on agreed-upon criteria. The essence: The learner initiates the style in which he or she will conduct the episode or a series of episodes. The learner has the option to select any style on the Spectrum. The learner must be familiar with the array of the styles offered by the Spectrum.

Style K: Self-teaching This style provides the learner the opportunity to make maximum decisions about his or her learning experience—without any direct involvement by the teacher. This style is rarely, if ever, used in school. It is more appropriate for developing a hobby or leisure activity. The very choice of this style is the learner's decision. The essence: The learner initiates his or her learning experience, designs it, performs it, and evaluates it. The learner decides how much teacher involvement to use. The teacher accepts the learner's decisions and provides general conditions for the learner's plans if performed in the school.

"LANDMARK" STYLES AND THE "CANOPY"

Styles A–K have been identified as "landmark" styles because of their mutually exclusive structure of decisions, and their significantly different T–L–O. However, in the gymnasium and the playing field, situations exist that fall between landmark styles. This situation arises when all the required decisions were not shifted in a particular episode. For example, a common condition in gymnastics is that the location of an apparatus determines the location of the activity; therefore, when style B is used, the learner does not make a location decision. Sometimes, an institution decides the attire and appearance (uniforms, etc.): Again, in style B the learner does not make this decision. These are not earthshaking realizations, but they identify different realities in terms of decisions.

Posture is always intrinsic to a given task's structure; therefore, in styles B–E this decision is not shifted to the learner. A written test is an example of a situation where a task is performed and the feedback is mostly delayed—it is not a stimulus-response episode (style A), nor is it practice time (B). The same is true in the case of a lecture. All these examples, by decision analysis, fall between A and B. They are said to be under the canopy of A or the canopy of B, depending on the proximity to the particular landmark style. Episodes conducted under the canopy of a given style help us to understand and to differentiate possibilities that exist in the classroom. Our ability to identify the decisions and the behavior of a style helps us to determine whether the action was congruent with the intent.

Certain words and terms have been used in education that do not fulfill these two criteria: (1) they do not identify the decisions made by the teacher and/or the learner, and (2) they do not specifically describe the behavior. Some of these terms are: *discussion, direct/indirect teaching, socialization, individualizing instruction,* and *teaching for thinking.* These terms are vague and give license to almost any activity. Often these terms represent educational slogans that are in vogue at a given moment.

Discussion can be conducted in style B and in style G, depending on the objectives of the episode; direct teaching can be conducted in styles A through E, and so on. General terms are not helpful in understanding the teaching-learning relationships.

CREATIVITY

Literature about creativity is very rich and available. Points of view vary, but we suggest that creativity is the capacity to see something new by engaging in a particular cognitive operation for a given period of time. One is not "just" creative; rather, one is creative in comparing, in categorizing, in solving, and in inventing for a given duration. The creative process flows by engaging in a particular cognitive operation for a given time.

This flow may shift from one cognitive operation to another, but only one operation can be triggered at one time. A teacher can be creative in designing episodes for the learner who will "practice" creativity in one cognitive operation or another. We are talking here about deliberate behavior and deliberate teaching, which is the hallmark of the Spectrum. Styles G–J represent this notion and process. Expressing the creative capacity—the final product—can take many forms. In fact, many products of the creative process are manifested and offered via a style A presentation.

Most public displays of dance, folk dance, or gymnastics performances are presented in unison, adhering to predetermined models. They are all style A episodes born and designed through style H, via a creative process. Activities like these that may seem a puzzling paradox turn into a unique combination of behaviors: a H/A relationship! With a little creative effort, many more insights could emerge.

THE GROUP

A group is a particular unit, a particular form of organizing people. A group is not a teaching style, although most styles can be done in a group. For example, style A can be done with one learner or with many. The same is true with styles B, D, E, and H. Style C requires at least one pair (the smallest possible group).

Although it is most efficient one-on-one, style F can be done with a group. All styles, then, (except C) when used with groups accommodate the organizational requirement of the class and the structure of a given sport or a particular social objective.

The size of the group, the task for each individual, and the nature of the social contact depend on the structure of the sport and the objective of the episode. Consider these dimensions when you analyze the group concept in an evening of social dances and a group of mountaineers attempting to reach a summit.

HOW TO SELECT A STYLE

"How will I teach my students in the next episode?" A teacher who is aware of students, the subject matter, and the objective of education is always con-

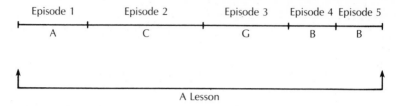

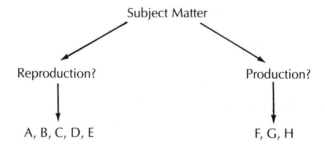

FIGURE 16–4   A lesson

sidering this question. When you become skilled in using all the styles, you must decide which one is appropriate for a given episode. It is a matter of deciding which style is most appropriate. The following series of steps serve as a guide for deliberately selecting a style.

1. Always think about the T–L–O. You must remember that this inextricable bond exists in every episode.
2. Always think about the *episodes* that comprise the lesson (see Figure 16-4).
3. What are your *objectives* for a given episode?

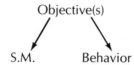

What would you like the learners to accomplish in the subject matter? What is the task? What is the standard for the performance?

What behavior are you trying to develop in the learner? Or, from your knowledge of the learner, which behavior does the learner need to examine?

Once you have answered these questions and are reasonably clear about your objectives for the ensuing episode, go on to the next step.

4. Have you selected a task in the subject matter (or a series of tasks) that requires *reproduction*? Or is it a task that invites the learner to discover or *produce* his or her own ideas?

If the task requires reproduction (meaning that it belongs on the left side of the Discovery Threshold) then you have five styles from which to choose plus the possible canopies—a rather large number of options!

If the task invites discovery and production of alternatives and examination of these ideas (meaning that it belongs on the right side of the Threshold) then styles F, G, and H are available to you.

Identifying and realizing the placement of the task on the appropriate side of the Threshold is a *crucial* step when selecting a style.

5. What behavior do you want to develop? Or, what behavior does the learner need to examine, experience, or develop? Are you seeking one of the following?
   a. Precision in performance?
   b. Synchronization?
   c. Replication of a model?
   d. Beginning of independence?
   e. Socialization? Which form?
   f. Self-assessment and feedback?
   g. Examining the self-perception?
   h. Developing options in subject matter?
   i. Designing? Inventing? Solving problems?
   j. Other?

Since each of these (or a cluster of these) can be developed by a particular style, you are ready now for the next step.

6. Match the objectives of the subject matter and the sought behavior, which will lead you to the selection of an appropriate style.

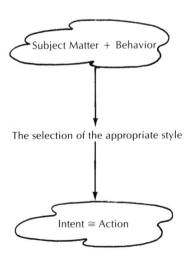

Subject Matter + Behavior

The selection of the appropriate style

Intent ≅ Action

In time, with reasonable experience in the Spectrum, your students will be able to participate in selecting styles for different episodes. When this occurs, your students demonstrate their capacity for mobility along the Spectrum and their willingness to expand beyond their past experiences.

To reap the benefits of any style, episodes must be of some duration. Like any other skill, both teacher and learner must practice the style. It takes time to learn the decisions, their relationships, and their implications. It takes time to internalize the behavior of the styles. Perhaps the only style where short episodes of a few minutes can produce the desired results is style A, but such episodes should still be done with some frequency. Duration and consistency, then, are necessary for successful development of deliberate teaching.

At times there is a tendency to associate a style with an entire sport (Gymnastics is best taught by style _____; swimming, by style _____; etc.). The previous guidelines for selecting styles should be helpful in avoiding this tendency. Different aspects of the sport (or activity) can (and should) be taught by different styles—depending on the objective.

RESEARCH POSSIBILITIES

The Spectrum offers new possibilities for research on teaching physical education because of the capacity to differentiate among different teaching behaviors (styles) and the capacity for consistency within each style. Some suggested research directions are:

1. Research within each style. Realizing the uniqueness of each T–L–O offers many possibilities for investigating these relationships within each style. This also implies that styles do not compete with each other for supremacy. Research that seeks to find which style is "best" is theoretically and practically futile.

2. Research within the cluster. The common characteristic of each style within a cluster offers many possibilities for finding out more about the relationships among the styles. Researchers should be aware that examining styles from one cluster against learning outcomes that belong to the other cluster will yield inappropriate and inaccurate results.

3. Research that examines assumptions made about the possible existing relationships between each style, the developmental channels, and various educational variables. A considerable amount of research has been conducted recently focusing on variables of time-on-task (or ALT-PE). There are ample data to substantiate the impact of this dimension on learning. If we are mainly concerned with this dimension and its contribution to physical development, then styles A and B will do the best job.

   However, if the broader goal of physical education is to develop many other human dimensions, then other styles must be studied in relationship to the developmental channels and other educational variables.

4. When research is conducted in the reality of the gymnasium where teaching is mostly arbitrary and idiosyncratic, the observed teaching behavior is usually studied as a "lump." The Spectrum offers concrete differentiation among the styles, allowing the fidelity of the teaching behavior in each style to be verified and replicated. The results of research in such conditions may yield significantly different results.

RELATIONSHIP WITH OTHER IDEAS ABOUT TEACHING

Over the years, many ideas about teaching have evolved. Many programs have been designed, models identified and tested, philosophies used as guides, and research developed to understand each of these. The question that arises is what is the relationship between each of these ideas and the Spectrum of Teaching Styles? Do all these programs and models stand apart from the Spectrum?

If every teaching episode has a decision structure, then by identifying these decisions in each program it becomes possible to place the program in the Spectrum. By knowing who makes which decisions, about what, and when, we can identify who makes decisions about the task, the nature of the task, who gives the feedback, and so on. In short, an identification of a T–L–O emerges for the models under observation. This T–L–O can be placed somewhere in the Spectrum—either with one of the landmark styles or under one of the canopies.

This placement helps identify the relationship between intent and action of the model or program and helps delineate their relationships to other models and programs. For example, "Mastery Learning" is an excellent example of style B operating over a long period of time. The different machines used for developing strength represent style D. Some of the episodes of the "Direct Teaching" proposals are styles A, $\widehat{A}$, B, $\widehat{B}$. All of these fall on the left side of the Discovery Threshold.

Inquiry programs, creative movement designs that focus on alternatives, searching processes that seek different strategies in ballgames—all of these represent various forms of style H and fall on the right side of the Threshold. Since the Spectrum represents a unified theory of teaching, then by decision analysis it can offer insight into the structure and implications of any teaching-learning episode.

CLOSURE

We have travelled a long way in the Spectrum. The invitation to be mobile, to expand our view of teaching behavior, is quite demanding. Values have to be examined, goals realized and procedures reorganized. Initially, learning and doing the styles in the Spectrum may be difficult or perhaps awkward. Everyone is anchored and comfortable in one behavior or another; everyone has preferences. The Spectrum calls for reexamination of this anchorage and for expansion of preferences. The Spectrum calls for a shift of paradigm in the way we look at teaching. It is demanding and at times painful; it takes time. The weaning process for both teacher and learner takes time, and only becomes possible when we believe that people can learn to move, in both directions, along the Spectrum of Teaching Styles—from command to discovery.

References

READING REFERENCES

The surge of research on teaching physical education has produced a considerable number of publications that are available in the professional literature. The reader is invited to study these publications and find out which ones offer support to the ideas offered by the Spectrum, which ones offer different insights, and which ones offer questions that stimulate further thought and study. The following is a list of some reading that might be helpful to the student of teaching physical education.

ANDERSON, W. G. *Analysis of Teaching Physical Education*. St. Louis: C.V. Mosby, 1980.

ASHWORTH, S. "A Comparison of Feedback Behavior of Teachers Trained in Mosston's Spectrum and Teachers Not Trained in the Spectrum." Unpublished doctoral dissertation, Temple University, 1983.

BRYANT, W. "Comparison of the Practice and Reciprocal Styles of Teaching." Unpublished project, Temple University, 1974.

CHAMBERLAIN, J. R. "The Effects of Mosston's Practice Style and Individual Program Teacher Design on Motor Skill Acquisition and Self-Concept of Fifth Grade Learners." Unpublished doctoral dissertation, Temple University, 1979.

CHEFFERS, J. T. "Validation of an Instrument Designed to Expand the Flanders System of Interaction Analysis to Describe Nonverbal Interaction, Different Varieties of Teacher Behavior, and Pupil Responses." Unpublished doctoral dissertation, Temple University, 1972.

DODDS, P.; RIFE, F.; and METZLER, M. "Academic Learning Time in Physical Education: Data Collection, Completed Research and Future Directions." Paper presented at the AIESEP Annual Meeting, Boston, August 1982.

DOUGHERTY, N. J. "A Comparison of the Effects of Command, Task, and Individualized Program Styles of Teaching in the Development of Physical Fitness and Motor Skills." Unpublished doctoral dissertation, Temple University, 1970.

GALLAHUE, D. L. *Developmental Physical Education for Today's Children*. Madison, WI: Brown and Benchmark Publishers, 1993.

GERNEY, P. E. "The Effects of Mosston's Practice Style and Reciprocal Style on Psychomotor Skill Acquisition and Social Development of Fifth Grade Students." Unpublished doctoral dissertation, Temple University, 1979.

GOLDBERGER, M.; GERNEY, P.; and CHAMBERLAIN, J. "The Effects of Three Styles of Teaching on the Psychomotor Performance and Social Skill Development of Fifth Grade Children." *Research Quarterly for Exercise and Sport* 53 (1982): 116–124.

GRAHAM, G. "Research on Teaching Physical Education: A Discussion with Larry Locke and Daryl Siedentop." *Journal of Teaching in Physical Education* 1 (1981): 3–15.

GRAHAM, G. *Teaching Children Physical Education: Becoming a Master Teacher.* Champaign, IL: Human Kinetics Books, 1992.

GRAHAM, G., and HEIMERER, E. "Research on Teaching Effectiveness: Implications for the Real World Teacher." Paper presented at the AAHPERD National Convention, Detroit, April 1981.

GRIFFEY, D. C. "What is the Best Way to Teach?" *Journal of Teaching in Physical Education* 1 (1981): 18–24.

HAAG, H., ed. *Physical Education and Evaluation: Proceedings of the XXII ICHPER World Congress Kiel.* West Germany, July 1979.

HARRISON, J. M. *Instructional Strategies for Secondary School Physical Education. 3rd ed.* Dubuque, IA: William C. Brown Publishers, 1992.

JACOBY, D. J. "A Comparison of the Effects of Command, Reciprocal, and Individual Styles of Teaching on the Development of Selected Sports Skills." Unpublished dissertation, Ohio University, 1975.

LOCKE, L. "Qualitative Research in Physical Education: Theory and Methods." Unpublished workshop materials for the Teaching Behavior Research Workshop, Ohio State University, June 1982.

LOCKE, L. "Research on Teaching Physical Education: New Hope for a Dismal Science." *Quest* 28 (1977): 2–16.

LOCKE, L. "Teaching and Learning Processes in Physical Activity: The Central Problem of Sport Pedagogy." Physical Education and Evaluation: Proceedings of the XXII ICHPER World Congress Kiel, edited by H. Haag. West Germany, July 1979.

LOCKE, L.; SIEDENTOP, D.; and MAND, C. *The Preparation of Physical Education Teachers: A Subject-Matter-Centered Model.* Undergraduate Physical Education Programs: Issues and Approaches, edited by H. Lawson. Washington, DC: AAHPERD, 1981.

MCCLEARY, E. "A Comparison of the Task and Problem-Solving Styles in Teaching Kindergarten and First Grade Students. A Unit on Self-Testing Activities." Unpublished project, Temple University, 1976.

METZLER, M. W. *Instructional Supervision for Physical Education.* Champaign, IL: Human Kinetics Books, 1990.

PICHERT, J. W.; ANDERSON, R. C.; ARMBRUSTER, B. V.; SURBER, J. R.; and SHIRLEY, L. L. *Final Report: An Evaluation of the Spectrum of Teaching Styles.* Urbana, IL: Laboratory for Cognitive Studies in Education, 1976.

PIERON, M. *Readings in Teaching Analysis.* Belgium: University of Liege, 1984.

PIERON, M., and MATHY, J. "Study of Teaching Physical Education; Teaching Effectiveness; Teacher Students Interactions and Related Subjects. A Bibliography." Belgium: University of Liege, 1981.

RINK, J. E. *Teaching Physical Education for Learning.* 2nd ed. St. Louis, MO: 1993.

SIEDENTOP, D. *Developing Teaching Skills in Physical Education.* 2nd ed. Palo Alto, CA: Mayfield Publishing Co., 1983.

SIEDENTOP, D. "Teaching Research: The Intervention View." *Journal of Teaching in Physical Education* 1 (1982): 46–50.

SIEDENTOP, D.; BIRDWELL, D.; and METZLER, M. "A Process Approach to Measuring

Teaching Effectiveness in Physical Education." Paper presented at the AAHPERD National Convention, New Orleans, March 1979.

SIEDENTOP, D.; MAND, C.; and TAGGART, A. *Physical Education: Teaching and Curriculum Strategies for Grades 5–12.* Palo Alto, CA: Mayfield Publishing Company, 1986.

SIEDENTOP, D.; TOUSIGNANT, M.; and PARKER, M. *Academic Learning Time—Physical Education Coding Manual.* Columbus, OH: Ohio State University, 1982.

TELAMA, R., et al., eds. *Research in School Physical Education.* Jyraskyla, Finland: The Foundation for Promotion of Physical Culture and Health, 1983.

VICKERS, J. N. *Instructional Design for Teaching Physical Activities.* Champaign, IL: Human Kinetics Books, 1990.

VIRGILIO, S. J. "The Effects of Direct and Reciprocal Teaching Strategies on the Cognitive, Affective, and Psychomotor Behavior of Fifth Grade Pupils in Beginning Archery." Unpublished dissertation, Florida State University, 1979.

YERG, B. J. "The Impact of Selected Presage and Process Behaviors on the Refinement of a Motor Skill." *Journal of Teaching in Physical Education* 1 (1981a): 38–46.

YERG, B. J. "Reflections on the Use of the RTE Model in Physical Education." *Research Quarterly for Exercise and Sport* 52 (1981b): 38–47.

YOUNG, J., and METZLER, M. "Correlations between ALT-PE and Student Achievement in a Novel Skill ETU." Paper presented at the AAHPERD National Convention, Houston, April 1982.

BIBLIOGRAPHY

ABELSON, PHILIP H. et al. "Creativity and Learning," *Daedalus* (Journal of the American Academy of Arts and Sciences). Cambridge, MA, 1965.

ABERCROMBIE, M. L. JOHNSON. *The Anatomy of Judgment.* New York: Basic Books, Inc., 1960.

ALLPORT, GORDON, W. *Becoming.* New Haven: Yale University Press, 1955.

ANDERSON, RICHARD C. "Learning in Discussion: A Resume of Authoritarian-Democratic Studies." *Harvard Educational Review* 29 (1959): 201–15.

ANDERSON, RICHARD C., and ANDERSON, R. M. "Transfer of Originality Training." *Journal of Educational Psychology* 54, no. 6 (1963): 300–304.

ANDERSON, RICHARD C., and AUSUBEL, DAVID P., eds. *Readings in the Psychology of Cognition.* New York: Holt, Rinehart, & Winston, Inc., 1965.

ANDREWS, GLADYS. *Physical Education for Today's Boys and Girls.* Boston: Allyn & Bacon, Inc., 1960.

ASHTON-WARNER, SYLVIA. *Teacher.* New York: Bantam Books, Inc., 1963.

ATKIN, MYRON J., and KARPLUS, ROBERT. "Discovery or Invention?" *The Science Teacher* 29 (1962): 45–69.

AUSUBEL, DAVID P. "Creativity, General Creative Abilities, and the Creative Individual." *Psychology in the Schools* 1 (1964): 344–47.

BERKSON, I. B. *Education Faces the Future.* New York: Harper & Row, Publishers, 1943.

BLOOM, BENJAMIN S., ed. *Taxonomy of Educational Objectives (Handbook I: Cognitive Domain).* New York: David McKay Co., Inc., 1956.

———. *Human Characteristics and School Learning.* New York: McGraw-Hill Book Co., 1976.

BORICH, GARY D. *The Appraisal of Teaching: Concepts and Process.* Reading, MA: Addison-Wesley Publishing Co., 1977.

BREHN, J. W., and COHEN, A. R. *Exploration in Cognitive Dissonance.* New York: John Wiley & Sons, Inc., 1962.

BROWN, GEORGE I. "A Second Study in the Teaching of Creativity." *Harvard Educational Review* 35, no. 1 (Winter 1965): 39–54.

BRUNER, JEROME S. "The Act of Discovery." *Harvard Educational Review* 31 (1961): 21–32.

———. "Needed: A Theory of Instruction." *Educational Leadership* 20 (1963): 523–32.

———. *On Knowing: Essays for the Left Hand.* Cambridge, MA: Harvard University Press, 1962.

———. *The Process of Education.* New York: Random House, Inc., 1963.

BRUNER, J. S.; GOODNOW, J. J.; and AUSTIN, G. A. *A Study of Thinking.* New York: John Wiley & Sons, Inc., 1960.

BUKH, NIELS. *Primary Gymnastics.* 6th ed. London: Methuen & Co., Ltd., 1941.

CARIN, A., and SUND, R. B. *Teaching Science Through Discovery.* Columbus, OH: Charles E. Merrill Books, Inc., 1964.

CHILDS, JOHN L. *Education and Morals.* New York: Appleton-Century & Appleton-Century-Crofts, Inc., 1950.

CHRISTIAN, ROGER W. "Guides to Programmed Learning." *Harvard Business Review,* November–December, 1962.

COLLINS, BARRY E., and GUETZKOW, HAROLD. *A Social Psychology of Group Processes for Decision-Making.* New York: John Wiley & Sons, Inc., 1964.

COPPERMAN, PAUL. *The Literacy Hoax.* New York: William Morrow & Co., Inc., 1978.

COWELL, C. C. *Scientific Foundations of Physical Education.* New York: Harper & Row, Publishers, 1953.

CRATTY, BRYANT J. *Movement Behavior and Motor Learning.* Philadelphia: Lea & Febiger, 1964.

DAVID, ELWOOD C., and WALLIS, EARL L. *Toward Better Teaching in Physical Education.* Englewood Cliffs, NJ: Prenctice Hall, Inc., 1961.

DEWEY, JOHN. *Democracy and Education.* New York: The Macmillan Company, 1916.

———. *Experience and Education.* New York: Collier Books, 1963.

———. *How We Think.* Boston: D. C. Heath & Company, 1933.

DIEM, LISILOTT. *Who Can?* Trans. with an intro. by H. Steinhous. Frankfurt am Main, Germany: W. Limpert, 1957.

DOUGHERTY, NEIL J., and BONANNO, DIANE. *Contemporary Approaches to the Teaching of Physical Education.* Minneapolis: Burgess Publishing Co., 1979.

DUNKIN, MICHAEL J., and BIDDLE, BRUCE J. *The Study of Teaching.* New York: Holt, Rinehart, & Winston, Inc., 1974.

FESTINGER, LEON. *The Theory of Cognitive Dissonance.* Evanston, IL: Row, Peterson, 1957.

FLANDERS, NED A. "Analyzing Teacher Behavior." *Educational Leadership* 19 (1961): 173–80.

———. *Analyzing Teaching Behavior.* Reading, MA: Addison-Wesley Publishing Co., 1970.

FLEISCHMAN, EDWIN A. *The Dimensions of Physical Fitness.* (Technical Report No.

4, Office of Naval Research, Department of Industrial Administration and Department of Psychology, Yale University.) New Haven, CT, 1962.

FORD, G. W., and PUGNO, L., eds. *The Structure of Knowledge and the Curriculum.* Chicago: Rand McNally & Co., 1964.

FRIEDLANDER, BERNARD Z. "A Psychologist's Second Thoughts on Concepts, Curiosity, and Discovery in Teaching and Learning." *Harvard Educational Review* 35, no. 1 (Winter 1965): 18–38.

GAGE, N. L. "Toward a Cognitive Theory of Teaching." *Teachers College Record* 65 (1964): 408–12.

———. *Teacher Effectiveness and Teacher Education: The Search for a Scientific Basis.* Palo Alto: Pacific Books, Publishers, 1972.

GAGNE, ROBERT M. *The Conditions of Learning.* New York: Holt, Rinehart, & Winston, Inc., 1965.

GAGNE, ROBERT M., and BROWN, L. T. "Some Factors in the Programming of Conceptual Learning." *Journal of Experimental Psychology* 62 (1961): 313–21.

GROSS, RONALD, ed. *The Teacher and the Taught.* New York: Dell Publishing Co., Inc., 1963.

GUILFORD, J. P. "Three Faces of Intellect." *The American Psychologist* 14 (1959): 469–79.

HALLMAN, RALPH J. "Can Creativity Be Taught?" *Educational Theory* 14 (1964): 15–23.

HALSEY, ELIZABETH. *Inquiry and Invention in Physical Education.* Philadelphia: Lea & Febiger, 1964.

HARLOW, H. F. "The Formation of Learning Sets." *Psychological Review* 56 (1949): 51–65.

HETHERINGTON, CLARK W. *School Program in Physical Education.* New York: World Book Company, 1922.

HYMAN, RONALD T. *Ways of Teaching.* Philadelphia: J. B. Lippincott Co., 1974. *Individualizing Instruction.* (Association for Supervision and Curriculum Development Yearbook.) Washington, DC, 1964.

INHELDER, BARBEL, and PIAGET, JEAN. *The Growth of Logical Thinking from Childhood to Adolescence.* New York: Basic Books, Inc., Publishers, 1958.

JOYCE, BRUCE, and WEIL, MARSHA. *Models of Teaching.* Englewood Cliffs, NJ: Prentice Hall, Inc., 1972.

KATONA, GEORGE. *Organizing and Memorizing.* New York: Columbia University Press, 1949.

KILPATRICK, W. H. *Philosophy of Education.* New York: The Macmillan Company, 1951.

KOZMAN, H. C.; CASSIDY, R.; and JACKSON, C. O. *Methods in Physical Education.* Philadelphia: W. B. Saunders Co., 1958.

KRATHWOHL, DAVID R.; BLOOM, BENJAMIN S.; and MASIA, BERTRAM B. *Taxonomy of Educational Objectives (Handbook II: Affective Domain).* New York: David McKay Co., Inc., 1956.

KUBIE, LAWRENCE S. *Neurotic Distortion of the Creative Process.* New York: The Noonday Press, 1961.

LINDHARD, J. *The Theory of Gymnastics.* 2nd ed. London: Methuen & Co., Ltd., 1939.

LOCKE, LAWRENCE F., and NIXON, JOHN E. *Research on Teaching Physical Education.* (Draft manuscript—for review only.)

MASLOW, ABRAHAM H. *Toward A Psychology of Being*. Princeton, NJ: D. Van Nostrand Co., Inc., 1962.

MILLER, A., and WHITCOMB, V. *Physical Education in the Elementary School Curriculum*. Englewood Cliffs, NJ: Prentice Hall, Inc., 1963.

MORRISON, RUTH. *Educational Gymnastics*. Liverpool: Speirs & Gledsdale Ltd., 1955.

MOSSTON, MUSKA. *Developmental Movement*. Columbus, OH: Charles E. Merrill Publishing Co., 1965.

MUSE, M. B. *Guiding Learning Experience*. New York: The Macmillan Company, 1950.

NASH, J. B., ed. *Interpretations of Physical Education, Vol. 1: Mind-Body Relationships*. New York: A. S. Barnes & Co., Inc., 1931.

———. *Physical Education: Interpretations and Objectives*. New York: A. S. Barnes & Co., Inc., 1948.

NEA. *Schools for the 60s*. New York: McGraw-Hill Book Company, 1963.

NEA Project on Instruction. *Deciding What to Teach*. Washington, DC, 1963.

NEILSON, N. P., and BRONSON, A. O. *Problems in Physical Education*. Englewood Cliffs, NJ: Prentice Hall, Inc., 1965.

NISSEN, HARTVIG. *A B C of the Swedish System of Educational Gymnastics*. New York, Boston, Chicago: Educational Publishing Company, 1892.

OXENDINE, JOSEPH B. *Psychology of Motor Learning*. New York: Appleton-Century-Crofts, 1968.

Perceiving, Behaving, Becoming. (Association for Supervision and Curriculum Development Yearbook.) Washington, DC, 1962.

PIAGET, JEAN, and INHELDER, BARBEL. *The Growth of Logical Thinking*. New York: Basic Books, 1958.

POLYA, G. *How to Solve It*. Garden City, NY: Doubleday & Company, Inc., 1957.

RATHS, LOUIS. "What Is a Good Teacher?" *Childhood Education* 40 (1964): 451–56.

RICCIO, A. C., and CYPHERT, F. R. *Teaching in America*. Columbus, OH: Charles E. Merrill Publishing Co., 1962.

ROGERS, CARL. *On Becoming a Person*. Boston: Houghton Mifflin, 1961.

SANBORN, M. A., and HARTMAN, B. G. *Issues in Physical Education*. Philadelphia: Lea & Febiger, 1964.

SCHWAB, JOSEPH J. "The Concept of the Structure of a Discipline." *The Educational Record* 43 (1962): 197–205.

SHAW, JOHN. "The Operation of a Value System in the Selection of Activities and Methods of Instruction in Physical Education." Fifty-Ninth Annual Proceedings (National College Physical Education Association). Daytona Beach, FL, 1956.

SHOBEN, EDWARD JOSEPH. "Viewpoints from Related Disciplines: Learning Theory." *Teachers College Record* 60 (1959): 272–82.

SINGER, ROBERT N. *Motor Learning and Human Performance: An Application to Physical Education Skills*. New York: The Macmillan Co., 1968.

SKINNER, B. F. "The Science of Learning and the Art of Teaching." *Harvard Educational Review* 24 (1954): 86–97.

SMITH, OTHANEL B. "A Conceptual Analysis of Instructional Behavior." *Journal of Teacher Education* 14 (1963): 294–98.

———. "The Need for Logic in Methods Courses." *Theory into Practice* 3 (1964): 5–7.

STEBBING, SUSAN L. *Thinking to Some Purpose*. Baltimore: Penguin Books, Inc., 1961.

TABA, HILDA, and ELZEY, FREEMAN F. "Teaching Strategies and Thought Processes." *Teachers College Record* 65 (1964): 524–34.

THOMSON, ROBERT. *The Psychology of Thinking.* Baltimore: Penguin Books, Inc., 1959.

TORRANCE, PAUL E. *Education and the Creative Potential.* Minneapolis: The University of Minnesota Press, 1963.

———. "What Research Says to the Teacher." *Creativity* 28. Washington, DC: National Education Association, 1963.

VANNIER, M., and FAIT, H. F. *Teaching Physical Education in Secondary Schools.* Philadelphia: W. B. Saunders, Co., 1964.

VANNIER, M., and FOSTER, M. *Teaching Physical Education in Elementary Schools.* Philadelphia: W. B. Saunders Co., 1963.

WESTON, ARTHUR. *The Making of American Physical Education.* New York: Appleton-Century & Appleton-Century-Crofts, 1962.

WOODRUFF, ASAHEL D. "The Uses of Concepts in Teaching and Learning." *Journal of Teacher Education* 15 (1964): 81–97.

Index

Note: Page numbers followed by (f) indicate figures; page numbers followed by (t) indicate tables.